12/10

THE SACRED LITERATURE SERIES

THE SPIRIT OF THE QUAKERS

THE SPIRIT OF THE
QUAKERS

SELECTED AND INTRODUCED BY

GEOFFREY DURHAM

PUBLISHED IN ASSOCIATION WITH
THE INTERNATIONAL SACRED LITERATURE TRUST

YALE UNIVERSITY PRESS
NEW HAVEN AND LONDON

For information about this and other Yale University Press publications please contact:
U.S. Office: sales.press@yale.edu   yalebooks.com
Europe Office: sales@yaleup.co.uk   www.yalebooks.co.uk

Set in Arno by IDSUK (DataConnection) Ltd
Printed in Great Britain by MPG Books, Bodmin, Cornwall

Library of Congress Cataloging-in-Publication Data

The spirit of the Quakers.
      p. cm. — (The sacred literature series)
    Includes index.
    ISBN 978-0-300-16736-8
    1. Society of Friends. 2. Society of Friends—History—Sources.
I. Durham, Geoffrey.
    BX7631.3.S65   2010
    289.609—dc22

                                                              2010029763

A catalogue record for this book is available from the British Library.

10 9 8 7 6 5 4 3 2 1

INTERNATIONAL
SACRED
LITERATURE
TRUST

The International Sacred Literature Trust was established to promote understanding and open discussion between and within faiths and to give voice in today's world to the wisdom that speaks across time and traditions.

What resources do the sacred traditions of the world possess to respond to the great global threats of poverty, war, ecological disaster, and spiritual despair?

Our starting-point is the sacred texts with their vision of a higher truth and their deep insights into the nature of humanity and the universe we inhabit. The publishing program is planned so that each faith community articulates its own teachings with the intention of enhancing its self-understanding as well as the understanding of those of other faiths and those of no faith.

The Trust especially encourages faiths to make available texts which are needed in translation for their own communities and also texts which are little known outside a particular tradition but which have the power to inspire, console, enlighten, and transform. These sources from the past become resources for the present and future when we make inspired use of them to guide us in shaping the contemporary world.

Our religious traditions are diverse but, as with the natural environment, we are discovering the global interdependence of human hearts and minds. The Trust invites all to participate in the modern experience of interfaith encounter and exchange which marks a new phase in the quest to discover our full humanity.

To the Quaker Quest Eleven with love and thanks

CONTENTS

PREFACE

The distinguished classical accompanist Gerald Moore called his autobiography *Am I Too Loud?* Having completed this anthology, I rather think I know how he felt. My aim has been to guide new readers down the hidden paths of Quaker literature in a logical way, based on my own experience and a sense of what they might want to know next. My fear, however, is that I may have pointed the route too clearly. If that proves to be the case for you, I hope you will simply ignore me and dip in wherever you wish. These writers are quite capable of telling you about their lives without my help.

What I care about passionately is that people read this great writing. Quakers went through a quiet period towards the end of the twentieth century, during which they spoke a good deal to each other but thought it better to say very little to the world. They are beginning to come out of that now, but there is some catching up to do. If this book opens the door of Quakerism to just one person, I shall be happy.

Quakers will, of course, think of many other extracts that they would have chosen. I can only say that I shall almost certainly agree with them. I hope that they appreciate what they do find here, and that I may perhaps occasionally have introduced to them a little jewel they had not encountered before.

One clear omission for those new to the Quakers, inevitable in an anthology, is a full exposition of their history. I have included a brief summary of the first vital years and a chronology of essential events, but I suggest that readers who want to know more should read

Portrait in Grey by John Punshon (London: Quaker Books, 2nd edition, 2006). It is an admirable account, which is both scholarly and readable.

Many people have helped as I have assembled this little collection. Malcolm Gerratt, both in his capacity as Director of the International Sacred Literature Trust and as editor and colleague, has been encouraging, thoughtful and meticulous. Richard Summers, Quaker and ISLT Trustee, has read every word and made perceptive suggestions. Val Ferguson and Mary Lou Leavitt, Quakers of great wisdom and erudition, have given me invaluable support. Wendy Tennant has deciphered my notes and typed the manuscript with skill and forbearance. I am grateful to them all.

I did much of the groundwork at Woodbrooke Quaker Study Centre in Birmingham, which is a researcher's paradise, because as well as being the friendliest of institutions it also has a superb library that never closes. Ian Jackson, its Librarian, has been unfailingly helpful. The staff of Friends' House Library in London, too, have done wonderful work in rooting out texts that I sometimes despaired of ever finding. I owe them all a great debt.

Numerous authors, copyright holders, owners of publishing rights and their representatives have generously permitted their work to be reproduced here and I would like to thank them warmly and alphabetically: Beth Allen, Robin Alpern, Rex Ambler, Brenda Bailey, Margaret Bearlin, David Boulton, Alison Burrell, Trish Carn, Dilawar Chetsingh, Joanna Clark, Mary Jo Clogg, Mary Anne Crowley, Deborah Curle, Jonathan Dale, Ben Pink Dandelion, Alec Davison, Shirley Dodson, Helen Drewery, Gilly Duff, John Dunston, George Ellis, Suzanne Finch, Simon Fisher, John Fitzgerald, Mary Fox, Diana Francis, Jonathan Fryer, David Gee, Harvey Gillman, Mark Gorman, Sarah Graham, Claire Gregory, Linley Gregory, Wright Horne, Michael Hutchinson, Peter Jarman, Ashok Jashapara, Jennifer Kavanagh, Judy Kirby, Diana Lampen, Mary Lou Leavitt, Alison Leonard, Marrianne McMullen, Tim Newell, Parker J. Palmer, Oriole Parker-Rhodes, Frank Parkinson, Judith Pembleton, Jai Penna, Andreas Priestland, John

Punshon, Jim Pym, Anne Rack, Mary Rowlands, Michael Rutter, Janet Scott, William Sessions, Gil Skidmore, Martha G. Smith, Elizabeth Stevenson, Tony Stoller, Frances Taber, Katie Terrell, Helen Garay Toppins, Catherine Trippett, Eva Tucker, Katie B. Wade, Simon Watson, Rowan Whittington, Alex Wildwood.

There is a small number of copyright holders who, despite my best efforts, I am still unable to find. Any who have yet to be approached for their permission are asked to get in touch, so that omissions may be put right in future editions of this book.

Geoffrey Durham

INTRODUCTION

This book is an anthology, a selection, a pot-pourri. It is also a narrative. Readers who care to take it in order will discover, I hope, that it forms an introduction to the faith and experience of members of The Religious Society of Friends.

The extracts in this book cover the three and a half centuries that Quakers have been in existence. During their formative years they produced a huge body of written work in a short time, some of it of great importance to their future development. For that reason, I have included a good deal of material produced by the visionaries who were active between 1650 and 1700. Two hundred years later, there began another golden age of Quaker writing which covered the whole of the twentieth century. I have chosen a considerable amount of that material, too. Between those two fruitful periods, the literature is sometimes less than helpful to modern audiences, but there are notable exceptions and John Woolman, Luke Cock and Elizabeth Fry, among others, have much to offer us today. They are also represented here.

I have had to rely on my own judgement and accept that everything in this book must be a personal choice; there is only a handful of 'standard' texts in Quakerism. My selection has inevitably been influenced by my own taste and background – I am a British Quaker who attends unprogrammed meetings – but I have tried to keep the range wide and there are pieces here by British, American, New Zealand and Australian writers of all varieties of witness and beliefs.

Anthologies are quite a tradition among Quakers. Each Yearly Meeting (a group of Quakers covering a large geographical area) has its own version of *Faith and Practice*, a collection of Quaker writing intended as a guide and *vade mecum* for the Quakers of that region. The British version, *Quaker Faith & Practice*, serves the United Kingdom, but also enjoys a world-wide readership. It is a treasure-trove of inspirational Quaker writing and warmly recommended to anyone who is interested in finding out more about the Quaker way.

This book is not intended as an alternative to that or any other of those indispensable collections, and is entirely different from them. The main distinction lies simply in the needs of its target audience. This volume is intended for newcomers: everything here is geared towards trying to make the rich variety of Quaker thought and inspiration accessible to enquirers. With that in mind, I have included closely argued pieces that have no place in a book intended for the use of Quakers alone. There is a good deal of 'first impression' material here as well, which I hope will be of interest to general readers. And I have taken advantage of the practice of Quaker journalling to feature four extensive extracts from great examples of that genre. Fox's *Journal* for 1652 provides an insight into the early days of a revolutionary movement. Mary Penington gives a female perspective, as well as revealing her doubts about the first Quakers she met. John Woolman, often thought of as the quintessential Quaker, shows the quiet persistence of a man not only doggedly truthful but also out of step with the society he lived in. Finally, Pierre Ceresole offers something else again: the thoughts of a devoted Quaker of the mid-twentieth century, wrestling with the ethical dilemmas of living in a world in turmoil.

The Quaker way is about the people who practise it and I hope that readers will start to notice which of the prolific writers they have most in common with and follow them through the book. I hope, too, that they will get a sense of the variety and depth of thought of this most eclectic group of worshippers and activists. I am confident that, as they read, they will begin to understand the faith of Quakers through their own words. However, I am also aware that those who know nothing of The Religious Society of Friends may need a little groundwork, so in the next paragraphs I shall try briefly to explain some of the key principles in order that newcomers may find themselves better equipped to join the dots.

Let us begin with belief. Most religions have creeds. There are teachings, certainties and essential truths which, despite the inevitable doubts, are nonetheless welcomed by all their members. That is not the Quaker way. Quakers joyfully profess an experience-based faith. They do not believe what they are told. There have been many changes and shifts of emphasis in Quakerism since the early 1650s when George Fox began his mission as a 'publisher of Truth', but those fundamentals have never varied. Quakers do not proclaim a set of beliefs which they have to follow, they do not preach and they do not insist that theirs is the only way. For Quakers, personal experience is the key. They have no formal creed.

It often happens that newcomers ask reasonable questions of Quakers which are impossible to answer. 'What is the Quaker position on life after death?' 'Do Quakers believe that Jesus was the Son of God?' 'What do they say about suffering?' These enquiries can never reach a satisfactory conclusion – though the ensuing discussion will undoubtedly be long and fascinating – because The Religious Society of Friends refuses to make general pronouncements on matters of faith. Individuals speak for themselves and they often agree with one other, but they remain open to new experience and are always prepared to change their minds.

In a twenty-first century world used to hearing religious faith expressed in the form of opposing dogmas, this may all seem weak, flaky and a little odd. We are accustomed to assurance. We worry about doubt. We want our questions answered clearly and succinctly, so that we can quickly make up our own minds. We fear that lack of certainty betrays a fundamental incoherence or paucity of thought. So a person who ponders long and hard before answering what seems to be a simple question may often be considered to be lacking in incisiveness.

Quakers who are asked if they believe in God, for example, are likely to be reluctant to give a straight yes or no; and it follows that, in an age hungry for information, their unwillingness to commit themselves will often be seen as evasive. But for many Friends, the question itself is simply fatuous and unhelpful: the point is not whether you believe in God, but whether you *encounter* the Divine. *And if so, how?* The answers will be different from person to person and they will lack absolute clarity. Crucially, they will determine the shape of every life and the ways in which each individual is led to live it. Quakerism is not about what we say, it is about what we find ourselves impelled to do. Therein lies its coherence and its strength.

Encounters – with God, with each other, with a fractured world – are at the heart of the Quaker faith. And if Quakers' freedom from universally expressed convictions makes it impossible to write a definitive catalogue of shared beliefs, we should not infer that Friends are without purpose or meaning in their lives. Nothing could be further from the truth. In fact, the nature of Quaker worship fuses meaning and purpose in a way that renders them inextricable from each other: meaning becomes purpose, purpose becomes meaning. Quakers' religious convictions and their commitment to action cannot be separated.

Let us see how this works in practice.

A newcomer to *The Religious Society of Friends (Quakers)* – the words 'Friend' and 'Quaker' are synonymous and interchangeable – will almost always start by visiting a Quaker Meeting House. The people who attend it regularly are called collectively a 'Meeting' and so, confusingly, is their collective act of worship. (This is one of those strange historical anomalies that appear entirely natural from the inside, but are unhelpful to an outside observer.) The members of the meeting, named for their area – Hampstead Meeting, say, or Skipton Meeting – will know each other well. They will meet regularly for worship, discussions and social time. Numbers will vary – Local Meetings can consist of anything from five or six people to two hundred and more – but it is likely that, however large or small the group, most members will be aware of the personal circumstances of the others. Every Quaker Meeting celebrates deep, long-lasting and resonant friendships.

No one is in charge, and great pains are taken to ensure that hierarchies cannot develop. Quakers' belief in equality runs very deep. All jobs, from the most important to the least significant, are done for three years at a time and then handed on: it is vital that people do not start to become protective of their roles in a Meeting. Thus, a small number will be asked for a period of three years to be Elders: they are given the task of looking after the spiritual needs of the Meeting. Others, called Overseers, undertake the pastoral care within the group. And then there are those who, again for three years only, look after the fabric of the building, run the library, administer the finances, edit the newsletter, organise social events, take care of activities for children and make the coffee – all familiar roles within any company of people united by one central activity. In the case of Quakers, that activity occupies a precious place in the life of each member: it can and does change people profoundly. It is a weekly shared practice that binds everyone together and gives them meaning and purpose. It is called Meeting for Worship.

Each Quaker tends to interpret the word 'worship' in his or her own way. Some are at pains to clarify and explain exactly what they are worshipping in meeting. Others go back to the core meaning of the word and emphasise that they are giving 'worth-ship' to the Divine. Still more return to a phrase used widely by early Quakers: 'standing in the Light'. Later in this book, all these views are explored by Quakers from different periods and perspectives.

Every Meeting House has an area which is used regularly for Quaker worship. It is not consecrated for the purpose – a meeting can take place anywhere – but the room needs to be big enough for each person to have a place to sit and for the chairs to be laid out in such a way that everybody in the room can see everyone else. This generally means a circular arrangement, but there are old Meeting Houses with two permanent banks of seating facing each other, or benches laid out in square formation. It doesn't matter how the furniture is set out, so long as nobody is sitting separately and everyone feels part of the group. Quaker worship is a communal activity.

In the centre of the room there is usually a table. It is not an altar and has no significance other than its utilitarian purpose. It often has flowers on it. It is likely, too, to have a copy of *Quaker Faith & Practice*, the essential anthology which is updated for every generation. *Advices & Queries* (see page 42) is always on the table and extracts are often read aloud. The Bible is also there, and some Meetings include works of non-Christian faiths. All these books are for the use of Quakers during the meeting.

Most people who have heard of The Religious Society of Friends know that Quakers meet in silence. They are quite right, of course, but if they go on to assume that silence is the point of the meeting, they are making a mistake. Quiet is important, but it is certainly not the purpose. It is an aid to what the meeting is really about, which is stillness.

'Still waiting on God' is the Quaker phrase for what Friends practise in a Meeting for Worship. As the group of worshippers sits in silence, a sense of unspoken community begins subtly to be felt by everybody present. The quiet becomes fuller. Some Quakers use the deepening stillness to examine themselves, to see their circumstances as they truly are, to stare out the issues in their lives. Sometimes their contemplations may go on to open up a wider, more unexpected picture to them. It might be that they are able to focus on the sheer fact of their existence, maybe they have a feeling of purpose that wasn't there before, or a renewed sense of community. Perhaps, for a few moments, they may glimpse the eternal.

Occasionally, a member of the meeting may feel moved to speak from a deep, unfamiliar place inside them. They stand and say what they can, often with no true sense of its meaning or purpose, always without preparation. Quakers call this 'ministry'. It is a rare gift, and is unlikely to happen to one person very often; weeks, months and years can go by before a Friend is moved again to speak in meeting. Helpful ministry stimulates thought and inspires imagination while at the same time contributing to the corporate stillness.

Many Quakers experience a beating heart before they speak, and some use that to test whether or not it is right for them to minister. Almost every Quaker feels the need to check mentally whether the message they are receiving is intended for them alone or for the meeting as a whole. There is nothing worse than sitting down after ministering with the sense that it was the wrong thing to do, or that ego may have been involved in the decision to speak. Sometimes, though, there is simply no choice – worshippers are suddenly moved to stand and say as best they can what is in their heart.

Often the spoken contributions to a meeting knit together and form an overall picture which begins, like a mosaic, to characterise that particular mix of people and to give meaning to the unique encounter. When this fails to happen, however, it certainly does not mean that the meeting is somehow 'less' or 'worse'. And many meetings naturally contain no speech at all. At these times, the silent ministry of all the participants gives the occasion a character which is entirely its own and a spiritual dimension which touches the participants. One thing is sure: no two meetings are ever alike.

When I first experienced a Quaker meeting, there was actually no quiet at all. Somebody was playing loud music on their radio just outside the window and it threatened to wreck everything. I was at a loss to know how this strange, disrupted hour could ever turn itself into a religious experience. Yet slowly, imperceptibly, the event reached a communal stillness of a kind which could almost be touched. It was miraculous. When that happens, and it occurs often both in noisy and the much more familiar silent meetings, Quakers have a word for it. They call it a 'covered' or 'gathered' meeting. Many Quakers believe, as Thomas Kelly makes clear on page 19, that what characterises a gathered meeting is the presence of the Divine. If he is right, then the still waiting on God of those Quakers on my first day did indeed fulfil its aim.

Meeting for Worship is the bedrock of Quaker faith and Quaker practice. It has to come first: no book on Quakerism can begin with the theology or the structures or even the work Quakers do in the world. The fundamental motivation, the cause, the reason for Quakerism, lies in the communal experience of silent worship – and it is, after all, a faith based on experience. Quakers did not invent it – it was widely practised by many of the small religious groups which sprang up in the aftermath of England's Civil War in the mid-seventeenth century – but they embraced it and recognised it for what it was: a means of transforming people and helping them to behave differently. For 350 years Quakers have been leaving their meetings not only refreshed, but also prompted to think again about their lives. Silent worship helps people to see who they are and become who they can be.

This fusion of meaning and purpose, for that is what it is, is also behind the often expressed Quaker belief that all of life is sacramental. It is a big statement and it needs some unpacking, but it goes a long way towards explaining how Quakers think. So, first of all, what is a sacrament? Dictionaries tell us that it is a word of Christian origin, signifying a religious act or ceremony which is seen as an outward and visible sign of inward and spiritual grace. Quakers, too, are of Christian origin, but they choose to express their faith without ritual. In doing so, they are not rejecting sacraments or sacramental living: on the contrary, they regard both as essential to their way of life. Nor are they abandoning the idea of inward and spiritual grace. They simply prefer not to manifest it through ceremonial and symbol.

For Quakers, there is no distinction between the sacred and the secular. To live sacramentally is to believe that all of life is sacred. Inseparable from that is the conviction that everyone can have an unmediated relationship with the Divine, that we are all the priests. Friends use many words for God, and there is no imposition of any view of the Divine, but the inescapable facts are that (1) Quakers acknowledge that they are led constantly by something outside themselves and that (2) they find it hard – most would say impossible – to define it.

Quakers believe that every day is holy. So no day is more special, important or significant than any other; and it follows from that, of course, that they feel no need to celebrate a Sabbath. In addition, early Friends refused to recognise the conventional titles given to days of the week and months of the year, derived as they were from the names of pagan gods and Roman emperors. Instead, they labelled them 'First-day',' First-month' and so on. This practice has all but died out in modern times, but evidence for it will be found in many of the extracts from George Fox, John Woolman and Elizabeth Fry later in this book. Quakers' rejection of church calendars and religious festivals, on the other hand, is still very much alive: they continue to commemorate the religious events that matter to them as individuals without designating a specific day to a particular occasion. Equally, Quakers are able to find something sacrosanct in every place – each lump of earth, blade of grass and busy street. So it follows, as we have seen, that they do not find the concept of hallowed or consecrated ground useful either. Quakers can and do hold their acts of worship anywhere and everywhere.

Quakers believe that every meal has a spiritual significance. They do not find it necessary to consecrate food and drink or use them in a religious ceremony, because they regard them as already blessed. Equally, they do not baptise new-born children, preferring simply to welcome them into their communities without the frame of a rite or symbol. And perhaps most importantly of all in their understanding of sacramental living, Quakers express their spiritual convictions through what they do, rather than what they say – demonstrating once more that, for them, meaning and purpose have become the same thing.

The actions taken by specific Quakers speak openly of their individual beliefs. Many share enthusiasms for common causes. Criminal justice, prison reform, peace building, conflict resolution are all bright in the minds of Quakers and they try to make a difference in the fields that mean most to them personally. As they contemplate their lives in their Meetings for Worship, they find their perspectives changing and they discover new ways of taking action that they have perhaps never considered before. Often, these initiatives are small: there is no

Quaker commandment that insists on everything being monumental or ground-breaking and the local, neighbourhood contribution is as much part of the Quaker way as an enterprise that grabs the headlines.

And none of it, of course, is compulsory. No one is forcing Quakers to do anything. But the truth is that if you try to live sacramentally, you often find yourself without any choice as to what you do next. Quakers take action because they feel the need to. And that is because they realise they can only be truly fulfilled by doing what they are spiritually led to do – there are those twin urges, meaning and purpose, again – and by allowing their lives to serve as a testimony to their most closely held beliefs. I use the word 'testimony' deliberately: it is an important one for Quakers. They use it often to describe action which they corporately affirm as being a defining, non-negotiable part of all their lives, either as an established fact or an aspiration. There have historically been many Quaker testimonies, but four crucial ones bear public witness to the lives of Friends in the twenty-first century: equality, peace, simplicity and truth.

Quakers have written a great deal on these four building blocks of their faith, and many of the extracts later in this book will reflect that. It is enough at this stage to acknowledge that without the four testimonies there would be no Quakers and no Quakerism. And the most influential is the testimony to equality. Indeed, it is the basis of the other three. One cannot, to take one simple example, do violence to a person without a sense that they are somehow 'other' (see the piece by Diana Francis on page 139). Equally basically, a simple life freely chosen (see Advice 41 on page 49) conserves resources which can be used for the benefit of one's equals. And a life founded on truth and integrity implies respect for one's fellows and (see Luke Cock's testimony on page 132) may be rewarded in the most unexpected of ways. There is much more to it than that, of course – everything that Quakers stand for is based around the same need to practise complete equality. Indeed, any person who chooses to take the notion of equality to its utmost, logical conclusion, who bases their life around it and begins to perceive it as a spiritual if not religious issue, is inevitably well on the way to becoming a Quaker.

The principles and customs of the Quaker faith are ingrained in the lives of Friends. They lapse readily into silence before meals and at the beginning and end of the most mundane of gatherings. The Quaker business method, also based on the silence of a Meeting for Worship, enables decisions to be taken without majority voting, using spiritual discernment to come to conclusions which are never pressed by individuals. Crucial to this way of conducting the Meeting's affairs is the role of the Clerk, an administrator and chair whose place is not to help to drive through resolutions, but rather to act as a channel through whom the Meeting's concerns and deliberations can pass. This is another of those roles which is undertaken for three years at a time before simply being passed on to another person. The Clerk often appears to be a figurehead and at times is the public face of the Meeting. Yet the principle of equality, combined with the desire of Quakers to ensure that everything is approached at a religious level, ensures that neither ego nor power can ever be part of the Clerk's agenda.

Quakers have had no leaders for centuries, but it was not always their way. During the first intense forty years or so of their development – from around 1652 to 1691 – there were some notable figures who captivated enquirers through preaching, publishing and causing a stir. George Fox, James Nayler, William Penn, Edward Burrough, Isaac Penington and many others put Quakerism on the map. They emerged from the wreckage of the English Civil War with a passionate realisation that all their priorities up to that time had been wrong. They believed that everyone could have a direct relationship with God and that priests, churches and the traditional structure of ecclesiastical life should be swept away.

They called themselves Friends of Truth. As if that were not provocative enough, they challenged people openly in the street and told them to change and repent. They referred disparagingly to churches as 'steeplehouses'. They refused to swear oaths on the principle, as the Bible says, that 'your yea be yea and your nay, nay'. They denied all double standards of truth. They were beaten up, tortured and frequently thrown into gaol for their beliefs. The general public, seeing the display of shaking and trembling that sometimes accompanied their devotions, derisively called them 'Quakers'. They were happy to accept that, and have used the nickname ever since.

In 1654, a group of Friends, often known to historians as The Valiant Sixty (though they were actually closer to seventy in number), spread out around the country, preaching their radical gospel and bringing this young, fresh way of thinking to people who had not experienced it before. They convinced many people of the rightness of their cause and also incited controversy wherever they went, usually being rewarded with further physical abuse and incarceration. They produced endless letters, sermons and pamphlets, which were generally matched by an equal amount of hastily produced, vituperative literature from their opponents, denouncing them as heretics and trouble-makers.

One of their number, George Fox, emerged gradually as a leader. He was a powerful speaker, thinker and organiser and he persuaded great numbers of people to join him. One of his converts, Margaret Fell, was married to a judge and, although he never became a Quaker himself, Thomas Fell provided food and shelter for Friends at his house, Swarthmoor Hall, near Ulverston in Cumbria. His patronage was a key factor in holding the movement together in the early years because, quite apart from the other help he was giving, his unspoken acceptance of Quakers made them for a brief period somewhat less likely, in that area at least, to be hauled before a court.

After Thomas Fell died in 1658, however, the beatings, ransackings and imprisonments continued unabated. Both Margaret Fell and George Fox spent considerable stretches in prison and endured much suffering. But Swarthmore Hall remained a centre of Quaker activity and eleven years after being widowed, Margaret Fell married George Fox and they set up home there together. More forced separations and inevitable incarcerations followed until, in 1675, Margaret and George were able at last to pass one year together in relative peace and tranquillity. They spent it drawing up an organisational system that would ensure that Quakers could continue to operate functionally as a religious group for the generations that were to follow them. With only a few changes, the model has survived and it is perhaps significant that one of the principal decision-making bodies of British Quakers is still, to this day, called Meeting for Sufferings, after the travails of the early Quakers whose affairs were being considered under its auspices.

In the early 1680s one of the leaders of Quakers in Britain, William Penn, an aristocrat who had been converted to Quakerism, was given an enormous plot of land in America by Charles ll, in settlement of a debt owed by the king to Penn's father. The tract amounted to some 45,000 square miles, south of New Jersey and north of Maryland. Penn already had links with the burgeoning Quaker movement in America and began to ship Friends out of Britain to his new estate, which was eventually called Pennsylvania. It became a home for persecuted minorities of many different faiths and Penn's 'holy experiment', as he called it, became the starting point of the Quaker movement in America, where it has had a continued presence ever since.

The impact of American Quakerism on the USA was considerable. John Woolman, an eighteenth-century American Quaker, was one of the first people to understand the full impact and iniquity of slavery. It can sometimes take a visionary to see something for the first time which, years later, becomes manifested as a universal human truth, accepted by all. Woolman wrote a pamphlet in 1753, *Some Considerations on the Keeping of Negroes*, more than a hundred years before the eventual abolition of slavery in his country. Part of his journal appears on page 169 of this book, and shows how the style of Quaker activism changed during the first century of its existence from the rabble-rousing style of George Fox to Woolman's subdued, persuasive waiting.

Quakers continue in that same quiet spirit today. In July 2009, British Friends agreed to carry forward the initiative that 'same sex marriages can be prepared, celebrated, witnessed, recorded and reported to the state, as opposite sex marriages are'. Here is another Quaker concern which has seemed outlandish to many critics in its own time, but which will doubtless be seen as a proclamation of a basic human right by future generations. Like all such issues, it went through a long process of discussion, discernment and prayer at a local level before a still Meeting for Worship of over 1,000 people agreed that it should be adopted. Quakers do not come to quick conclusions and they ponder every decision at great length to ensure that it becomes the considered wish of the meeting. Once they finally have absolute clarity, Quakers apply themselves patiently to seeing the matter through.

The work goes on. Quakers have permanent offices at the United Nations in both Geneva and New York. They work for peace, they campaign against the arms trade, they are passionate about climate change, they are heavily involved in social action at a local level, they are deeply committed to all forms of conflict resolution. Any list of what Quakers do to 'mend the world' is long and quickly becomes superannuated, but it is always there and always growing.

Modern Quakerism is a direct descendant of the religious faith of seventeenth-century Friends, but it is not the same. Advice 7 (see page 43) suggests that we should be 'open to new light'. That has always been the Quaker way. It follows that any description of the faith of Friends can never be definitive, all-embracing or final. The Quaker impulse will always be to 'do what love requires of you'. This book attempts to cast light on the nature of that love in the words of the Quakers themselves.

A SHORT QUAKER CHRONOLOGY

1649	Execution of Charles I and the institution of the Commonwealth. Four years later, in 1653, Oliver Cromwell becomes Lord Protector of England, Scotland and Ireland.
1624–1691	Life of George Fox.
1644–1651	Fox begins his work as an itinerant preacher, attracting both enthusiastic followers and angry detractors.
1652	The year from which Quakers generally date their foundation. The Friends of Truth are by now well established in the midlands and north of England.
1654	Quaker evangelists begin to move south, experiencing welcome and opposition in roughly equal measure. Many are imprisoned, usually for vagrancy, interrupting church services or refusing to pay tithes.
c1655	Quakers begin to spread their message to other countries. Over the next few years, they visit Holland, Germany, America and Barbados, as well as meeting both the Pope and the Turkish Sultan.
1660	The monarchy is restored: Charles ll comes to the throne. George Fox is imprisoned for the fifth time. Quakers make their declaration (see page 144) that they unequivocally refuse to take up arms.
1661–1662	Around 4,200 Quakers in prison.
1644–1718	Life of William Penn.
1680	An estimated 66,000 people in Britain (around 1 in 130 of the total population) are now Quakers.

1682	Penn sails for America and eventually founds Pennsylvania, where freedom of conscience and worship are guaranteed to all.
1689	The Act of Toleration in Britain. This leads over the next few years to the release of prisoners, fewer incarcerations and a tendency to quietism among British Quakers, who feel less impelled to convert others.
1773	Opposition to slavery is minuted by Pennsylvania Monthly Meeting. Three years later, Philadelphia Quakers prohibit their members from owning slaves.
1796	William Tuke opens The Retreat in York, England, pioneering humane care for the mentally ill.
1780–1845	Life of Elizabeth Fry. From 1816 to her death, she works to improve the lot of prisoners in Newgate Gaol and elsewhere, clothing them, educating the children, campaigning against the severest punishments and introducing after-care.
c1820–c1890	Differences among Quakers in America lead to the development of a number of strands of Quakerism in that country. As a result, American Friends today tend to describe themselves as belonging to either the 'programmed', 'evangelical', 'conservative' or 'unprogrammed' traditions.
1870	Quakers undertake relief work during the Franco-Prussian War.
1902	American missionaries visit Kenya and establish a Quaker presence. A hundred years later, one third of all Quakers worldwide live there.
1914	Friends Ambulance Unit (see p. 85) founded.
1920–1930	American missionaries bring Quakerism to South America, where it becomes particularly strong in Bolivia and Peru.
1920–present	The first World Conference of Friends is held, after which they are mounted approximately once a generation. Under the auspices of Friends World Committee for Consultation, founded in 1937, the fifth conference is planned for Kenya in 2012.

1939–1945   Quakers undertake large-scale relief work during World
                 War Two.

1942–present   Quakers participate in the foundation of a large number
                 of key charities and pressure groups worldwide,
                 including Oxfam, Amnesty International and
                 Greenpeace.

1947   The Nobel Prize for Peace is awarded jointly to Friends
                 Service Council in Britain and the American Friends
                 Service Committee in the USA, in recognition of their
                 relief work for victims of war.

1947–present   Friends Service Council (later called Quaker Peace and
                 Social Witness) and American Friends Service
                 Committee continue to support initiatives promoting
                 peace education, conflict transformation, mediation
                 and restorative justice in their own countries and
                 throughout the world. Among their many other active
                 concerns are housing, prisons, education and the
                 environment. Quaker Peace and Social Witness also
                 manages the UK/Ireland Ecumenical Accompaniment
                 Programme (an initiative of the World Council of
                 Churches) in Israel and Palestine.

1948   Friends World Committee for Consultation, in
                 recognition of the aims shared by Quakers and the
                 United Nations, gains consultative status with the
                 UN Economic and Social Council. Quaker United
                 Nations offices open in New York and Geneva,
                 enabling their representatives to work for human
                 rights, peace and disarmament, refugees, and global
                 economic issues.

1963   A small group of British Quakers publishes *Towards a
                 Quaker View of Sex*, widely seen as controversial
                 because of its refusal to take judgemental attitudes
                 (*'God can enter any relationship in which there is a
                 measure of selfless love'*).

1960s–present   British Quakers join protests and hold peace vigils at
                 numerous military and nuclear weapons establishments,
                 including Aldermaston, Faslane, Fylingdales and

	Greenham Common. In 1985, *The Gates of Greenham*, an oratorio by Alec Davison and Tony Biggin, produces the largest gathering of British Quakers in the twentieth century when it is premiered at London's Royal Festival Hall.
1980–present	The Quaker United Nations Office submits recommendations on the use of child soldiers to the UN's 36th session of the Commission on Human Rights. After years of complex negotiations, the UN General Assembly declares in 2000 that 'states shall not recruit persons under the age of eighteen'.
2009	The annual business meeting of British Quakers expresses support for same sex marriages and seeks to lobby the British government for changes to the law.

QUAKER MEETING FOR WORSHIP

Friends, meet together and know one another in that which is eternal, which was before the world was.

George Fox, 1657

What is the ground and foundation of the gathered meeting? In the last analysis, it is, I am convinced, the Real Presence of God.

Thomas R. Kelly, 1940

Let no one go to Friends' meetings with the expectation of finding everything to his taste.

Caroline Stephen, 1890

If ever there were a perfect example of the whole being greater than the sum of its parts, it must surely be the Quaker Meeting for Worship. While it is certainly true that some people are able only to see its fundamental components – a circle of people saying little or nothing, followed by a hand-shake at the end – for many more, it proves to be life-changing. To them, Quaker meetings provide direct religious experiences of a kind that other groups use symbols to express.

Robert Barclay, the seventeenth-century Quaker who was the first to attempt an analysis of Quaker theology, describes the effect on him of his first meeting.

When I came into the silent assemblies of God's people, I felt a secret power among them, which touched my heart, and as I gave way unto it, I found the evil weakening in me, and the good raised up, and so I became thus knit, and united unto them, hungering more and more after the increase of this power and life, whereby I might feel myself perfectly redeemed.

Robert Barclay, 1678

At the time that Barclay became attracted to Quakerism, meetings were open-ended and could last for three or four hours and more. Today, a Meeting for Worship usually has an allotted time span – maybe an hour – and ends when two Quakers, who have been previously asked to do so, close the proceedings by shaking hands. They will try to discern the right time to finish, perhaps by considering the pattern of short statements which may have been expressed vocally, or by listening carefully to the progression of the silent worship.

Apart from their length, however, very little has changed since Quakers held their first gatherings. Here are four descriptions by visitors to Quaker Meetings experiencing worship for the first time. They span the last 330 years.

And this is the manner of their worship. They are to wait upon the Lord, to meet in the silence of flesh, and to watch for the stirrings of his life, and the breaking forth of his power amongst them. And in the breakings forth of that power they may pray, speak, exhort, rebuke, sing, or mourn, &c. according as the Spirit teaches, requires, and gives utterance. But if the Spirit do not require to speak, and give to utter, then every one is to sit still in his place (in his heavenly place I mean), feeling his own measure, feeding thereupon, receiving therefrom, into his spirit, what the Lord giveth. Now, in this is edifying, pure edifying, precious edifying; his soul who thus waits, is hereby particularly edified by the Spirit of the Lord at every meeting. And then also there is the life of the whole felt in every vessel that is turned to its measure: insomuch as the warmth of life in each vessel doth not only warm the particular, but they are like a heap of fresh and living coals, warming one another, insomuch as a great strength, freshness, and vigour of life flows into all. And if any be burthened, tempted, buffeted, distressed, &c., the estate of such is felt in Spirit, and secret cries, or open (as the Lord pleaseth), ascend up to the Lord for them, and they many times find ease and relief, in a few words spoken, or without words, if it be the season of their help and relief with the Lord.

Isaac Penington, published 1680

Some seventeen years ago, I first found myself within reach of a Friends' meeting, and, somewhat to my surprise, cordially made welcome to attend it. The invitation came at a moment of need, for I was beginning to feel with dismay that I might not much longer be able conscientiously to continue to join in the Church of England service; not for want of appreciation of its unrivalled richness and beauty, but from doubts of the truth of its doctrines, combined with a growing recognition that to me it was as the armour of Saul in its elaboration and in the sustained pitch of religious fervour for which it was meant to provide an utterance. Whether true or not in its speculative and theoretical assumptions, it was clear to me that it was far from true as a periodical expression of my own experience, belief, or aspiration. The more vividly one feels the force of its eloquence, the more, it seems to me, one must hesitate to adopt it as the language of one's own soul, and the more unlikely is it that such heights and depths of feeling as it demands should be ready to fill its magnificent channels every Sunday morning at a given hour. The questionings with which at that period I was painfully struggling were stirred into redoubled activity by the dogmatic statements and assumptions with which the Liturgy abounds, and its unbroken flow left no loophole for the utterance of my own less disciplined, but to myself far more urgent, cries for help. Thus the hour of public worship, which should have been a time of spiritual strengthening and calming, became to me a time of renewed conflict, and of occasional exaltation and excitement of emotion, leading but too surely to reaction and apathy.

I do not attempt to pass any judgement on this mental condition. I have described it at some length because I cannot believe it to be altogether exceptional, or without significance. At any rate, it was fast leading me to dread the moment when I should be unable either to find the help I needed, or to offer my tribute of devotion in any place of worship amongst my fellow-Christians. When lo, on one never-to-be-forgotten Sunday morning, I found myself one of a small company of silent worshippers, who were content to sit down together without words, that each one might feel after and draw near to the Divine Presence, unhindered at least, if not helped, by any human utterance. Utterance I knew was free, should the words be given; and before the meeting was over, a sentence or two were uttered in great simplicity by an old and apparently untaught man, rising in his place amongst the rest of us. I did not pay much attention to the words he spoke, and I have no recollection of their purport. My whole soul was filled with the unutterable peace of the undisturbed opportunity for communion with God, with the sense that at last I had found a place where I might, without the faintest suspicion of insincerity, join with others in simply seeking His presence. To sit down in silence could at the least pledge me to nothing; it might open to me (as it did that morning) the very gate of heaven. And since that day, now more than seventeen years ago, Friends' meetings have indeed been to me the greatest of outward helps to a fuller and fuller entrance into the spirit from which they have sprung; the place of the most soul-subduing, faith-restoring, strengthening and peaceful communion, in feeding upon the bread of life, that I have ever known.

Caroline Stephen, 1890

Some Friends are able to recall with clarity the first occasion on which they attended a Quaker meeting. While I cannot remember when or where I did so, I do have a vivid recollection of the meeting which I began to attend regularly.

It was held in a rather hideous building: the meeting room was dingy. We sat on rickety chairs that creaked at the slightest move-ment. The whole place gave little hope that those who worshipped there might catch a glimpse of the vision of God. It was in stark contrast to the splendour of the Anglican churches to which I had been accustomed, where through dignified ritual the beauty of holiness was vividly portrayed.

However, it was in this unlikely setting that I came to know what I can only describe as the amazing fact of Quaker worship. It was in that uncomfortable room that I discovered the way to the interior side of my life, at the deep centre of which I knew that I was not alone, but was held by a love that passes all understanding. This love was mediated to me, in the first place, by those with whom I worshipped. For my journey was not solitary, but one undertaken with my friends as we moved towards each other and together travelled inwards. Yet I knew that the love that held me could not be limited to the mutual love and care we had for each other. It was a signal of transcendence that pointed beyond itself to the source of all life and love.

In that ordinary room a group of ordinary people entered quietly into a new dimension in which everyday life was transformed and transcended, as we found a depth of loving communion that was infinite and eternal in its quality. This was achieved by waiting together in stillness without the assistance of a trained leadership, ritual acts or programmed worship.

There was a remarkable sense of freedom among us for we were not bound by dogma nor restricted by the negative side of credal statements. At the same time we were supported by a strong awareness of trust in life as having meaning and purpose. Our experience drew from us the conviction that love was the nature of this meaning and purpose.

The experience could be described at many levels, and interpreted in many ways. At the lowest it could be seen as a human activity and expressed in secular language. At the highest it could be seen as the breaking in of divinity to be described in transcendent or religious language. The range of outlook and attitudes held by the group was wide. The experience of individuals varied enormously. At the extreme poles it would seem that the one must contradict the other – yet at the still centre we found unity not conflict . [. . .]

All life was present in that shabby room which Sunday after Sunday was silently transformed into a gateway to transcendence. Together we knew the simple happiness of living: the essential goodness and meaning of life. Together we experienced moments of despair and depression when truth, love and goodness seemed to be obliterated by the evil in ourselves and in the world around us. But terrifying as were those black periods when '... there was an ocean of darkness and death', we, like George Fox also saw '... an infinite ocean of light and love, which flowed over the ocean of darkness'. Also like George Fox we saw in the darkness and the light 'the infinite love of God'. For all of us had looked at our world and had been drawn to interpret its meaning as love. To this interpretation we had committed ourselves and by its light we tried to live.

The experience of my first encounter with Quaker worship was not misleading. It has been repeated over and over again in countless other meetings I have known. Sometimes I have come across Friends and others who feel that to interpret religious experience basically in terms of love is too simple and easy. Religion, they say, is something that makes fundamental claims upon our obedience. All I can say in reply is that to love another person really and in depth is the hardest demand that can be made upon us. It transcends all law and moral obligation and calls for a response from the whole of our personality. It is a costly, sacrificial activity, the true nature of which was dramatically shown by the death of Jesus on the cross.

The more we respond in love to others and accept their love for us, the greater our capacity for love becomes. This extraordinary character of love which is inherently creative urges us to see that love is the meaning, truth and reality of life. At this point we find ourselves responding warmly to the developing awareness of the nature of God recorded in the pages of the Bible which culminated in the explicit New Testament statement that God is love.

Quakerism is essentially empirical rather than theoretical in its approach to religion. Quakers come to it not by way of argument about transcendence or love or the existence of God, but by putting themselves in a position where they can be open to experience. So the essential life of the Society of Friends is to be seen in the repeated activity of worship. Here Quakers continually re-affirm the worth of love, and through dwelling silently in the presence of this love, know the presence of God, not as theory but as fact.

George Gorman, 1973

So here I was, sitting on a bench in a Friends meeting for the first time in my life, not knowing at all what to expect. There was nothing to look at, nothing to occupy my mind, nothing to appeal to my senses, nothing to sing, nothing to join in with, in fact, absolutely nothing whatever to do, and a whole hour to fill.

I imagine that nearly everybody feels like this at their first unprogrammed meeting, for this manner of worship is exceptional. However, one does not have to move for very long in Quaker circles to find that it can speak to the condition of Friends and non-Friends alike. There is a common pattern of experience, whatever the outward religious loyalty of those who come. People will say that at first the silence is highly demanding, but after a while it becomes a source of peace and spiritual nourishment. Those who find they are unable to do without it naturally tend to become Friends. Those who like to come sometimes, but prefer other kinds of worship, are usually friends of Friends. Sitting on my bench, it was not yet clear whether I would fall into either of those groups, for I had no experience of silence whatsoever. So what did I do?

First, I suppose, I did not actually do anything, but something happened. It was not terribly sensational. It was simply the consequence of being well brought up and put in a social situation in which I did not want to make an exhibition of myself. There was no opportunity to stand up and stretch, chat to my neighbour, chuckle, yawn, snore, snort, wriggle, stretch out on the bench, keep turning round to see who was behind me, or do anything that might make a noise and disturb the other people in whatever it was they were doing. I knew they were supposed to be worshipping God, but there was precious little evidence of that happening. Being deprived of movement, and not a little frightened lest I be responsible for a grunt or a squeak or a sniff that would draw all the eyes in the meeting house upon me, I settled myself as comfortably as I could for a long wait and began to take stock of my surroundings. In the years that followed I was to become completely at home in the atmosphere I experienced that day, but on the first occasion I don't think I did very much worshipping.

I was not used to sitting totally still for a long period of time, so the meeting was quite an experience for me. I remember my astonishment at how I seemed far more aware than usual of all the messages my senses were giving me. It also dawned on me that these messages were there all the time, but I was normally far too busy to pay attention to them.

I was surprised to find the light remarkable, and I do not mean the spiritual variety Quakers like to go on about. After a good few years of membership in the Society of Friends, I have clocked up a pretty fair total of meeting houses attended, and I get the feeling that there is something about the windows that are very important. In meeting houses, they tend to be high up in the eaves, so that shafts of sunlight cascade to the floor, warming the worshipping Friends, colouring the posy of flowers on the central table, or burnishing the gold lettering on the spine of the Bible which also lies there.

Whether or not it was felt in former times that if you had windows to gaze out of, you would lose the art of inward retirement and spend too much time admiring the creation to take notice of the creator, I don't know. When the day is grey or dim, as it usually is in England, and the meeting house has a pitched roof or ceiling, you look up not to obscurity, but to as much clarity as the architecture can scoop out of the day. I do not now remember the state of the weather the day I first went to meeting, but I certainly noticed the light.

John Punshon, 1987

John Punshon's assertion that 'Those who find they are unable to do without it naturally tend to become Friends' is unquestionably true. There is something attractive, almost addictive for many people in the unplanned balance of silence and speech which makes up a Quaker meeting. Since every gathering is utterly distinct from every other, there is rarely anything predictable or stale, and a powerful meeting defies analysis. Quaker writers have often had success, however, in examining the constituent parts. In particular, they have written a good deal about ministry which, as we saw in the Introduction, is the word given by Quakers to the spontaneous speaking which often takes place during Meeting for Worship.

The meeting for worship is, however, not all silence. The silence is preparation. One listens before one speaks. There is a quickening power in living silence, though, of course, dead silence tends to kill out freshness and spontaneity. Where the temperature and atmosphere of the group are right, the one who prays or speaks is not just a solitary individual saying words. He becomes in some real sense a voice for the cooperating group. There is more in his words than he consciously knows or explicitly thinks out. There is a certain team-effect, a cumulative power, such as one often sees when the expectant attitude of an audience in some moment of crisis suddenly raises an orator to a height of eloquence which he could never reach by himself and perhaps never does reach on any other occasion.

Rufus M. Jones, 1927

Ministry is what is on one's soul, and it can be in direct contradiction to what is on one's mind. It's what the Inner Light gently pushes you toward or suddenly dumps in your lap. It is rooted in the eternity, divinity, and selflessness of the Inner Light; not in the worldly, egoistic functions of the conscious mind.

Marrianne McMullen, 1987

The first time I was led to minister I felt I was being battered with pillows; I did not follow the leading, and came away from Meeting utterly drained by the effort of resisting. Over the years the leading became more understandable: the words were there and would not go away, and my heart beat faster; I learned only to minister when I truly felt led. There is no one single way of testing this leading. Because we operate in varied ways we feel the nudge in different ways and have to learn our own signals. For example, I have never 'found myself on my feet' in the way that some Friends have described. For me there is always a conscious choice. I think that our experience of following leadings develops; more recently I have only felt the beating heart after I've spoken, which is rather disconcerting; I now have to test the leading less physically and more inwardly.

Beth Allen, 2007

I saw by the Light and Spirit of Christ Jesus that a minister of the word of God must wait for the word and counsel of God, and have the word before he can minister to edification and comfort of the people. I saw likewise by the same spirit that if a minister did not keep down in his mind to the word of life and dwell with it he would be liable to receive false conceptions, and have false impressions on his mind, and so take hold of the wrong thing and be deceived. For Satan transforms himself to the likeness of an angel of light to cast mists and fogs over the understanding, and he endeavours to blind the mind that the light of the glorious gospel should not be perceived. I likewise saw that, if a minister waited for the word, and had the word of the Lord, he would speak such things as were suitable to the states of the people he minis-tered among, his doctrine would be understood and his words would be felt by them, and they would be benefited, for in the word of life there is food for all states and growths of Christians.

Josiah Langdale, c1723

Brevity, earnestness, sincerity – and frequently a lack of polish – char-acterize the best Quaker speaking. The words should rise like a shaggy crag upthrust from the surface of silence, under the pressure of river power and yearning, contrition, and wonder. But on the other hand the words should not rise up like a shaggy crag. They should not break the silence, but continue it. For the Divine Life who is ministering through the medium of silence is the same Life as is now ministering through words. And when such words are truly spoken 'in the Life', then when such words cease, the uninterrupted silence and worship continue, for silence and words have been of one texture, one piece. Second and third speakers only continue the enhancement of the moving Presence, until a climax is reached, and the discerning head of the meeting knows when to break it.

Thomas R. Kelly, 1940

As the meeting continues in this gathered, receptive state, someone may be moved to rise and speak a few words or offer a prayer. If we allow the 'magic' of the gathered meeting to do its work in us, even our listening takes on a different quality as we absorb the words rather than merely hearing and reacting to them. It is not uncommon for the message to parallel or to complement our own stream of thought or for it to speak directly to some problem or question within us. Perhaps the message may help to gather and focus us so that we may enter even more deeply into the transforming communion which surrounds us. Sometimes the message is difficult to hear; perhaps the speaker is saying something we would rather not think about. Yet, if we absorb the words rather than react to them, we may discover that God is using these words to open us to some blind spot or prejudice or lack of faithfulness – and that can be painful. Even if the message is long and tedious, or if it seems inappropriate to us, we can still remain in that special state of consciousness which allows us to stay focused on God while at the same time surrounding the speaker and the rest of the meeting with love and light.

William Taber, 1992

And the end of words is to bring men to the knowledge of things beyond what words can utter. So, learn of the Lord to make a right use of the Scriptures: which is by esteeming them in their right place, and prizing that above them which is above them.

Isaac Penington, undated letter

We do not regard those who have the gift of 'ministry' as infallible, or even as necessarily closer to God than many of the silent worshippers who form the great majority in every congregation. We feel that the gift is from above, and that on all of us lies the responsibility of being open to it, willing to receive it, should it be bestowed, and to use it faithfully while entrusted with it. But we fully recognise that to do this perfectly requires a continual submission of the will, and an unceasing watchfulness. We know that to 'keep close to the gift' is not an easy thing. We know that the singleness of eye which alone can enable any one always to discern between the immediate guidance of the Divine Spirit and the mere promptings of our own hearts, is not attained without much patience, and a diligent and persevering use of all the means of instruction provided for us. We recognise the value of such corrections even as may come through the minds of others; for, although the servant is responsible only to his own Master, and we desire earnestly to beware of any dependence on each other in such matters, yet it has (as I have already mentioned) been thought right that some Friends should be specially appointed to watch over the ministers in the exercise of their gift. The 'elders', to whom this task is entrusted, do in fact often offer not only encouragement or counsel, but at times admonition and even rebuke, when they believe it to be needed. It is thus clear that the Society has always held with the Apostle Paul that 'the spirits of the prophets are subject to the prophets'. The great care and caution shown in all the arrangements of the Society with respect to ministry bear witness to its recognition of the deep truth, that, the more precious the treasure, the more serious the risks to which the earthen vessels enclosing it are exposed.

Caroline Stephen, 1890

The last extract was written at a time when those who ministered in Quaker meetings were appointed to do so for fixed periods. It is different now. Anyone can minister in a Meeting for Worship, be they

Friend, friend or visitor. Quakers hold, too, that ministry is not limited to those who actually speak. The ministry of the silent worshippers is as vital as that of the vocal ones. This truly is a communal event.

And what of the participants of the meeting? How do they sit? Are they always able easily to centre themselves? What are they thinking about? Are there any rules?

I began to get still. But I had no more commenced than a perfect pandemonium of voices reached my ears, a thousand clamouring notes from without and within, until I could hear nothing but their noise and din. Some of them were my own voice, some were my own questions, some of them were my very prayers. Others were the suggestions of the tempter, and the voices of the world's turmoil. Never before did there seem to be so many things to be done, to be said, to be thought; and in every direction I was pushed and pulled, and greeted with noisy acclamations of unspeakable unrest. It seemed necessary for me to listen to some of them, and to answer some of them, but God said, 'Be still, and know that I am God'. Then came the conflict of thoughts for the morrow, and its duties and cares; but God said 'Be still'. And as I listened, and slowly learnt to obey, and shut my ears to every sound, I found, after a while, that when the other voices ceased, or I ceased to hear them, there was a still, small voice in the depths of my being that began to speak with an inexpressible tenderness, power and comfort.

John Edward Southall (attributed), c1900

And now I must be honest and admit to much of what I actually do in meeting. Certainly I pray and meditate, but I also do many other things. I daydream. I sing silently or hum inaudible tunes. On occasion I have gone to sleep, so I suppose slumber would be one of my meeting activities. I carry a little Bible in my jacket pocket, and though it is for reference, I must own up to reading it. There are other things Friends read, but that is my bag.

I often get bored. I fidget. I have to cope with my own body and its periodic discomfort. I shut my eyes and then open them and then shut them again for no very good reason. I wonder whether X wears a wig or what brand of toothpaste Y prefers or whatever induced K and L to marry. I think about work, about other people, about personal problems and relationships. I grumble a bit to myself, since I talk to myself a lot anyway. I periodically attempt to clear my mind, but much of the time I simply think. I speculate about theology but usually manage to make it subservient to my worship. I also think about the government and the state of the world, and I make it a principle to give serious and sympathetic consideration to all the spoken ministry.

So beginners and visitors to Friends meetings who are unaccustomed to the silence need to realise that the Quakers are doing just what they are doing. There is no secret way of coping with silence. You just get on with it. I do not wish to leave the impression that this is all there is, though. That would be very far from the truth. But we do not need to enter murky theological waters, we need simply to register that if meeting were nothing more than sitting in silence having pleasant but wandering thoughts, Quaker worship would be a wool-gathering farce.

John Punshon, 1987

Some think, through a mistaken judgment, that they must be doing something every meeting, (like the preachers of the letter, who must either be singing, preaching or praying all the time) and by such a conduct they lose their interest and place in the hearts of friends by too long and too frequent appearing in both preaching and prayer: For the avoiding of which, keep close to thy gift, intently waiting to know thy place, both when to speak and when to be silent; and when thou speakest, begin under a sense of divine influence, whether it be in preaching or praying; and without it, do not either preach or pray.

Samuel Bownas, 1750

The intent of all speaking is to bring into the life, and to walk in, and to possess the same, and to live in and enjoy it, and to feel God's presence.

George Fox, 1657

Heed not distressing thoughts when they rise ever so strongly in thee; fear them not, but be still awhile, not believing in the power which thou feelest they have over thee, and it will fall on a sudden. It is good for thy spirit and greatly to thy advantage to be much and variously exercised by the Lord. Thou dost not know what the Lord hath already done and what he is yet doing for thee therein.

Isaac Penington, undated letter

In the gathered meeting the sense is present that a new Life and Power has entered our midst. And we know not only that we stand erect in the holy Presence, but also that others sitting with us are experiencing the same exaltation and access of power. We may not know these our neighbours in any outwardly intimate sense, but we now know them, as it were, from within, and they know us in the same way, as souls now alive in the same areas and as blended into the body of Christ, which is His church. Again and again this community of life and guidance from the Presence in the midst is made clear by the way the spoken words uttered in the meeting join on to one another and to our inward thoughts. This, I presume, has been a frequent experience for us all, as a common life and current sweeps through all. We are in communication with one another because we are being communicated to, and through, by the Divine Presence. Such indeed is a taste of 'the communion of saints'.

John Hughes once told of two Friends sitting side by side in such a gathered meeting. The secret currents of worship flowed with power and then encountered a check. One man moved nervously but did not rise to his feet. Finally the other Friend arose and spoke a few words of searching power, and the meeting proceeded in a sense of covering. After the meeting had broken, the man who had spoken nudged his silent neighbour and said, 'Next time, Henry, say it yourself'.

But our interest in the gathered meeting is not in such striking side-phenomena as lift eyebrows of doubting Thomases, but in the central fact of the over-shadowing presence of the Eternal One. For it is God Himself who graciously reveals Himself in such holy times. The gathered meeting, as group mysticism, shows all the four characteristics which William James applies to mystic states, namely, indescribability, a knowledge-quality, transiency, passivity.

The experience is ineffable, it is not completely describable in words. We live through such hours of expanded vision, yet never can we communicate to another all that wonder and power and life and recreation which we knew when swept along in the immediacy of the Divine Presence. To an absent friend we can only say what Philip said to Nathaniel concerning Jesus, 'Come and see'. And such must always be the report of any experience of God, by individuals or in groups. 'He is wonder and joy, judgment and power. And he is more than all these. Come and see.'

Thomas R. Kelly, 1940

There are customs, but certainly no rules. It is generally agreed that a person will not minister more than once in a meeting. It is accepted that a period of silence will always follow a vocal contribution – this is no place for riposte, argument, conversation or debate. And worshippers sit exactly as they wish, with eyes open or closed depending on their mood.

Some people find it helps to have a model, a guide to centring down, so here is a useful suggested practice – by no means the only one – described by Diana Lampen:

Be sure you are sitting comfortably. It is good to have a straight back – 'straight', not rigid. Plant your feet flat on the floor. Rest your hands loosely in your lap. Then go through the body, starting with the feet, and tighten then release each part in turn. Check that you are not frowning or tensing your jaw. When you have gone through the whole body, mentally visit each part again and check that it is still relaxed. Pay special attention to your 'tension trouble spots' such as the shoulders.

Then bring your awareness to just outside your nostrils and simply feel the breath. Don't interfere at all, just observe each breath come and each breath go, noting the stronger sensation of the cooler in-breath in the nostrils, the more subtle sensation of the warmer out-breath, and the pauses. The mind will still wander at first. Don't be annoyed – that sets up tension! Just let the thought go, focus on the breath again and continue watching.

When you have mastered this watching with total attention, try to be also aware of the slight movements in the body caused by the breath, holding in your awareness at the same time the ebb and flow of air in the nostrils and the gentle body movements. Can you now become aware too of the stillness in the body?

[...] Once you are able to focus with full attention on the breath, you can add unspoken words which you 'say' in time to each breath: one word or syllable on the inhalation, another on the exhalation. I often recommend the phrase 'Be still'. [...] In your mind say 'Be' as you inhale, and "still" as you breathe out. Do this again and again until you realise you can let go of the words and open yourself to the Light.

Diana Lampen, 2008

People sometimes confuse the quiet stillness of a Meeting for Worship with meditation. While meditative techniques are often used by Friends in meeting, the communal nature of the activity and the frequent use of speech make it qualitatively different. And, self-evidently, it is impossible to hold a Quaker meeting on your own.

As many candles lighted, and put in one place, do greatly augment the light, and make it more to shine forth, so when many are gathered together into the same life, there is more of the glory of God, and his power appears, to the refreshment of each individual; for that he partakes not only of the light and life raised in himself, but in all the rest.

Robert Barclay, 1678

Nevertheless, many Friends use their Meeting for Worship for personal prayer. Quakers have not written a great deal about this subject, and no two members of the Religious Society of Friends are likely to approach prayer in exactly the same way.

Prayer is an exercise of the spirit, as thought is of the mind. To pray about anything is to use the powers of the spirit on it, just as to think clearly is to use our mental powers. For the best solution of every problem, the best carrying out of every action, both thought and prayer are necessary. [...] To pray about any day's work does not mean to ask success in it. It means, first, to realise my own inability to do even a familiar job, as it truly should be done, unless I am in touch with eternity, unless I do it 'unto God', unless I have the Father with me. It means to see 'my' work as part of a whole, to see 'myself' as not mattering much, but my faith, the energy, will and striving, which I put into the work, as mattering a great deal. My faith is the point in me at which God comes into my work; through faith the work is given dignity and value. And if, through some weakness of mine, or fault of others, or just 'unavoidable circumstances', the work seems a failure, yet prayer is not wasted when it is unanswered, any more than love is wasted when it is unreturned.

Mary F. Smith, 1936

One of the questions which often worries newcomers and established Quakers alike is that of prayer. What is prayer and what do we do when we pray?

Isaac Penington described prayer as the 'breathing of the child to the Father which begat it'. It may be described as a human response to the world around; an awareness of ourselves, of others, of that power most of us call God, working in the world, loving it, transforming it, and empowering us. The problem is that we often think of prayers in the plural rather than prayer in general. Prayers seem to be formulas, words we recite; prayer on the contrary is a state of awareness where not even words may be necessary.

I once met a Benedictine monk who was interested in the Religious Society of Friends. His problem was that he was tired of the repetition of words. There is a Catholic form of spirituality which believes that prayer is like a boat and that we can sail upon the words, even when we feel we should prefer to remain in port. The words help us along. There is good insight in this. But there are times when weariness takes over. This monk and I agreed that it would be nice if there could be a sort of silent mass. After all, what are the ingredients of the mass? There is a general preparation and awareness of our shortcomings (confession), prayers to the glory of God, ministry of the word, the creed, prayers on behalf of the world and the people, sharing of the peace, the preparation of gifts and thanksgiving for them, prayers of consecration, communion, thanksgiving for communion, and the dismissal.

Yet, however formal all these may appear, they have their counterpart in everyday life. We prepare ourselves for meeting, aware of how we have not lived up to our ideals during the week. We open ourselves up to the world of creation, often with no more than a 'thank you', just as in confession we may have been able to utter no more than 'I'm sorry, I've done it again'. We bring to mind the needs of our friends, problems in the world, we think of people who have meant much to us. Thinking lovingly is a form of prayer. Of course Quakers do not recite creeds, even silent ones, but they are mindful of their basic convictions, their place in the world, and how the world might be made more holy by their actions and their love.

Harvey Gillman, 1988

The place of prayer is a precious habitation; for I now saw that the prayers of the saints were precious incense; and a trumpet was given to me that I might sound forth this language; that the children might hear it and be invited together to this precious habitation, where the prayers of the saints, as sweet incense, arise before the throne of God and the Lamb. I saw this habitation to be safe, to be inwardly quiet when there were great stirrings and commotions in the world.

John Woolman, published 1772

In worship we have our neighbors to right and left, before and behind, yet the Eternal Presence is over all and beneath all. Worship does not consist in achieving a mental state of concentrated isolation from one's fellows. But in the depth of common worship it is as if we found our separate lives were all one life, within whom we live and move and have our being.

Thomas R. Kelly, 1938

Be still and cool in thy own mind and spirit from thy own thoughts, and then thou wilt feel the principle of God to turn thy mind to the Lord God, whereby thou wilt receive his strength and power from whence life comes, to allay all tempests, against blusterings and storms. That is it which moulds up into patience, into innocency, into soberness, into stillness, into stayedness, into quietness, up to God, with his power.

George Fox, published 1694

I have sometimes thought that at the end of a Meeting, Friends rather resemble an audience leaving a concert hall after a musical recital. One notices the same stretching of muscles, mental as well as physical, the same sense of coming back to earth, with tacit agreement that something worthwhile has been satisfactorily completed. Of course there is one obvious difference: no applause. That is because there is no distinction between audience and performers; we were all involved. (Quakers didn't abolish the priesthood [. . .] – they abolished the laity.)

Smiles are passed around, while the Clerk reads out the notices that bring us back to everyday practicalities. As Friends stand up and start to leave the room a few words may be exchanged about the ministry (or the music), as if to confirm that an experience has been shared, and it was in some sense a valid one (or perhaps not). Not many words though, because the experience cannot be captured in words, it may easily be distorted, and that too is recognised. A dispassionate critique might come later, if at all. Just now, as we all make our way towards coffee and sociability, the music, the silence, is still with us. Was it grandiloquent Verdi today, or provocative Mahler, delicately intricate Chopin or rumbustuous Gershwin? There are so many different kinds of enrichment in the concert hall, and in the Meeting House.

Let's not exaggerate. Not every Meeting for Worship is a powerful experience. When we are held by the silent music we feel it and are grateful, but we do not expect to feel it for the whole hour every Sunday. For that matter I don't suppose each churchgoer comes away from every Communion or Mass overwhelmed by the Transcendental Mystery of the Body and Blood of Christ. Not every meal is a banquet. Sometimes a Meeting that for one person is intensely moving has little or no impact on the person sitting adjacent. But there are other occasions when the whole gathering seems to be feeling and experiencing something together, in unity. Those are the unforgettable Meetings. They are what we call a 'Gathered Meeting'.

Philip Rack, 2002

The religious experiences in meetings which Philip Rack refers to as 'unforgettable' are difficult to explain. Here is Thomas Kelly, a mystical American writer whose concise, penetrating descriptions of the religious life have become classics of Quaker literature. He perhaps comes closer than anyone to conveying the heady feeling of a 'gathered' or 'covered' meeting.

In the practice of group worship on the basis of silence come special times when the electric hush and solemnity and depth of power steals over the worshippers. A blanket of divine covering comes over the room, a stillness that can be felt is over all, and the worshippers are gathered into a unity and synthesis of life which is amazing indeed. A quickening Presence pervades us, breaking down some part of the special privacy and isolation of our individual lives and blending our spirits within a superindividual Life and Power.

An objective, dynamic Presence enfolds us all, nourishes our souls, speaks glad, unutterable comfort within us, and quickens us in depths that had before been slumbering. The Burning Bush has been kindled in our midst, and we stand together on holy ground.

Thomas R. Kelly, 1940

When a Meeting for Worship comes to an end, we must hope that those who have attended it have found meaning. As they leave the meeting house, that meaning can turn to purpose. And so, with meaning and purpose in their lives, Quakers find themselves not just willing, not just able, but impelled to work for change in the world. For them, through the Meeting for Worship, meaning has become purpose and purpose has become meaning. Later in this book, we explore the results of such God-given resolve.

Friends, keep your meetings in the power of God, and in his wisdom, (by which all things were made), and in the love of God, that by that ye may order all to his glory. And when Friends have finished their business, sit down and continue awhile quietly, and wait upon the Lord to feel him: and go not beyond the power, but keep in the power, by which God Almighty may be felt among you. For the power will bruise the head of the serpent, and all false and contrary heads; this blessed seed, as he is the head of the church, so he is also the head of every member of his body. And so, by the power of the Lord ye come to love truth, and love Jesus Christ, and love holiness; and by the power ye come to love God, and praise him, and bless him, and magnify him, who lives forevermore. For the power of the Lord will work through all, if that ye follow it.

George Fox, undated epistle

ADVICES AND QUERIES

As we have seen, Quakers have no creed. There is no dotted line that a newcomer has to sign, no statement of belief, no exam. They do not proclaim a better life for you if you follow them. What Quakers offer is a journey: a voyage of spiritual discovery undertaken with friends, which is reflected in turn in their journeys. They offer a faith which is based on personal experience, and which contains no dogma.

It follows from all this that Quakers are unlikely to take kindly to a rule book, or to an agreed prescription for the maintenance of an unsullied life. Yet, perhaps surprisingly, Friends do publish a pocket-sized volume which many carry around with them and which they find to be of great personal help. It is a set of forty-two paragraphs containing thoughtful advice and some distinctly awkward questions. Its introduction declares it to be 'for the comfort and discomfort of Friends'. It is called *Advices & Queries* and Quakers love it.

Open it anywhere, and this little book's shrewdness, wisdom and religious intelligence sparkle on the page. All Friends have their favourite passages, often culled from the queries, echoing George Fox's 'What canst thou say?' Quotations from *Advices & Queries* tend to pepper Quaker conversation: 'live adventurously'; 'a simple lifestyle freely chosen is a source of strength'; 'come to meeting for worship with heart and mind prepared'; 'think it possible that you may be mistaken'. Friends do not believe that anyone can achieve total adherence to the principles expressed here, but a lot of them like to try.

Advices & Queries in its present form is rewritten and updated every thirty or forty years, so it is less likely to become irrelevant or out of touch. Each country has its own version of the book, and there are some gems in the *A & Qs*, as Quakers tend to call them, of other editions. The version which follows is British. It has been current among Friends in Britain since 1995.

1. Take heed, dear Friends, to the promptings of love and truth in your hearts. Trust them as the leadings of God whose Light shows us our darkness and brings us to new life.

2. Bring the whole of your life under the ordering of the spirit of Christ. Are you open to the healing power of God's love? Cherish that of God within you, so that this love may grow in you and guide you. Let your worship and your daily life enrich each other. Treasure your experience of God, however it comes to you. Remember that Christianity is not a notion but a way.

3. Do you try to set aside times of quiet for openness to the Holy Spirit? All of us need to find a way into silence which allows us to deepen our awareness of the divine and to find the inward source of our strength. Seek to know an inward stillness, even amid the activities of daily life. Do you encourage in yourself and in others a habit of dependence on God's guidance for each day? Hold yourself and others in the Light, knowing that all are cherished by God.

4. The Religious Society of Friends is rooted in Christianity and has always found inspiration in the life and teachings of Jesus. How do you interpret your faith in the light of this heritage? How does Jesus speak to you today? Are you following Jesus' example of love in action? Are you learning from his life the reality and cost of obedience to God? How does his relationship with God challenge and inspire you?

5. Take time to learn about other people's experiences of the Light. Remember the importance of the Bible, the writings of Friends and all writings which reveal the ways of God. As you learn from others, can you in turn give freely from what you have gained? While respecting the experiences and opinions of others, do not

be afraid to say what you have found and what you value. Appreciate that doubt and questioning can also lead to spiritual growth and to a greater awareness of the Light that is in us all.

6. Do you work gladly with other religious groups in the pursuit of common goals? While remaining faithful to Quaker insights, try to enter imaginatively into the life and witness of other communities of faith, creating together the bonds of friendship.

7. Be aware of the spirit of God at work in the ordinary activities and experience of your daily life. Spiritual learning continues throughout life, and often in unexpected ways. There is inspiration to be found all around us, in the natural world, in the sciences and arts, in our work and friendships, in our sorrows as well as in our joys. Are you open to new light, from whatever source it may come? Do you approach new ideas with discernment?

8. Worship is our response to an awareness of God. We can worship alone, but when we join with others in expectant waiting we may discover a deeper sense of God's presence. We seek a gathered stillness in our meetings for worship so that all may feel the power of God's love drawing us together and leading us.

9. In worship we enter with reverence into communion with God and respond to the promptings of the Holy Spirit. Come to meeting for worship with heart and mind prepared. Yield yourself and all your outward concerns to God's guidance so that you may find 'the evil weakening in you and the good raised up'.

10. Come regularly to meeting for worship even when you are angry, depressed, tired or spiritually cold. In the silence ask for and accept the prayerful support of others joined with you in worship. Try to find a spiritual wholeness which encompasses suffering as well as thankfulness and joy. Prayer, springing from a deep place in the heart, may bring healing and unity as nothing else can. Let meeting for worship nourish your whole life.

11. Be honest with yourself. What unpalatable truths might you be evading? When you recognise your shortcomings, do not let that discourage you. In worship together we can find the

assurance of God's love and the strength to go on with renewed courage.

12. When you are preoccupied and distracted in meeting let wayward and disturbing thoughts give way quietly to your awareness of God's presence among us and in the world. Receive the vocal ministry of others in a tender and creative spirit. Reach for the meaning deep within it, recognising that even if it is not God's word for you, it may be so for others. Remember that we all share responsibility for the meeting for worship whether our ministry is in silence or through the spoken word.

13. Do not assume that vocal ministry is never to be your part. Faithfulness and sincerity in speaking, even very briefly, may open the way to fuller ministry from others. When prompted to speak, wait patiently to know that the leading and the time are right, but do not let a sense of your own unworthiness hold you back. Pray that your ministry may arise from deep experience, and trust that words will be given to you. Try to speak audibly and distinctly, and with sensitivity to the needs of others. Beware of speaking predictably or too often, and of making additions towards the end of a meeting when it was well left before.

14. Are your meetings for church affairs held in a spirit of worship and in dependence on the guidance of God? Remember that we do not seek a majority decision nor even consensus. As we wait patiently for divine guidance our experience is that the right way will open and we shall be led into unity.

15. Do you take part as often as you can in meetings for church affairs? Are you familiar enough with our church government to contribute to its disciplined processes? Do you consider difficult questions with an informed mind as well as a generous and loving spirit? Are you prepared to let your insights and personal wishes take their place alongside those of others or be set aside as the meeting seeks the right way forward? If you cannot attend, uphold the meeting prayerfully.

16. Do you welcome the diversity of culture, language and expressions of faith in our yearly meeting and in the world community of Friends? Seek to increase your understanding and to gain from this rich heritage and wide range of spiritual insights. Uphold your own and other yearly meetings in your prayers.

17. Do you respect that of God in everyone though it may be expressed in unfamiliar ways or be difficult to discern? Each of us has a particular experience of God and each must find the way to be true to it. When words are strange or disturbing to you, try to sense where they come from and what has nourished the lives of others. Listen patiently and seek the truth which other people's opinions may contain for you. Avoid hurtful criticism and provocative language. Do not allow the strength of your convictions to betray you into making statements or allegations that are unfair or untrue. Think it possible that you may be mistaken.

18. How can we make the meeting a community in which each person is accepted and nurtured, and strangers are welcome? Seek to know one another in the things which are eternal, bear the burden of each other's failings and pray for one another. As we enter with tender sympathy into the joys and sorrows of each other's lives, ready to give help and to receive it, our meeting can be a channel for God's love and forgiveness.

19. Rejoice in the presence of children and young people in your meeting and recognise the gifts they bring. Remember that the meeting as a whole shares a responsibility for every child in its care. Seek for them as for yourself a full development of God's gifts and the abundant life Jesus tells us can be ours. How do you share your deepest beliefs with them, while leaving them free to develop as the spirit of God may lead them? Do you invite them to share their insights with you? Are you ready both to learn from them and to accept your responsibilities towards them?

20. Do you give sufficient time to sharing with others in the meeting, both newcomers and long-time members, your understanding of worship, of service, and of commitment to the Society's witness?

Do you give a right proportion of your money to support Quaker work?

21. Do you cherish your friendships, so that they grow in depth and understanding and mutual respect? In close relationships we may risk pain as well as finding joy. When experiencing great happiness or great hurt we may be more open to the working of the Spirit.

22. Respect the wide diversity among us in our lives and relationships. Refrain from making prejudiced judgments about the life journeys of others. Do you foster the spirit of mutual understanding and forgiveness which our discipleship asks of us? Remember that each one of us is unique, precious, a child of God.

23. Marriage has always been regarded by Friends as a religious commitment rather than a merely civil contract. Both partners should offer with God's help an intention to cherish one another for life. Remember that happiness depends on an understanding and steadfast love on both sides. In times of difficulty remind yourself of the value of prayer, of perseverance and of a sense of humour.

24. Children and young people need love and stability. Are we doing all we can to uphold and sustain parents and others who carry the responsibility for providing this care?

25. A long-term relationship brings tensions as well as fulfilment. If your relationship with your partner is under strain, seek help in understanding the other's point of view and in exploring your own feelings, which may be powerful and destructive. Consider the wishes and feelings of any children involved, and remember their enduring need for love and security. Seek God's guidance. If you undergo the distress of separation or divorce, try to maintain some compassionate communication so that arrangements can be made with the minimum of bitterness.

26. Do you recognise the needs and gifts of each member of your family and household, not forgetting your own? Try to make your home a place of loving friendship and enjoyment, where all who live or visit may find the peace and refreshment of God's presence.

27. Live adventurously. When choices arise, do you take the way that offers the fullest opportunity for the use of your gifts in the service of God and the community? Let your life speak. When decisions have to be made, are you ready to join with others in seeking clearness, asking for God's guidance and offering counsel to one another?

28. Every stage of our lives offers fresh opportunities. Responding to divine guidance, try to discern the right time to undertake or relinquish responsibilities without undue pride or guilt. Attend to what love requires of you, which may not be great busyness.

29. Approach old age with courage and hope. As far as possible, make arrangements for your care in good time, so that an undue burden does not fall on others. Although old age may bring increasing disability and loneliness, it can also bring serenity, detachment and wisdom. Pray that in your final years you may be enabled to find new ways of receiving and reflecting God's love.

30. Are you able to contemplate your death and the death of those closest to you? Accepting the fact of death, we are freed to live more fully. In bereavement, give yourself time to grieve. When others mourn, let your love embrace them.

31. We are called to live 'in the virtue of that life and power that takes away the occasion of all wars'. Do you faithfully maintain our testimony that war and the preparation for war are inconsistent with the spirit of Christ? Search out whatever in your own way of life may contain the seeds of war. Stand firm in our testimony, even when others commit or prepare to commit acts of violence, yet always remember that they too are children of God.

32. Bring into God's light those emotions, attitudes and prejudices in yourself which lie at the root of destructive conflict, acknowledging your need for forgiveness and grace. In what ways are you involved in the work of reconciliation between individuals, groups and nations?

33. Are you alert to practices here and throughout the world which discriminate against people on the basis of who or what they are

or because of their beliefs? Bear witness to the humanity of all people, including those who break society's conventions or its laws. Try to discern new growing points in social and economic life. Seek to understand the causes of injustice, social unrest and fear. Are you working to bring about a just and compassionate society which allows everyone to develop their capacities and fosters the desire to serve?

34. Remember your responsibilities as a citizen for the conduct of local, national, and international affairs. Do not shrink from the time and effort your involvement may demand.

35. Respect the laws of the state but let your first loyalty be to God's purposes. If you feel impelled by strong conviction to break the law, search your conscience deeply. Ask your meeting for the prayerful support which will give you strength as a right way becomes clear.

36. Do you uphold those who are acting under concern, even if their way is not yours? Can you lay aside your own wishes and prejudices while seeking with others to find God's will for them?

37. Are you honest and truthful in all you say and do? Do you maintain strict integrity in business transactions and in your dealings with individuals and organisations? Do you use money and information entrusted to you with discretion and responsibility? Taking oaths implies a double standard of truth; in choosing to affirm instead, be aware of the claim to integrity that you are making.

38. If pressure is brought upon you to lower your standard of integrity, are you prepared to resist it? Our responsibilities to God and our neighbour may involve us in taking unpopular stands. Do not let the desire to be sociable, or the fear of seeming peculiar, determine your decisions.

39. Consider which of the ways to happiness offered by society are truly fulfilling and which are potentially corrupting and destructive. Be discriminating when choosing means of entertainment and information. Resist the desire to acquire possessions or income through unethical investment, speculation or games of chance.

40. In view of the harm done by the use of alcohol, tobacco and other habit-forming drugs, consider whether you should limit your use of them or refrain from using them altogether. Remember that any use of alcohol or drugs may impair judgment and put both the user and others in danger.

41. Try to live simply. A simple lifestyle freely chosen is a source of strength. Do not be persuaded into buying what you do not need or cannot afford. Do you keep yourself informed about the effects your style of living is having on the global economy and environment?

42. We do not own the world, and its riches are not ours to dispose of at will. Show a loving consideration for all creatures, and seek to maintain the beauty and variety of the world. Work to ensure that our increasing power over nature is used responsibly, with reverence for life. Rejoice in the splendour of God's continuing creation.

QUAKER JOURNALS 1: GEORGE FOX

It was customary among Friends during the seventeenth and eighteenth centuries to write religious autobiographies. They called them journals, though they bore little resemblance either to diaries or to the practice of 'journalling' which is common today. They were often quite short and were intended for publication as a record of the spiritual development of the writer. There was rarely much in the way of personal detail – spouses and children were often left out entirely – because what mattered was to set down the author's journey in the spirit from infancy to the present.

Journals often appeared in diary form, but were invariably put together retrospectively and can contain a good deal of the wisdom of hindsight. The best of them, though, are outstanding documents, plainly written and epitomising their writers' commitment to simplicity in everything. Many contain deep spiritual insights couched in an honest and intimate style. Their insistence on truth can be very disarming.

The *Journal* of George Fox (1624–1691) was a big, impressive volume. Its original edition weighed in at four and a half pounds. Dictated during the last fifteen years of his life, it was published in 1694, three years after his death, and has never been out of print since. It paints a vivid image of the public man, and if we never quite meet in its pages the individual described by William Penn as 'meek, contented, modest, easy, steady, tender', we certainly do encounter 'an original, being no man's copy', as the same writer also characterised Fox. He was a man convinced he was right, and he could be intolerant, arrogant and uncompromising in his proclamation of the Quaker message.

Analysts have suggested that he may have been a depressive, and there are, at the very least, signs of eccentricity in the following extract from the

Journal, which is his entire entry for 1652, the year from which Quakers usually date their foundation. Perhaps the most important event of all takes place at the very beginning; Fox climbs to the top of Pendle Hill near Burnley in Lancashire and is profoundly moved by the sheer numbers of people whom he needs to convince of the Quaker message. Yet this seminal event merits not quite one paragraph. Small, almost insignificant happenings, on the other hand, are remembered with absolute clarity twenty-five years or more later – like the man in Kendal who offers him a smoke: 'I accepted his love, but did not receive his tobacco.'

If there is a theme running right through this year of Fox's life, it is the violence to which he is constantly subjected. Hardly a day goes by, it seems, without some outraged bruiser seeing fit to beat George up. Significantly, he does not fight back. He never trumpets his commitment to nonviolence in the *Journal*, yet his pacifism glows from every page. And we are left to wonder if the conversion of James Lancaster's wife, who bombards the founder of Quakerism with stones one day and yet suddenly seems convinced that he is right the next, may perhaps have had something to do with Fox's impressive lack of resistance to her onslaught.

Fox was not a typical Quaker, either then or now. He could be self-righteous, pig-headed and unbending. (It is difficult to imagine another Quaker describing anyone – which he does the priest called Lampitt here – as 'full of filth'.) Yet as a result of his energy, Friends began to travel away from Lancashire and Cumbria, where the movement began, and to proclaim their message across the whole country. Many of them were in their early twenties, a good number of them were women, and their vision had a freshness that was appealing in the turmoil following the English Civil War. Within thirty years, around one person in 130 in Britain was a Quaker.

As we travelled we came near a very great hill, called Pendle Hill, and I was moved of the Lord to go up to the top of it; which I did with difficulty, it was so very steep and high. When I was come to the top, I saw the sea bordering upon Lancashire. From the top of this hill the Lord let me see in what places he had a great people to be gathered. As I went down, I found a spring of water in the side of the hill, with which I refreshed myself, having eaten or drunk but little for several days before.

At night we came to an inn, and declared truth to the man of the house, and wrote a paper to the priests and professors, declaring the day of the Lord, and that Christ was come to teach people Himself, by His power and Spirit in their hearts, and to bring people off from all the world's ways and teachers, to His own free teaching, who had bought them, and was the Saviour of all them that believed in Him. The man of the house spread the paper abroad, and was mightily affected with the truth. Here the Lord opened unto me, and let me see a great people in white raiment by a river side, coming to the Lord; and the place that I saw them in was about Wensleydale and Sedbergh.

The next day we travelled on, and at night got a little fern or bracken to put under us, and lay upon a common. Next morning we reached a town, where Richard Farnsworth parted from me; and then I travelled alone again. I came up Wensleydale, and at the market town in that Dale, there was a lecture on the market-day. I went into the steeple-house; and after the priest had done I proclaimed the day of the Lord to the priest and people, warning them to turn from darkness to the Light, and from the power of Satan unto God, that they might come to know God and Christ aright, and to receive His teaching, who teacheth freely. Largely and freely did I declare the Word of life unto them, and had not much persecution there.

Afterwards I passed up the Dales, warning people to fear God, and preaching the everlasting gospel to them. In my way I came to a great house, where was a schoolmaster; and they got me into the house. I asked them questions about their religion and worship; and afterwards I declared the truth to them. They had me into a parlour, and locked me in, pretending that I was a young man that was mad, and had run away from my relations; and that they would keep me till they could send to them. But I soon convinced them of their mistake, and they let me forth, and would have had me to stay; but I was not to stay there.

Then having exhorted them to repentance, and directed them to the Light of Christ Jesus, that through it they might come unto Him and be saved, I passed from them, and came in the night to a little ale-house on a common, where there was a company of rude fellows drinking. Because I would not drink with them, they struck me with their clubs; but I reproved them, and brought them to be somewhat cooler; and then I walked out of the house upon the common in the night.

After some time one of these drunken fellows came out, and would have come close up to me, pretending to whisper to me; but I perceived he had a knife; and therefore I kept off him, and bade him repent, and fear God. So the Lord by His power preserved me from this wicked man; and he went into the house again. The next morning I went on through other Dales, warning and exhorting people every-where as I passed, to repent and turn to the Lord: and several were convinced. At one house that I came to, the man of the house (whom I afterwards found to be a kinsman of John Blakelin's) would have given me money, but I would not receive it.

The next day I went to a meeting at Justice Benson's, where I met a people that were separated from the public worship. This was the place I had seen, where a people came forth in white raiment. A large meeting it was, and the people were generally convinced; and they continue still a large meeting of Friends near Sedbergh; which was then first gathered through my ministry in the name of Jesus.

In the same week there was a great fair, at which servants used to be hired; and I declared the day of the Lord through the fair. After I had done so, I went into the steeple-house yard, and many of the people of the fair came thither to me, and abundance of priests and profes-sors. There I declared the everlasting truth of the Lord and the Word of life for several hours, showing that the Lord was come to teach His people Himself, and to bring them off from all the world's ways and teachers, to Christ, the true teacher, and the true way to God. I laid open their teachers, showing that they were like them that were of old condemned by the prophets, and by Christ, and by the apostles. I exhorted the people to come off from the temples made with hands; and wait to receive the Spirit of the Lord, that they might know themselves to be the temples of God.

Not one of the priests had power to open his mouth against what I declared: but at last a captain said, 'Why will you not go into the church? this is not a fit place to preach in.' I told him I denied their church. Then stood up Francis Howgill, who was preacher to a congregation. He had not seen me before; yet he undertook to answer that captain; and he soon put him to silence. Then said Francis Howgill of me, 'This man speaks with authority, and not as the scribes.'

After this, I opened to the people that that ground and house were no holier than another place; and that the house is not the Church, but the people, of whom Christ is the head. After awhile the priests came up to me, and I warned them to repent. One of them said I was mad; so they turned away. But many were convinced there that day, who were glad to hear the truth declared, and received it with joy. Amongst these was Captain Ward, who received the truth in the love of it, and lived and died in it.

The next First-day I came to Firbank chapel in Westmoreland, where Francis Howgill and John Audland had been preaching in the morning. The chapel was full of people, so that many could not get in. Francis said he thought I looked into the chapel, and his spirit was ready to fail, the Lord's power did so surprise him: but I did not look in. They made haste, and had quickly done, and they and some of the people went to dinner; but abundance stayed till they came again. John Blakelin and others came to me, and desired me not to reprove them publicly; for they were not parish-teachers, but pretty tender men. I could not tell them whether I should or no, though I had not at that time any drawings to declare publicly against them; but I said they must leave me to the Lord's movings.

While others were gone to dinner, I went to a brook, got a little water, and then came and sat down on the top of a rock hard by the chapel. In the afternoon the people gathered about me, with several of their preachers. It was judged there were above a thousand people; to whom I declared God's everlasting truth and Word of life freely and largely for about the space of three hours. I directed all to the Spirit of God in themselves; that they might be turned from darkness to Light, and believe in it; that they might become the children of it, and might be turned from the power of Satan unto God, and by the Spirit of truth might be led into all truth, and sensibly understand the words of the prophets, of Christ, and of the apostles; and might all come to know Christ to be their teacher to instruct them, their counsellor to direct them, their shepherd to feed them, their bishop to oversee them, and their prophet to open divine mysteries to them; and might know their bodies to be prepared, sanctified, and made fit temples for God and Christ to dwell in. In the openings of heavenly life I explained unto them the prophets, and the figures and shadows, and directed them to Christ, the substance. Then I opened the parables and sayings of Christ, and things that had been long hid.

Now there were many old people who went into the chapel and looked out at the windows, thinking it a strange thing to see a man preach on a hill, and not in their church, as they called it; whereupon I was moved to open to the people that the steeple-house, and the ground whereon it stood were no more holy than that mountain; and that those temples, which they called the dreadful houses of God were not set up by the command of God and of Christ; nor their priests called, as Aaron's priesthood was; nor their tithes appointed by God, as those amongst the Jews were; but that Christ was come, who ended both the temple and its worship, and the priests and their tithes; and that all should now hearken unto Him; for He said, 'Learn of me'; and God said of Him, 'This is my beloved Son, in whom I am well pleased; hear ye Him.'

I declared unto them that the Lord God had sent me to preach the everlasting gospel and Word of life amongst them, and to bring them off from all these temples, tithes, priests, and rudiments of the world, which had been instituted since the apostles' days, and had been set up by such as had erred from the Spirit and power the apostles were in.

Very largely was I opened at this meeting, and the Lord's convincing power accompanied my ministry, and reached the hearts of the people, whereby many were convinced; and all the teachers of that congregation (who were many) were convinced of God's everlasting truth.

At Kendal a meeting was held in the Town-hall. Several were convinced and many were loving. One whose name was Cock met me in the street and would have given me a roll of tobacco, for people were then much given to smoking. I accepted his love, but did not receive his tobacco.

Thence I went to Underbarrow, and several people going along with me, great reasonings I had with them, especially with Edward Burrough.

At night the priest and many professors came to the house; and a great deal of disputing I had with them. Supper being provided for the priest and the rest of the company, I had not freedom to eat with them; but told them that if they would appoint a meeting for the next day at the steeple-house, and acquaint the people with it, I might meet them. They had a great deal of reasoning about it; some being for, and some against it.

In the morning, after I had spoken to them again concerning the meeting, as I walked upon a bank by the house, there came several poor travellers, asking relief, who I saw were in necessity; and they gave them nothing, but said they were cheats. It grieved me to see such hard-heartedness amongst professors; whereupon, when they were gone in to their breakfast, I ran after the poor people about a quarter of a mile, and gave them some money.

Meanwhile some that were in the house, coming out, and seeing me a quarter of a mile off, said I could not have gone so far in such an instant, if I had not had wings. Hereupon the meeting was like to have been put by; for they were filled with such strange thoughts concerning me that many of them were against having a meeting with me.

I told them that I had run after those poor people to give them some money; being grieved at the hardheartedness of those who gave them nothing.

Then came Miles and Stephen Hubbersty, who, being more simple-hearted men, would have the meeting held. So to the chapel I went, and the priest came.

A great meeting there was, and the way of life and salvation was opened; and after awhile the priest fled away. Many of Crook and Underbarrow were convinced that day, received the Word of life, and stood fast in it under the teaching of Christ Jesus.

After I had declared the truth to them for some hours, and the meeting was ended, the chief constable and some other professors fell to reasoning with me in the chapel yard. Whereupon I took a Bible and opened the Scriptures, and dealt tenderly with them, as one would do with a child. They that were in the Light of Christ and Spirit of God knew when I spake Scripture, though I did not mention chapter and verse, after the priest's form, to them.

Then I went to an ale-house, to which many resorted betwixt the time of their morning and afternoon preaching, and had a great deal of reasoning with the people, declaring to them that God was come to teach His people, and to bring them off from the false teachers, such as the prophets, Christ, and the apostles cried against. Many received the Word of life at that time, and abode in it.

Thence I went to Ulverston, and so to Swarthmore to Judge Fell's; whither came up one Lampitt, a priest, who was a high notionist. With him I had much reasoning; for he talked of high notions and perfection, and thereby deceived the people. He would have owned me, but I could not own nor join with him, he was so full of filth. He said he was above John; and made as though he knew all things. But I told him that death reigned from Adam to Moses; that he was under death, and knew not Moses, for Moses saw the paradise of God; but he knew neither Moses nor the prophets nor John; for that crooked and rough nature stood in him, and the mountain of sin and corruption; and the way was not prepared in him for the Lord.

He confessed he had been under a cross in things; but now he could sing psalms, and do anything. I told him that now he could see a thief, and join hand in hand with him; but he could not preach

Moses, nor the prophets, nor John, nor Christ, except he were in the same Spirit that they were in.

Margaret Fell had been absent in the day-time; and at night her children told her that priest Lampitt and I had disagreed, which somewhat troubled her, because she was in profession with him; but he hid his dirty actions from them. At night we had much reasoning, and I declared the truth to her and her family. The next day Lampitt came again, and I had much discourse with him before Margaret Fell, who then clearly discerned the priest. A convincement of the Lord's truth came upon her and her family.

Soon after a day was to be observed for a humiliation, and Margaret Fell asked me to go with her to the steeple-house at Ulverston, for she was not wholly come off from them. I replied, 'I must do as I am ordered by the Lord.' So I left her, and walked into the fields; and the Word of the Lord came to me, saying, 'Go to the steeple-house after them.'

When I came, Lampitt was singing with his people; but his spirit was so foul, and the matter they sung so unsuitable to their states, that after they had done singing, I was moved of the Lord to speak to him and the people. The word of the Lord to them was, 'He is not a Jew that is one outwardly, but he is a Jew that is one inwardly, whose praise is not of man, but of God.'

As the Lord opened further, I showed them that God was come to teach His people by His Spirit, and to bring them off from all their old ways, religions, churches, and worships; for all their religions, worships, and ways were but talking with other men's words; but they were out of the life and Spirit which they were in who gave them forth.

Then cried out one, called Justice Sawrey, 'Take him away'; but Judge Fell's wife said to the officers, 'Let him alone; why may not he speak as well as any other?' Lampitt also, the priest, in deceit said, 'Let him speak.' So at length, when I had declared some time, Justice Sawrey caused the constable to put me out; and then I spoke to the people in the graveyard.

From thence I went into the island of Walney; and after the priest had done I spoke to him, but he got away. Then I declared the truth to the people, but they were something rude. I went to speak with the priest at his house, but he would not be seen. The people said he went to hide himself in the haymow; and they looked for him there, but could not find him. Then they said he was gone to hide himself in the standing corn, but they could not find him there either. I went to James Lancaster's, in the island, who was convinced, and from thence returned to Swarthmore, where the Lord's power seized upon Margaret Fell, her daughter Sarah, and several others.

Then I went to Baycliff, where Leonard Fell was convinced, and became a minister of the everlasting gospel. Several others were convinced there, and came into obedience to the truth. Here the people said they could not dispute; and would fain have put some other to hold talk with me; but I bade them fear the Lord, and not in a light way hold a talk of the Lord's words, but put the things in practice.

I directed them to the Divine Light of Christ, and His Spirit in their hearts, which would let them see all the evil thoughts, words, and actions that they had thought, spoken, and acted; by which Light they might see their sin, and also their Saviour Christ Jesus to save them from their sins. This I told them was their first step to peace, even to stand still in the Light that showed them their sins and transgressions; by which they might come to see they were in the fall of old Adam, in darkness and death, strangers to the covenant of promise, and without God in the world; and by the same Light they might see Christ that died for them to be their Redeemer and Saviour, and their way to God.

Soon after, Judge Fell being come home, Margaret Fell, his wife, sent to me, desiring me to return thither; and feeling freedom from the Lord so to do, I went back to Swarthmore. I found the priests and professors, and that envious Justice Sawrey, had much incensed Judge Fell and Captain Sands against the truth by their lies; but when I came to speak with him I answered all his objections, and so thoroughly satisfied him by the Scriptures that he was convinced in his judgment. He asked me if I was that George Fox of whom Justice Robinson spoke so much in commendation amongst many of the Parliament men? I told him I had been with Justice Robinson, and with Justice Hotham in Yorkshire, who were very civil and loving to me; and that they were convinced in their judgment by the Spirit of God that the principle to which I bore testimony was the truth; and they saw over and beyond the priests of the nation, so that they, and many others, were now come to be wiser than their teachers.

After we had discoursed some time together, Judge Fell himself was satisfied also, and came to see, by the openings of the Spirit of God in his heart, over all the priests and teachers of the world, and did not go to hear them for some years before he died: for he knew it was the truth that I declared, and that Christ was the teacher of His people, and their Saviour. He sometimes wished that I were a while with Judge Bradshaw to discourse with him.

There came to Judge Fell's Captain Sands before-mentioned, endeavouring to incense the Judge against me, for he was an evil-minded man, and full of envy against me; and yet he could speak high things, and use the Scripture words, and say, 'Behold, I make all things new.' But I told him, then he must have a new God, for his God was his belly. Besides him came also that envious justice, John Sawrey. I told him his heart was rotten, and he was full of hypocrisy to the brim. Several other people also came, of whose states the Lord gave me a discerning; and I spoke to their conditions. While I was in those parts, Richard Farnsworth and James Nayler came to see me and the family; and Judge Fell, being satisfied that it was the way of truth, notwithstanding all their opposition, suffered the meeting to be kept at his house. A great meeting was settled there in the Lord's power, which continued near forty years, until the year 1690, when a new meeting-house was erected near it.

On the market-day I went to Lancaster, and spoke through the market in the dreadful power of God, declaring the day of the Lord to the people, and crying out against all their deceitful merchandise. I preached righteousness and truth unto them, which all should follow after, walk and live in, directing them how and where they might find and receive the Spirit of God to guide them thereinto.

After I had cleared myself in the market, I went to my lodging, whither several people came; and many were convinced who have since stood faithful to the truth.

The First-day following, in the forenoon, I had a great meeting in the street at Lancaster, amongst the soldiers and people, to whom I declared the Word of life, and the everlasting truth. I opened unto them that all the traditions they had lived in, all their worships and religions, and the profession they made of the Scriptures, were good for nothing while they lived out of the life and power which those were in who gave forth the Scriptures. I directed them to the Light of Christ, the heavenly man, and to the Spirit of God in their own hearts, that they might come to be acquainted with God and Christ, receive Him for their teacher, and know His kingdom set up in them.

In the afternoon I went to the steeple-house at Lancaster, and declared the truth to the priest and people, laying open before them the deceit they lived in, and directing them to the power and Spirit of God which they wanted. But they haled me out, and stoned me along the street till I came to John Lawson's house.

Another First-day I went to a steeple-house by the waterside, where one Whitehead was priest. To him and to the people I declared the truth in the dreadful power of God. There came a doctor so full of envy that he said he could find it in his heart to run me through with his rapier, though he were hanged for it the next day; yet this man came afterwards to be convinced of the truth so far as to be loving to Friends. Some were convinced thereabouts who willingly sat down under the ministry of Christ, their teacher; and a meeting was settled there in the power of God, which has continued to this day.

After this I returned into Westmoreland, and spoke through Kendal on a market-day. So dreadful was the power of God upon me, that people flew like chaff before me into their houses. I warned them of the mighty day of the Lord, and exhorted them to hearken to the voice of God in their own hearts, who was now come to teach His people Himself. When some opposed, many others took my part. At last some fell to fighting about me; but I went and spoke to them, and they parted again. Several were convinced.

After I had travelled up and down in those countries, and had had great meetings, I came to Swarthmore again. And when I had visited Friends in those parts, I heard of a great meeting the priests were to have at Ulverston, on a lecture-day. I went to it, and into the steeple-house in the dread and power of the Lord. When the priest had done, I spoke among them the Word of the Lord, which was as a hammer, and as a fire amongst them. And though Lampitt, the priest of the place, had been at variance with most of the priests before, yet against the truth they all joined together. But the mighty power of the Lord was over all; and so wonderful was the appearance thereof, that priest Bennett said the church shook, insomuch that he was afraid and trembled. And when he had spoken a few confused words he hastened out for fear it should fall on his head. Many priests got together there; but they had no power as yet to persecute.

When I had cleared my conscience towards them, I went up to Swarthmore again, whither came four or five of the priests. Coming to discourse, I asked them whether any one of them could say he had ever had the word of the Lord to go and speak to such or such a people. None of them durst say he had; but one of them burst out into a passion and said that he could speak his experiences as well as I.

I told him experience was one thing; but to receive and go with a message, and to have a Word from the Lord, as the prophets and apostles had had and done, and as I had done to them, this was another thing. And therefore I put it to them again, 'Can any of you say you have ever had a command or word from the Lord immediately at any time?' but none of them could say so.

Then I told them that the false prophets, the false apostles, and the antichrists, could use the words of the true prophets, the true apostles, and of Christ, and would speak of other men's experiences, though they themselves never knew or heard the voice of God or Christ; and that such as they might obtain the good words and experiences of others. This puzzled them much, and laid them open.

At another time, when I was discoursing with several priests at Judge Fell's house, and he was by, I asked them the same question, – whether any of them had ever heard the voice of God or Christ, to bid him go to such and such a people, to declare His word or message unto them. Any one, I told them, that could but read, might declare the experiences of the prophets and apostles, which were recorded in the Scriptures. Thereupon Thomas Taylor, an ancient priest, did ingenuously confess before Judge Fell that he had never heard the voice of God, nor of Christ, to send him to any people; but that he spoke his experiences, and the experiences of the saints in former ages, and that he preached. This very much confirmed Judge Fell in the persuasion he had that the priests were wrong; for he had thought formerly, as the generality of people then did, that they were sent from God.

Now began the priests to rage more and more, and as much as they could to stir up persecution. James Nayler and Francis Howgill were cast into prison in Appleby jail, at the instigation of the malicious priests, some of whom prophesied that within a month we should be all scattered again, and come to nothing. But, blessed for ever be the worthy name of the Lord, His work went on and prospered; for about this time John Audland, Francis Howgill, John Camm, Edward Burrough, Richard Hubberthorn, Miles Hubbersty, and Miles Halhead, with several others, being endued with power from on high, came forth in the work of the ministry, and approved themselves faithful labourers therein, travelling up and down, and preaching the gospel freely; by means whereof multitudes were convinced, and many effectually turned to the Lord.

On a lecture-day I was moved to go to the steeple-house at Ulverston, where were abundance of professors, priests, and people. I went near to priest Lampitt, who was blustering on in his preaching. After the Lord had opened my mouth to speak, John Sawrey, the justice, came to me and said that if I would speak according to the Scriptures, I should speak. I admired him for speaking so to me, and told him I would speak according to the Scriptures, and bring the Scriptures to prove what I had to say; for I had something to speak to

Lampitt and to them. Then he said I should not speak, contradicting himself, for he had said just before that I should speak if I would speak according to the Scriptures. The people were quiet, and heard me gladly, till this Justice Sawrey (who was the first stirrer-up of cruel persecution in the north) incensed them against me, and set them on to hale, beat, and bruise me. But now on a sudden the people were in a rage, and fell upon me in the steeple-house before his face, knocked me down, kicked me, and trampled upon me. So great was the uproar, that some tumbled over their seats for fear.

At last he came and took me from the people, led me out of the steeple-house, and put me into the hands of the constables and other officers, bidding them whip me, and put me out of the town. They led me about a quarter of a mile, some taking hold by my collar, some by my arms and shoulders; and they shook and dragged me along.

Many friendly people being come to the market, and some to the steeple-house to hear me, diverse of these they knocked down also, and broke their heads so that the blood ran down from several; and Judge Fell's son running after to see what they would do with me, they threw him into a ditch of water, some of them crying, 'Knock the teeth out of his head.'

When they had haled me to the common moss-side, a multitude following, the constables and other officers gave me some blows over my back with their willow rods, and thrust me among the rude multitude, who, having furnished themselves with staves, hedge-stakes, holm or holly bushes, fell upon me, and beat me on my head, arms, and shoulders, till they had deprived me of sense; so that I fell down upon the wet common.

When I recovered again, and saw myself lying in a watery common, and the people standing about me, I lay still a little while, and the power of the Lord sprang through me, and the eternal refreshings revived me; so that I stood up again in the strengthening power of the eternal God, and stretching out my arms toward them, I said, with a loud voice, 'Strike again; here are my arms, my head, and my cheeks.'

There was in the company a mason, a professor, but a rude fellow, who with his walking rule-staff gave me a blow with all his might just over the back of my hand, as it was stretched out; with which blow my hand was so bruised, and my arm so benumbed, that I could not draw it to me again. Some of the people cried, 'He hath spoiled his hand for ever having the use of it any more.' But I looked at it in the love of God (for I was in the love of God to all that persecuted me), and after awhile the Lord's power sprang through me again, and through my hand and arm, so that in a moment I recovered strength in my hand and arm in the sight of them all.

Then they began to fall out among themselves. Some of them came to me, and said that if I would give them money they would secure me from the rest. But I was moved of the Lord to declare the Word of life, and showed them their false Christianity, and the fruits of their priest's ministry, telling them that they were more like heathens and Jews than true Christians.

Then was I moved of the Lord to come up again through the midst of the people, and go into Ulverston market. As I went, there met me a soldier, with his sword by his side. 'Sir,' said he to me, 'I see you are a man, and I am ashamed and grieved that you should be thus abused'; and he offered to assist me in what he could. I told him that the Lord's power was over all; and I walked through the people in the market, none of whom had power to touch me then. But some of the market people abusing some Friends in the market, I turned about, and saw this soldier among them with his naked rapier; whereupon I ran, and, catching hold of the hand his rapier was in, bid him put up his sword again if he would go along with me.

About two weeks after this I went into Walney island, and James Nayler went with me. We stayed one night at a little town on this side, called Cockan, and had a meeting there, where one was convinced.

After a while there came a man with a pistol, whereupon the people ran out of doors. He called for me; and when I came out to him he snapped his pistol at me, but it would not go off. This caused the people to make a great bustle about him; and some of them took hold of him, to prevent his doing mischief. But I was moved in the Lord's power to speak to him; and he was so struck by the power of the Lord that he trembled for fear, and went and hid himself. Thus the Lord's power came over them all, though there was a great rage in the country.

Next morning I went over in a boat to James Lancaster's. As soon as I came to land there rushed out about forty men with staves, clubs, and fishing-poles, who fell upon me, beating and punching me, and endeavouring to thrust me backward into the sea. When they had thrust me almost into the sea, and I saw they would knock me down in it, I went up into the midst of them; but they laid at me again, and knocked me down, and stunned me.

When I came to myself, I looked up and saw James Lancaster's wife throwing stones at my face, and her husband, James Lancaster, was lying over me, to keep the blows and the stones off me. For the people had persuaded James Lancaster's wife that I had bewitched her husband, and had promised her that if she would let them know when I came thither they would be my death. And having got knowledge of my coming, many of the town rose up in this manner with clubs and staves to kill me; but the Lord's power preserved me, that they could not take away my life.

At length I got up on my feet, but they beat me down again into the boat; which James Lancaster observing, he presently came into it, and set me over the water from them; but while we were on the water within their reach they struck at us with long poles, and threw stones after us. By the time we were come to the other side, we saw them beating James Nayler; for whilst they had been beating me, he walked up into a field, and they never minded him till I was gone; then they fell upon him, and all their cry was, 'Kill him, kill him.'

When I was come over to the town again, on the other side of the water, the townsmen rose up with pitchforks, flails, and staves, to keep me out of the town, crying, 'Kill him, knock him on the head, bring the cart; and carry him away to the churchyard.' So after they had abused me, they drove me some distance out of the town, and there left me.

Then James Lancaster went back to look after James Nayler; and I being now left alone, went to a ditch of water, and having washed myself (for they had besmeared my face, hands, and clothes with miry dirt), I walked about three miles to Thomas Hutton's house, where lodged Thomas Lawson, the priest that was convinced.

When I came in I could hardly speak to them, I was so bruised; only I told them where I left James Nayler. So they took each of them a horse, and went and brought him thither that night. The next day Margaret Fell hearing of it, sent a horse for me; but I was so sore with bruises, I was not able to bear the shaking of the horse without much pain.

When I was come to Swarthmore, Justice Sawrey, and one Justice Thompson, of Lancaster, granted a warrant against me; but Judge Fell coming home, it was not served upon me; for he was out of the country all this time that I was thus cruelly abused. When he came home he sent forth warrants into the isle of Walney, to apprehend all those riotous persons; whereupon some of them fled the country.

James Lancaster's wife was afterwards convinced of the truth, and repented of the evils she had done me; and so did others of those bitter persecutors also; but the judgments of God fell upon some of them, and destruction is come upon many of them since. Judge Fell asked me to give him a relation of my persecution; but I told him they could do no otherwise in the spirit wherein they were, and that they manifested the fruits of their priest's ministry, and their profession and religion to be wrong. So he told his wife I made light of it, and that I spoke of it as a man that had not been concerned; for, indeed, the Lord's power healed me again.

The time for the sessions at Lancaster being come, I went thither with Judge Fell, who on the way told me he had never had such a matter brought before him before, and he could not well tell what to do in the business. I told him, when Paul was brought before the rulers, and the Jews and priests came down to accuse him, and laid many false things to his charge, Paul stood still all that while. And when they had done, Festus, the governor, and king Agrippa, beckoned to him to speak for himself; which Paul did, and cleared himself of all those false accusations, so he might do with me.

Being come to Lancaster, Justice Sawrey and Justice Thompson having granted a warrant to apprehend me, though I was not apprehended by it, yet hearing of it, I appeared at the sessions, where there appeared against me about forty priests. These had chosen one Marshall, priest of Lancaster, to be their orator; and had provided one young priest, and two priests' sons, to bear witness against me, who had sworn beforehand that I had spoken blasphemy

When the justices were sat, they heard all that the priests and their witnesses could say and charge against me, their orator Marshall sitting by, and explaining their sayings for them. But the witnesses were so confounded that they discovered themselves to be false witnesses; for when the court had examined one of them upon oath, and then began to examine another, he was at such loss he could not answer directly, but said the other could say it. Which made the justices say to him, 'Have you sworn it, and given it in already upon your oath, and now say that he can say it? It seems you did not hear those words spoken yourself, though you have sworn it.'

There were then in court several who had been at that meeting, wherein the witnesses swore I spoke those blasphemous words which the priests accused me of; and these, being men of integrity and reputation in the country, did declare and affirm in court that the oath which the witnesses had taken against me was altogether false; and that no such words as they had sworn against me were spoken by me at that meeting. Indeed, most of the serious men of that side of the country, then at the sessions, had been at that meeting; and had heard me both at that and at other meetings also.

This was taken notice of by Colonel West, who, being a justice of the peace, was then upon the bench; and having long been weak in body, blessed the Lord and said that He had healed him that day; adding that he never saw so many sober people and good faces together in all his life. Then, turning himself to me, he said in the open sessions, 'George, if thou hast anything to say to the people, thou mayest freely declare it.'

I was moved of the Lord to speak; and as soon as I began, priest Marshall, the orator for the rest of the priests, went his way. That which I was moved to declare was this: that the holy Scriptures were given forth by the Spirit of God; and that all people must come to the Spirit of God in themselves in order to know God and Christ, of whom the prophets and apostles learnt: and that by the same Spirit all men might know the holy Scriptures. For as the Spirit of God was in them that gave forth the Scriptures, so the same Spirit must be in all them that come to understand the Scriptures. By this Spirit they might have fellowship with the Father, with the Son, with the Scriptures, and with one another: and without this Spirit they can know neither God, Christ, nor the Scriptures, nor have a right fellowship one with another.

I had no sooner spoken these words than about half a dozen priests, that stood behind me, burst into a passion. One of them, whose name was Jackus, amongst other things that he spake against the Truth, said that the Spirit and the letter were inseparable. I replied, 'Then every one that hath the letter hath the Spirit; and they might buy the Spirit with the letter of the Scriptures.'

This plain discovery of darkness in the priest moved Judge Fell and Colonel West to reprove them openly, and tell them that according to that position they might carry the Spirit in their pockets as they did the Scriptures. Upon this the priests, being confounded and put to silence, rushed out in a rage against the justices, because they could not have their bloody ends upon me. The justices, seeing the witnesses did not agree, and perceiving that they were brought to answer the priests' envy, and finding that all their evidences were not sufficient in law to make good their charge against me, discharged me.

After Judge Fell had spoken to Justice Sawrey and Justice Thompson concerning the warrant they had given forth against me, and showing them the errors thereof, he and Colonel West granted a supersedeas [a writ] to stop the execution of it. Thus I was cleared in open sessions of those lying accusations which the malicious priests had laid to my charge: and multitudes of people praised God that day, for it was a joyful day to many. Justice Benson, of Westmoreland, was convinced; and Major Ripan, mayor of the town of Lancaster, also.

It was a day of everlasting salvation to hundreds of people: for the Lord Jesus Christ, the way to the Father, the free Teacher, was exalted and set up; His everlasting gospel was preached, and the Word of eternal life was declared over the heads of the priests, and all such lucrative preachers. For the Lord opened many mouths that day to speak His Word to the priests, and several friendly people and professors reproved them in their inns, and in the streets, so that they fell, like an old rotten house: and the cry was among the people that the Quakers had got the day, and the priests were fallen.

FAITH IN ACTION

What a long time it can take to become the person one has always been!
How often in the process we mask ourselves in faces that are not our
own. How much dissolving and shaking of ego we must endure before
we discover our deep identity – the true self within every human being
that is the seed of authentic vocation.

Parker J. Palmer, 2000

True godliness don't turn men out of the world but enables them to live
better in it and excites their endeavours to mend it.

William Penn, 1682

To turn all the treasures we possess into the channel of universal love
becomes the business of our lives.

John Woolman, 1763

One apparently minor event which took place over 350 years ago still has
the power to move Quakers profoundly.

It happened in 1652, as the fledgling Quaker movement was
beginning to take wing. George Fox, iconoclastic and inspirational
proclaimer of Truth, attended a church in Ulverston – he would have
referred to it as a 'steeplehouse' – and proceeded to stand up on his seat
in the middle of the service. He asked if he could speak to the congregation. The priest gave him permission and here is part of what Fox said, as
reported forty-two years later by his wife:

You will say, Christ saith this, and the apostles say this; but what canst thou say? Art thou a child of Light and hast walked in the Light, and what thou speakest is it inwardly from God?

Reported by Margaret Fox, 1694

There are four vital questions in that little passage, all asked directly of the priest. The first is so important to Quakers that the remainder are often forgotten, but they were all part of the same thought process for Fox, and we shall return to it. For now, let us look at those celebrated four words at the end of his initial query: 'What canst thou say?' They are among the most frequently recalled in all Quakerism, beaten only for sheer quotability by the last six of another George Fox extract, this time from his Journal:

Be patterns, be examples in all countries, places, islands, nations, wherever you come, that your carriage and life may preach among all sorts of people and to them; then you will come to walk cheerfully over the world, answering that of God in every one.

George Fox, published 1694

George Fox is making demands. He disturbed the service in Ulverston and now he is disturbing us. *What can you say?* It is a direct challenge to the priest and to you and to me. Will you speak for yourself or from received wisdom? Are we to believe what we have been told? Tell us your experience of the Divine.

Answer that of God in everyone. This is a much tougher assignment than it may at first appear. Fox does not say, as we might be led to think by those who hanker after a Quaker creed, '*Believe there is that of God in everyone*'. He takes that as read and goes one, two, perhaps three steps further. Believe it. Find it. Answer it. That means finding and answering that of God in Adolph Hitler, in Charles Manson, in Saddam Hussein. It means that everyone on this planet is truly equal. It suggests a way in which we really can begin to love our enemies.

In 1652, that was radical stuff and for many of us it is no less so now. But, as we have seen, the Quaker Meeting for Worship can give unexpected energy and resolve to those who commit to it. It enables many to do what they could not have done before. It has the power to render passive people active and active people more so. It gives meaning and purpose through the sense that all of life is holy, that there is no distinction between the sacred and the secular, that all of life is sacramental.

To live sacramentally is to make thousands of little daily decisions. Whether we keep any spare money, and, if so, where? Which bank? Or other institution? What sort of investments? All the decisions we make about what we buy. Do we need it at all? Have we considered where it comes from? The nature of the regime; the transport implications? The fairness or otherwise of trade? Whether the firm has a good record in terms of employment policies, environmental responsiveness? Is it wasteful in packaging? The decisions we take about how often and how and where to go on holiday: What impact for good or ill does our part in the tourist trade have on the country concerned? Should we offer our financial support to an unacceptable regime?

Rather than finding the range of these issues daunting, we should see them as a standing invitation to a contemporary adventure of the spirit. Do we sense every area of our lives to be one where our spiritual discernment is exercised? Are we centred down in those decisions as in meeting for worship? Once again we are able to see how reflection on our experience of testimony is bound up with our spiritual condition. The most direct route to a deepening spirituality would be for more and more of us to share with each other how our state of soul is conditioned by every last aspect of how we live our lives. Spiritual renewal may well need to encounter mutual accountability.

Jonathan Dale, 2002

There can be no division between the secular and the sacred. Quaker beliefs exist only in terms of Quaker practice. There are no formal observances or rituals and Quakerism is not a 'Sunday religion'.

Rather, there is an onus on all of us to show sincerity in all that we do, with our beliefs put into practice in all aspects of our lives – private and public. Of course, many of us frequently fall short of that ideal but, still, the notion of individual responsibility and of an expectation that we be judged by what we do rather than by what we believe is central to Quakerism. There is an assumption of the universality of the spiritual element so that no aspect of life can be accepted as outside the responsibility of religious beliefs.

[. . .] That assumption creates an expectation that Friends show an active social concern, both as individuals and as a corporate body. For many years this has been, and still is, represented in the work of Friends in the peace movement, in work in prisons, and in race relations – to mention but three major concerns that have stood the test of time. Also, of course, it is reflected in the relatively high proportion of Friends in the caring professions, in the commitment of many to voluntary work in youth clubs or in organisations such as the Samaritans, and in various forms of relief work at home and overseas. Clearly, there is no agreement among Friends on any particular political solution to society's problems. Indeed, many of us have had the same reluctance to accept political dogma as religious dogma. [. . .]

Nevertheless, it has been said that: 'the quiet, grey, unobtrusive Quakers can be dangerously radical. . . . Quakers are a threat to the established order of society . . . because there is no knowing when they will hear the still, small voice counselling them to a course which may have far-reaching consequences' (Geoffrey Hubbard: *Quaker by Convincement*). Historically, this threat has been evident in Friends' willingness to go to prison for their religious beliefs, including conscientious objection to military service, and by their opposition to slavery. It is evident still today in Friends' insistence on speaking out on a variety of matters regarding which they share a concern. It would be hard, indeed, to be a Quaker without some involvement in the social issues of the day. On the other hand, Quaker participation in social action has certain features that tend to differentiate it from that of others. Most importantly, it starts with the principle that violence is not an acceptable means to any end, and that social actions should not bring harm or hurt to others. That principle has meant that Quakers are unlikely to be involved in revolutionary movements that work towards violent over-throw of government, however worthy the purpose. Put in the positive, it is to be expected that there will be an emphasis on reconciliation and on change by convincement rather than on 'victory' by force or by weight of numbers.

Michael Rutter, 1983

We need to guard against under-valuing the material expressions of spiritual things. It is easy to make a form of our very rejection of forms. And in particular, we need to ask ourselves whether we are endeavouring to make all the daily happenings and doings of life which we call 'secular' minister to the spiritual. It is a bold and colossal claim that we put forward – that the whole of life is sacramental, that there are innumerable 'means of grace' by which God is revealed and communicated – through nature and through human fellowship and through a thousand things that may become the 'outward and visible sign' of 'an inward and spiritual grace'.

A. Barratt Brown, 1932

Quakerism is far from a comfortable faith. It is full of queries. Are you? Have you? Then as one grows in the silence and in the development of the craft of Hope, there comes the realisation of another thorny growth – the inability to avoid responsibility for the suffering of others. 'Let your lives speak!' The challenge George Fox threw out three hundred years ago has not lost its barb. Do I? Am I? Should I? There are no easy answers in the Quaker way.

Elizabeth Stevenson, 1993

If this all seems a little overwhelming, consider a simpler approach in the next extract from the journal of Pierre Ceresole, in which he makes a direct connection between everyday life and the Divine in a concise but still uncompromising expression of the Quaker concept of sacramental living.

You say: 'But with the best will in the world, I can't get to the point of believing in God'. Well then, if you want to believe in him, if you feel something great behind it all and not just words, well, work for God, and you will see not only that it comes to the same thing as believing in him, but something infinitely more alive, more real, more powerful which fills you and satisfies you more than anything you might vaguely imagine under the name of 'real and living faith' – a reality, a life and not words.

Pierre Ceresole, published 1954

Newcomers to Quakerism often worry that too much will be expected of them, that they may have to give up their jobs or perform some life-changing task which they regard as lying outside their capabilities. There is no need for them to be anxious. Quaker faith in action involves the minutiae of life just as much as the big issues, the apparently insignificant deed no less than the grand gesture. Indeed, much of the most effective Quaker work is done on a small scale, at local level and in neighbourhood communities. For some, it starts with a simple change of attitude.

Do not look for such great matters to begin with; but be content to be a child, and let the Father proportion out daily to thee what light, what power, what exercises, what straits, what fears, what troubles he sees fit for thee; and do thou bow before him continually in humility of heart. [. . .] Thou must join in with the beginnings of life, and be exercised with the day of small things, before thou meet with the great things, wherein is the clearness and satisfaction of the soul. The rest is at noonday; but the travels begin at the breakings of day, wherein are but glimmerings or little light, wherein the discovery of good and evil are not so manifest and certain; yet there must the traveller begin and travel; and in his faithful travels [...] the light will break in upon him more and more.

Isaac Penington, 1665

If we believe in that of God in everyone, we must treat all as we would be treated, with love, respect and intelligent concern, no matter what they have done or are doing. We must remember that their bad actions are not themselves; that whatever they do, they are grounded in the divinity that is the sole reality. We must try to help them move from ignorance to knowledge, from hatred to love. We may have to prevent them in their ill-doing, but if we act with love, there could be no greater service; we may hope that others may so act towards us.

If we hold a different view of human nature, believing it to be intrinsically evil, steeped in original sin, violent, 'animal', imperfect, or a Manichean mixture of good and bad, our behaviour will certainly differ in dealing with unpeaceful relations. The emphasis will shift from acknowledging the divine essence in those whose actions are unpeaceful, and acting to restore them to an understanding of their true selves, to changing those actions. Depending on circumstances we would try to persuade, manipulate, or control, even to intimidate, restrain forcibly, or to kill. This would be impossible to those who recognised our shared heritage, our unity as beings made in the image and likeness of God. But to those who do not, or do so half-heartedly, the desire to alter material circumstances may legitimise such action in the name of maintaining or restoring peace.

Adam Curle, 1981

Do rightly, justly, truly, holy, equally to all people in all things; and that is according to that of God in every man, and the witness of God, and the wisdom of God, and the life of God in yourselves; and there ye are serviceable in your generation, labouring in the thing that is good, which doth not spoil, nor destroy, nor waste the creation upon the lusts.

[...] All husbandmen, and dealers about husbandry whatsoever, cattle, or ground, to you all this is the word of the Lord God: do rightly, holily, justly, honestly, plainly, and truly to all men and people, whomsoever ye have to deal withal; wrong not any in any case, though it be never so much to your advantage. Deny yourselves, and live in the cross of Christ, the power of God, for that destroys injustice; and 'without holiness none can ever see the Lord; and out of righteousness there is no true peace'. Therefore all, of what sort so ever, or what calling so ever, do justly, (whether ye be masters or servants, fathers or mothers, sons or daughters), to one another, and to all, do that which is just and righteous, uprightly and holily; in that you will have peace, and see God.

[. . .] So speak the truth, whether merchants or tradesmen, and all sorts of people whatsoever, in all your occasions, and in all your tradings, dealings, and doings, speak the truth, act in the truth, and walk in the truth; and this brings righteousness forth.

[. . .] And all, of what trade or calling so ever, keep out of debts; owe to no man anything but love. Go not beyond your estates, lest ye bring yourselves to trouble, and cumber, and a snare; keep low and down in all things ye act. For a man that would be great and goes beyond his estate, lifts himself up, runs into debt, and lives highly of other men's means; he is a waster of other men's, and a destroyer. He is not serviceable to the creation, but a destroyer of the creation and creatures, and cumbereth himself and troubleth others, and is lifted up, who would appear to be somebody; but being from the honest, the just, and good, falls into the shame. Therefore dwell every one of you under your own vine, (that know redemption from the earth), and seek not to be great, but in that, and dwell in the truth, justice, righteousness, and holiness; and there is the blessing enlarged.

George Fox, undated epistle

As we have seen, nobody is in charge of a Quaker meeting. Quakers have no priests. However, many embrace the concept of 'the priesthood of all believers'. It is a phrase much used by Friends, encapsulating the idea that, with no hierarchy, Quakers are, all of them, fulfilling the same role as do priests of other faiths – living in the Spirit, experiencing a direct, unmediated relationship with the Divine, declaring their witness, representing The Religious Society of Friends in all they do. There is a well-loved Quaker saying, possibly first coined by D. Elton Trueblood in 1935 (and quoted by Philip Rack on page 38), that Quakers have not abolished the priesthood: instead, they have abolished the laity.

If we believe in the priesthood of all believers then we are all, as Quakers, involved in, and responsible for our religion. Quakerism is not a spectator sport – it is a vocation.

Faith is not what we assert, but what we are prepared to act upon. It is not a statement of belief, but a trust in, and a dependence on God that affects the whole way in which we live. It is both a venture and an adventure.

In fulfilling our vocation, we have two helpers, the grace of God and the community of fellow-seekers. We live in a triangular relationship of self – God – community. In this we should reflect the two New Testament commandments that we love God with all our heart, soul and strength, and that we love our neighbour as ourselves.

The first principle of Quakerism is integrity – integrity of word, worship and action. Worship is at the heart of our faith. If our worship is right, words will spring from it and reflect truth; action will spring from it and reflect love.

Quakerism is a religion of roots and fruits. We are all familiar with the story of the enquirer attending meeting for worship for the first time, who asked a neighbour 'When does the service begin?' and received the answer 'When the meeting ends'. This is true but only a half truth. For the service is already there in the worship. The service has to be God's service. In our worship, we place God at the centre so that we can see people and events through God's eyes and can act as God's hands. Only the knowledge of God enables us to act with love and truth.

Janet Scott, 1982

If our concern is with the love of a creating, sustaining, sanctifying, indwelling Spirit for the life and wholeness of the world, we will be caught up and enlivened by images of the Spirit, desiring to break through in reconciling, whole-making love between all people, all beings and all things in the universe. This God is within us, empowering us, flowing out from, to, between us and all things – both immanent and transcendent.

To live in the Spirit is to act in the belief that love is stronger than death; in the belief that if we act in goodwill toward another we overcome our fear of them and their fear of us. And in such action is the proclamation of peace.

To live in the Spirit will mean moving towards being open to those modes of being, thinking, deciding and acting that are empowering from within rather than controlling from without for ourselves and for our neighbours.

Margaret Bearlin, 1984

The active life takes many forms, among them work, creativity and caring. The three are not mutually exclusive and are often intertwined, but it will be helpful to name the main traits of each of them. By understanding each type of action, and how each differs from the others, we will be able to appreciate more about the range of issues raised by the active life.

Work is action driven by external necessity or demand. We work because we need to make a living, because we need to solve a problem, because we need to surmount or survive. I do not mean that we are mere robots when we work, totally determined by factors outside ourselves; we may choose whether to work, when to work, how to work. But work, as I use the word here, always involves the element of necessity, and that element leads to the characteristic dilemmas of this form of the active life.

Creativity, in contrast, is driven more by inner choice than by outer demand. An act cannot be creative if it is not born of freedom. In creative action, our desire is not to 'solve' or 'succeed' or 'survive' but to give birth to something new; we want, for a while, to be less creaturely and more like the creator. If work reveals something of how we transcend it – and that fact gives rise to the dilemmas of creativity.

Caring is also action freely chosen. But in caring we aim not at giving birth to something new; we aim at nurturing, protecting, guiding, healing, or empowering something that already has life. The energy behind caring is compassion for others which, in turn, is energized by the knowledge that we are all in this together, that the fate of other beings has implications for our own fate. Caring may take a personal form, for instance, when we comfort a grieving friend. But it can also take form through movements for political and economic justice, in speaking on behalf of strangers whose oppression diminishes us all.

In the midst of these definitions we need to remember two things. First, these three forms of action are found together as well as apart. [. . .] Work can be creative, creativity can be caring, and caring can be a quality of work.

Second, though these definitions may feel airy and abstract, remember that the active life is embodied life, everyday life – so ordinary we hardly notice it. We work in offices, farms, and homes. We act creatively in everything from gardening to raising children to writing a poem. We care by visiting a sick neighbour and by marching for peace. One way or another, most of us are involved in the active life day in and day out.

But for me, and for many people that I know, these ordinary activities contain an extraordinary mix of blessing and curse. The blessing is obvious, especially when we lose the chance or the capacity to do these ordinary things: the active life makes it possible for us to discover ourselves and our world, to test and extend our powers, to connect with other beings, to co-create a common reality. The joys of action are known to everyone who has done a job well, made something of beauty, given time and energy to a just cause. Take away the opportunity to work, to create, or to care – as our society does to too many people – and you have deprived someone of a chance to feel fully human.

But the active life also carries a curse. Many of us know what it is to live lives not of action but of frenzy, to go from day to day exhausted and unfulfilled by our attempts to work, create, and care. Many of us know the violence of active life, a violence we sometimes inflict on ourselves and sometimes inflict on our world. In action, we project our spirits outside ourselves. Sometimes we project shadows which do damage to others, and sometimes we project light that others want to extinguish. Action poses some of our deepest spiritual crises as well as some of our most heartfelt joys.

Parker J. Palmer, 1990

Living in the Spirit can give strength at times of danger and difficulty. William Dewsbury was one of many Quakers who were imprisoned during the first fifty years in the life of The Religious Society of Friends.

For this I can say, I [. . .] joyfully entered prisons as palaces, telling mine enemies to hold me there as long as they could: and in the prison-house I sung praises to my God, and esteemed the bolts and locks put upon me as jewels, and in the Name of the eternal God I always got the victory, for they could keep me there no longer than the determined time of my God.

If any one has received any good or benefit through this vessel, called William Dewsbury, give God the glory; I'll have none, I'll have none, I'll have none.

William Dewsbury, 1688

Some of the work that has been achieved by Quakers during the last 350 years has been big, important and remarkable. Much has become famous, and the constant Quaker presence at the Union Nations bears witness to the respect in which Friends and their skills in conflict resolution are often held. The following extracts are from members of just two of the myriad important initiatives: Quakers played a vital role in the reforming of

prisons during the nineteenth century; and Quaker conscientious objectors during World Wars One and Two formed The Friends Ambulance Unit
to relieve the suffering of the combatants.

Elizabeth Fry (1780–1845) was a celebrity in her lifetime and is still
remembered for her pioneering work for prison reform. The religious life
which inspired her is perhaps not so well known. The following short
extracts from her diary for 1817 show clearly the uneasy balance between
her family life and her work with prisoners in Newgate Gaol.

Mildred's Court, 2nd month, 24th I have lately been much occupied in
forming a school in Newgate, for the children of the poor prisoners, as
well as the young criminals, which has brought much peace and satisfaction with it; but my mind has also been deeply affected in attending
a poor woman who was executed this morning. I visited her twice; this
event has brought me into much feeling, attended by some distress-
ingly nervous sensations in the night, so that this has been a time of
deep humiliation to me, thus witnessing the effect and consequences
of sin. This poor creature murdered her baby; and how inexpressibly
awful now to have her life taken away! The whole affair has been truly
afflicting to me; to see what poor mortals may be driven to, through
sin and transgression, and how hard the heart becomes, even to the
most tender affections. How should we watch and pray, that we fall
not by little and little, become hardened, and commit greater sins. I
had to pray for these poor sinners this morning, and also for the
preservation of our household from the evil there is in the world.

Mildred's Court, 3rd month, 7th My mind and time have been much
taken up with Newgate and its concerns. I have been encouraged
about our school, but I find my weak nature and proneness to be so
much affected by the opinions of man, brings me into some peculiar
trials and temptations: in the first place, our Newgate visiting could
no longer be kept secret, which I endeavoured that it should be, and
therefore I am exposed to praise that I do not the least deserve; also
to some unpleasant humiliations – for in trying to obtain helpers, I
must be subject to their various opinions; and also, being obliged to

confer at times with strangers, and men in authority, is to me a very unpleasant necessity. I have suffered much about the hanging of the criminals, having had to visit another poor woman, before her death; this again tried me a good deal, but I was permitted to be much more upheld and not so distressed as the time before.

Mildred's Court, 3rd month, 11th My mind too much tossed by a variety of interests and duties – husband, children, household, accounts, Meetings, the Church, near relations, friends and Newgate – most of these things press a good deal upon me. I hope I am not undertaking too much, but it is a little like being in the whirlwind, and in the storm; may I not be hurt in it, but enabled quietly to perform that which ought to be done; and may it all be done so heartily unto the Lord, and through the assistance of His grace, that if consistent with His Holy Will, His blessing may attend it, and if ever any good be done, that the glory of the whole work may be given where it is alone due.

4th month, 12th I have found in my late attention to Newgate, a peace and prosperity in the undertaking, that I seldom, if ever, remember to have done before. A way has very remarkably been opened for us, beyond all expectations, to bring into order the poor prisoners; those who are in power are so very willing to help us, in short the time appears come to work amongst them. Already, from being like wild beasts, they appear harmless and kind. I am ready to say, in the fullness of my heart, surely 'it is the Lord's doing, and marvellous in our eyes'; so many are the providential openings of various kinds.

7th month, 28th I am alone at home with my nine children, a great and very precious charge; at times they appear too much for me, at others I greatly enjoy them; I desire that the anxiety for their welfare and to have them in order, should not prevent my enjoying thankfully, the blessing of being surrounded by so sweet a flock. I sometimes think of these words, 'The fruit of the womb is his reward'; and having borne them through much fear and at times much tribulation, I believe I should thankfully enjoy them; not improperly resting in the precious gift. How I delight to see the springings of goodness in them, the blessed seed appearing, as well as mourn when the evil shows itself. Most gracious Lord, be pleased to be with them and bless them; strengthen the good, I beseech Thee, and weaken the evil in their hearts.

8th month, 4th My having been brought publicly forward in the newspapers, respecting what I have been instrumental in doing at Newgate, has brought some anxiety with it; in the first place, as far as I am concerned, that it may neither raise me too high, nor cast me too low, that having what may appear my good works thus published, may never lead me or others to give either the praise or glory where it is not due.

Elizabeth Fry, 1817

The Friends Ambulance Unit was formed in 1914 and continued in active service in France and Belgium until it was dissolved in 1919. Reformed in 1939, it consisted, during World War Two, of around 1,300 people, not all Quakers, some serving as ambulance drivers and medical orderlies in London during the Blitz, others working in a further eighteen war-torn countries in Europe and the Middle East. After World War Two, it continued as The Friends Ambulance Unit (Post-War Service) until 1959.

Here, three members of the FAU between 1939 and 1945, all conscientious objectors (or 'conchies'), reflect on their experiences.

My pacifist convictions came slowly, and they were more developed at the end of the war. I was quite dismayed with some of the chaps who said 'Well, that's the end of being a conchie. . .'. My feelings over the years as I got deeper into being a Quaker were that there are various grades of enlightenment, almost as in Buddhism. We had chosen not to fight, but there were Quakers who had decided to fight and put this man Hitler down. There is room for those two grades of people to be in unity. When Quakers go round with banners saying 'Quakers say no to all war' and we feel good, we ignore the person who feels he has to fight – his is as honest and tender a conscience as ours. It is over the years, sitting in the quiet as it were, that I have learned that the true Quaker witness is simply to say: our prime object must be the positive side, not the negative side, saying 'What can we do to help bring the Kingdom of God into being on this earth?' And positive work, like relief work is what is important, to reconstruct the damage that has been done. But further than that, following the lead of Jesus simply to help each other on the spiritual road, not just the material. One of the lessons learnt in well over a hundred years of Quaker relief work is that when you take the bread to those in need, they are most thankful but especially if in addition to the bread, they get a bit of you, or your love for them as a fellow human being. In the Lord's Prayer we say 'Give us this day our daily bread'. This doesn't just mean give us a crust, we're hungry, it means feed us spiritually.

I try not to be depressed with what is going on in the world today. It doesn't help to entertain negative thoughts. It was the prophet Micah who said 'they shall beat their swords into ploughshares and nation shall not lift up a sword against nation' – that is engraved in the entrance hall to the United Nations building. And although some are predicting that the millennium of Armageddon is nigh, I don't believe that things are moving so fast. The scale of bombing and destruction in Iraq (1991) has made many ordinary people say 'This is a ridiculous situation. It does no good'. I'm optimistic enough to think that war is ruling itself out as a useful way of solving disputes – there will still be minor wars, but I'm doubtful that we'll see another major war.

John Bailey, 1998

I was determined to think it out for myself and when war was declared I walked the Lake District mountains, thinking of peace and war and what I should do. Later, whilst living in digs in Birmingham, I continued to work things through for myself – this was during a lonely time of my life. [. . .] By the time my call-up was due, I had applied to join the FAU and was actually training when my Tribunal [to register as a conscientious objector] came up. At my Tribunal, I was careful not to mention that I was a Quaker because I think that Quakers had preferential treatment, especially in the Birmingham area where they were well known. I wanted them to judge me on the basis of my statement:

'I believe that a man's first duty is to his conscience rather than to his country or state. I consider war to be something which is wrong. It is contrary to Christian ideals and although I have great sympathy for the cause for which our country is fighting, I feel I must conscientiously object to taking any part in the propagation of this war. I feel that when there so many people in the world suffering as a result of the war, my duty lies towards them and I therefore intend to do my utmost to assist them. I would like to do ambulance work under civilian control or some other kind of relief work.'

I felt that by saying one was a Quaker, one was almost trying to take advantage of the situation and I think some who weren't Quakers were given a much tougher time with much more gruelling questioning. But when I was asked what I was doing and said 'the FAU' I was asked whether I was a Quaker and said 'yes'.

Chris Barber, 1998

There is this whole idea of living with a conscience and that we had to go on living with it. You know, I think I've lived with it ever since. And it is a permanent partner: a little, quiet, second identity that goes along with you – a little conscience, a little box. And I think I am a conchie for life.

Donald Swann, 1998

Donald Swann's 'little, quiet, second identity' will chime with many Friends. It impels them into action and enables them to achieve results in all kinds of fields, both large and small, often entirely unexpectedly.

Here are two early Friends, one energetically urging Quakers to put their heads above the parapet (where we can see the full context of Fox's celebrated 'that of God in everyone' phrase mentioned earlier) and the other illuminating that quiet second identity which enables them to do so.

Friends,

In the power of life and wisdom, and dread of the Lord God of life, and heaven, and earth, dwell, that in the wisdom of God over all ye may be preserved, and be a terror to all the adversaries of God, and a dread, answering that of God in them all, spreading the Truth abroad, awakening the witness, confounding deceit, gathering up out of transgression into the life, the covenant of light and peace with God. Let all nations hear the word by sound or writing. Spare no place, spare not tongue nor pen; but be obedient to the Lord God and go through the work and be valiant for the Truth upon earth; tread and trample all that is contrary under. [. . .] Keep in the wisdom of God that spreads over all the earth, the wisdom of the creation, that is pure. Live in it; that is the word of the Lord God to you all, do not abuse it; and keep down and low; and take heed of false joys that will change.

Bring all into the worship of God. Plough up the fallow ground. . . . And none are ploughed up but he who comes to the principle of God in him which he hath transgressed. Then he doth service to God; then the planting and the watering and the increase from God cometh. So the ministers of the Spirit must minister to the spirit that is transgressed and in prison, which hath been in captivity in every one; whereby with the same spirit people must be led out of captivity up to God, the Father of spirits, and do service to him and have unity with him, with the Scriptures and one with another. And this is the word of the Lord God to you all, and a charge to you all in the presence of the living God, be patterns, be examples in all countries, places, islands, nations, wherever you come; that your carriage and life may preach among all sorts of people, and to them. Then you will come to walk cheerfully over the world, answering that of God in every one; whereby in them ye may be a blessing, and make the witness of God in them to bless you. Then to the Lord God you will be a sweet savour and a blessing.

Spare no deceit. Lay the sword upon it; go over it; keep yourselves clear of the blood of all men, either by word, or writing, or speaking. And keep yourselves clean, [. . .] that nothing may rule nor reign but power and life itself, and that in the wisdom of God ye may be preserved in it.

George Fox, published 1694

Love is the hardest lesson in Christianity; but, for that reason, it should be most our care to learn it.

William Penn, 1693

GOD, THE SPIRIT AND THE LIGHT WITHIN

Give over thine own willing, give over thy own running, give over thine own desiring to know or be anything and sink down to the seed which God sows in the heart, and let that grow in thee and be in thee and breathe in thee and act in thee; and thou shalt find by sweet experience that the Lord knows that and loves and owns that, and will lead it to the inheritance of Life, which is its portion.

Isaac Penington, 1661

It is not opinion, or speculation, or notions of what is true, or assent to or the subscription of articles or propositions, though never so soundly worded, that [. . .] makes a man a true believer or a true Christian. But it is a conformity of mind and practice to the will of God, in all holiness of conversation, according to the dictates of this Divine principle of Light and Life in the soul which denotes a person truly a child of God.

William Penn, 1692

I was under great temptations sometimes, and my inward sufferings were heavy; but I could find none to open my condition to but the Lord alone, unto whom I cried night and day. And I went back into Nottinghamshire, and there the Lord shewed me that the natures of those things which were hurtful without, were within in the hearts and minds of wicked men. [. . .] And I cried to the Lord, saying, Why should I be thus, seeing I was never addicted to commit those evils? And the Lord answered that it was needful I should have a sense of all conditions, how else should I speak to all conditions; and in this I saw the infinite love of

God. I saw also that there was an ocean of darkness and death, but an
infinite ocean of light and love, which flowed over the ocean of darkness.
And in that also I saw the infinite love of God; and I had great openings.
George Fox, published 1694

Quakers in the twenty-first century are often reluctant to talk about the Divine. Many use the word 'God', but others prefer 'the Light', 'the Truth', 'the Seed' or 'the Spirit'. All these words were used constantly by early Friends, but they had quite specific meanings for them, none of which, as far as we can tell, exactly signified 'God'. Those original Quakers had discovered something which they urgently needed to express: that everybody can have a direct experience of the Divine, that they had no need for priests or intermediaries of any kind. In order to explain that weighty message and to make sense of the powerful experience of their Meetings for Worship, they created a new religious vocabulary. Modern Quakers have tended to use the same words, but in ways that make sense to them personally and without reference to their original significance to Friends. Some modern Quakers talk of 'the Holy Spirit', for example, often describing their lives as 'spirit-led', where others might use the word 'God' to mean exactly the same. This can be confusing, and not only to outsiders.

The word 'Light', of all those used by seventeenth century Friends, has possibly the greatest significance for their twenty-first century counterparts. 'The Light within', 'the inner Light' and 'standing in the Light' are all familiar expressions among modern Quakers, who continue to be inspired by George Fox's 'infinite ocean of light and love, which flowed over the ocean of darkness'.

Some Quakers today reject traditional notions of God and use the word 'nontheist' to express their position. Their view should not, however, be confused with an atheist one.

The basis of my understanding is that there is one life, one source, one being, one energy, which manifests physically as the universe we identify as planets, people, animals, rocks, water, air, etc. This means that I hurt when you hurt; I am uplifted when you are. It means I can hold someone in the Light, by focusing my attention on our innate connection, at a time when they may be feeling separate.

I care very much that this one stuff that makes up the universe *not* be identified as God. The notion of God is so old and freighted, so storified, that it stands in the way of my being present 'in the life', as early Quakers said.

I view meeting for worship as a precious opportunity to become very present to the oneness of all humans, of all existence. I come there to rest in the peace available when I share space and time with people who are not busy talking and doing, and who are collectively, consciously, aiming to lift our hearts and minds as high as they'll go. I bring my concerns, knowing that sometimes, in the warmth and safety of meeting, something intractable will melt. There is a quality of our quiet togetherness that I recognize instantly, whether I am at home, or visiting for the first time in a Meeting across the country. In Paris [. . .], where I spoke the language imperfectly, I still *knew* that human huddle.

Robin Alpern, 2006

Friends do not readily use words to express the ineffable. In this message from a group of elders (quoting St Paul in 2 Corinthians 3:6), they once again use those words 'light' and 'spirit' which mean so much to Quakers.

Dearly Beloved Friends, these things we do not lay upon you as a rule or form to walk by, but that all, with the measure of light which is pure and holy, may be guided; and so in the light walking and abiding, these may be fulfilled in the Spirit, not from the letter, for the letter killeth, but the Spirit giveth life.

Elders from Balby, 1656

This 'light' has nothing to do with will or ego. In fact, it is the reverse. It searches us out, and shows us who we are. It illuminates our shortcomings and gives us the strength to renew ourselves. Our task is to face it. In this passage from one of George Fox's epistles, he explains in detail how the practice works:

Friends, – Whatever ye are addicted to, the tempter will come in that thing; and when he can trouble you, then he gets advantage over you, and then ye are gone. Stand still in that which is pure, after ye see yourselves; and then mercy comes in. After thou seest thy thoughts, and the temptations, do not think, but submit; and then power comes. Stand still in that which shows and discovers; and there doth strength immediately come. And stand still in the light, and submit to it, and the other will be hushed and gone; and then content comes. And when temptations and troubles appear, sink down in that which is pure, and all will be hushed, and fly away. Your strength is to stand still, after ye see yourselves; whatsoever ye see yourselves addicted to, temptations, corruption, uncleanness, &c. Then ye think ye shall never overcome. And earthly reason will tell you, what ye shall lose; hearken not to that, but stand still in the light that shows them to you, and then strength comes from the Lord, and help contrary to your expectation. Then ye grow up in peace, and no trouble shall move you. [. . .] Come to stay your minds upon that spirit which was before the letter; here ye learn to read the scriptures aright. If ye do any thing in your own wills, then ye tempt God; but stand still in that power which brings peace.

George Fox, 1652

Let us look again at a quotation from Fox which we have already seen in another context (see page 72). When Fox stood on the pew in Ulverston Church in 1652 and asked the priest his searching questions, he was querying the authenticity of an apparently religious person who might lack true self-understanding, who could be ego-driven, who might not, as he so often put it, have 'stood still'.

You will say, Christ saith this, and the apostles say this; but what canst thou say? Art thou a child of Light and hast walked in the Light, and what thou speakest is it inwardly from God?

Reported by Margaret Fox, 1694

Here is a short extract from the work of Rex Ambler, who has done valuable work on the life-changing effect of Quaker worship on early Friends. Those Quakers used their Meetings for Worship to make profound personal changes to themselves. Ambler has used the same techniques in his own spiritual life and revealed a transforming practice that can enhance and deepen the experience of silent worship.

It began to dawn on me that I had at last found what I had been looking for all these years. But not in the way I had expected to. I had expected, or at least hoped, to find an idea, an interpretation of Quaker faith that I could then put into practice. But it came the other way round. I found a practice, and out of this arose the faith. Not that I produced the faith myself, for the practice was and is a matter of opening myself to what is already there, receiving what is offered, responding to what is revealed to me. The faith was produced in me by something much deeper in me than my conscious ego, but something that made itself felt by twinges of conscience that told me that all was not well with me. As I responded to these and allowed myself to be shown what was really going on in my life, I became aware of the self-deceptions that made me think that 'I', this conscious ego, was the centre of my being and my world – and aware of the truth, that my life was rooted in a reality way beyond my ken, but a reality that I could nevertheless trust. I had to use the word 'God' to signal this other-than-me which gave me my being, though I was aware intellectually of the impossibility of using the word in a logically consistent way. Paradoxical though it would be, I had to say that God was the source of my new-found freedom and joy.

Rex Ambler, 2002

While experience of the Divine often begins with Meeting for Worship, it certainly does not end there. Quakers are led, as Ambler puts it, by an 'other-than-me', and despite the reluctance of most to put their experiences into words, some have done so with telling effect.

Friends have always been cautious about using the name of God too easily, and today many are more acutely aware of this hesitation for a number of reasons. One of their main difficulties is that the word God has often been identified with misleading and false ideas, many of them highly coloured with superstition. A further difficulty is that the word God is frequently used as a kind of intellectual concept, whereas for Quakers their awareness of God is discovered in response and commitment to the deep meaning of life. Quakers also hesitate to use the word too freely because, while completely convinced that [people] everywhere can know this experience in the depth of their being, they also realise that the ways in which this experience is discovered and expressed by people will vary greatly. The attempt to press this living response into a word or words is liable to limit and distort it. This becomes obvious when we consider how inadequate words are to express and define any profound human experience. When a man says to a woman 'I love you', we recognise that the words themselves are quite unable to convey the full power and depth intended. But despite all these legitimate hesitations, and the impossibility of knowing exactly what the word God means, there is in the end no other word in human language that can finally convey the awareness of an encounter that confronts [people] at the centre of their being.

George Gorman, 1969

I do believe that there is a power which is divine, creative and loving, though we can often only describe it with the images and symbols that rise from our particular experiences and those of our communities. This power is part and parcel of all things, human, animal, indeed all that lives. Its story is greater than any one cultural version of it and yet

it is embodied in all stories, in all traditions. It is a power that paradoxically needs the human response. Like us it is energised by the reci-
procity of love.

Harvey Gillman, 1988

The most simple reality, God, is the one which humanity has striven
hardest to complicate. It has become the battle-ground of terrible
conflicts, the cause of fratricidal wars. God, through the fault of
people, has ceased to be a bond which unites and has become a flag to
be raised on fields of battle.

God is dead, we hear today. This conclusion was inevitable after so
many years of sectarianism. If He is really dead, dead in the hearts and
minds of people, it is because He has been crushed under the weight
of indigestible abstractions and interminable discussions.

To avoid adding new errors to the old ones, let us give the name
Silence to what others call The Word.

Speech tends to divide, people cling to words rather than to their
meaning. Words give rise to religions, to churches which break up the
great family of simple souls, for whom loving worship should be
enough, into rival sovereign fragments.

Words split apart, Silence unites. Words scatter, Silence gathers
together. Words stir up, Silence brings peace. Words engender denial,
Silence invites even the denier to find fresh hope in the confident
expectation of a mystery which can be accomplished within.

In my active silence, I shall prepare myself to hear the Silence
of God.

Pierre Lacout, 1969

So one approaches, by efforts which call for the deepest resources of
one's being, to the condition of true silence; not just of sitting still, not
just of not speaking, but of a wide awake, fully aware non-thinking.

It is in this condition, found and held for a brief instant only, that I
have experienced the existence of something other than myself. The
thinking me has vanished, and with it vanishes the sense of separation,

of unique identity. One is not left naked and defenceless, as one is, for example, by the operations of the mind in self-analysis. One becomes instead aware, one is conscious of being a participant in the whole of existence, not limited to the body, or the moment. This sounds like a description of a hallucinated state, and certainly it is an alarming experience when first encountered. But it differs from what I understand to be the condition induced by hallucinogenic drugs such as LSD (conditions which I would recognize as an opening, but a limited opening, of the identical doors of perception) in that the condition acquired without drugs is under control; one can leave it at the ring of a telephone bell, however reluctantly; it does not restrict or inhibit action, it does not accentuate the pre-existent mood, lifting the optimist to heaven and plunging the depressive into hell, and, most important of all, it carries a conviction of its essential truth which persists and enriches life outside the brief experience.

It is in this condition that one understands the nature of the divine power, its essential identity with love, in the widest sense of that much misused word. And the experience rings true; once we have gone so far we are bound to recognize the nature of our experience and there is no hiding from its implications.

Geoffrey Hubbard, 1974

Religion is living with God. There is no other kind of religion. Living with a Book, living with or by a Rule, being awfully high-principled are not in themselves religion, although many people think they are and that that is all there is to it. Religion has got a bad name through being identified with an outward orderliness. But an outward orderliness can be death, dullness and masochism. Doing your duty may be admirable stoicism; it isn't religion.

To find religion itself you must look inside people and inside yourself. And there, if you find even the tiniest grain of true love, you may be on the right scent. Millions of people have it and don't know what it is that they have. God is their guest, but they haven't the faintest idea that he is in the house. So you mustn't only look where God is confessed and acknowledged. You must look everywhere, to find the real religion. Nor must you look, in others or in yourself, for great spooky visions and revelations. Such visions and revelations come to many, a great deal oftener than we think; and to those to whom they come they are sun, moon and stars. But in most people who know God, and in all such people most of the time, living with God is not an apparition but a wordless and endless sureness. Like the silence of two friends together. Like the silence of lovers.

God is waiting to live like that in every single person in the world.

Bernard Canter, 1962

What is love?

Answer: What shall I say of it, or how shall I in words express its nature! It is the sweetness of life; it is the sweet, tender, melting nature of God, flowing up through his seed of life into the creature, and of all things making the creature most like unto himself, both in nature and operation. It fulfils the law, it fulfils the gospel; it wraps up all in one, and brings forth all in the oneness. It excludes all evil out of the heart, it perfects all good in the heart. A touch of love doth this in measure; perfect love doth this in fullness. But how can I proceed to speak of it! Oh that the souls of all that fear and wait on the Lord might feel its nature fully! And then would they not fail of its sweet, overcoming operations, both towards one another, and towards enemies. The great healing, the great conquest, the great salvation is reserved for the full manifestation of the love of God. His judgments, his cuttings, his hewings by the word of his mouth, are but to prepare for, but not to do, the great work of raising up the sweet building of his life, which is to be done in love, and in peace, and by the power thereof. And this my soul waits and cries after, even the full springing up of eternal love in my heart, and in the swallowing of me wholly into it, and the bringing of my soul wholly forth in it, that the life of God in its own perfect sweetness may fully run forth through this vessel, and not be at all tinctured by the vessel, but perfectly tincture and change the vessel into its own nature; and then shall no fault be found in my soul before the Lord, but the spotless life be fully enjoyed by me, and become a perfectly pleasant sacrifice to my God.

Oh! How sweet is love! How pleasant is its nature! How takingly doth it behave itself in every condition, upon every occasion, to every person, and about every thing! How tenderly, how readily, doth it help and serve the meanest! How patiently, how meekly, doth it bear all things, either from God or man, how unexpectedly soever they come, or how hard soever they seem! How doth it believe, how doth it hope, how doth it excuse, how doth it cover even that which seemeth not to be excusable, and not fit to be covered! How kind is it even in its interpretations and charges concerning miscarriages! It never overchargeth, it never grates upon the spirit of him whom it reprehends; it never hardens, it never provokes; but carrieth a meltingness and power of conviction with it. This is the nature of God; this, in the vessels capacitated to receive and bring it forth in its glory, the power of enmity is not able to stand against, but falls before, and is overcome by.

Isaac Penington, 1663

There is a spirit which I feel that delights to do no evil, nor to revenge any wrong, but delights to endure all things, in hope to enjoy its own in the end. Its hope is to outlive all wrath and contention, and to weary out all exaltation and cruelty, or whatever is of a nature contrary to itself. It sees to the end of all temptations. As it bears no evil in itself, so it conceives none in thoughts to any other. If it be betrayed, it bears it, for its ground and spring is the mercies and forgiveness of God. Its crown is meekness, its life is everlasting love unfeigned; it takes its kingdom with entreaty and not with contention, and keeps it by lowliness of mind. In God alone it can rejoice, though none else regard it, or can own its life. It's conceived in sorrow, and brought forth without any to pity it, nor doth it murmur at grief and oppression. It never rejoiceth but through sufferings; for with the world's joy it is murdered. I found it alone, being forsaken. I have fellowship therein with them who lived in dens and desolate places in the earth, who through death obtained this resurrection and eternal holy life.

James Nayler, 1660

It's a funny thing about God, which I still haven't understood. If you say with all your heart: he isn't there, then oddly he isn't. He seems to withdraw. In the same way, just not noticing produces the same results. He doesn't come thrusting himself into your life if you don't want him there. (I recognise that some people will want to say that's exactly how God came to them, but I think this is a different matter.) Yet if we say: God, I need you, then he moves closer to us. If we start the conversation, surprisingly it does not simply seem to fade into empty space. A sense of presence gradually begins to make itself felt.

Now I really don't know how I'm going to convince you of that. I also hear people telling me: I've tried that and it doesn't work. And that's also perfectly true, as we all painfully know from our own experiences. I know it's true and a very blank feeling it is when we have it. Yet I also know that the presence of God is as real, as the absence is negating. I begin to recognise that ultimately it is not for any intellectual reasons that I believe in God, nor even possibly as a result of my emotional state, but simply from the growing sense that when I call he answers.

I don't find it easy to write this, for I also need to overcome the sense that you will find what I say faintly ridiculous. However, it seems worth the risk, because the alternative is rather bleak – that there is, after all, no converse with God, because we do not begin the conversations. All I want to say is that once the conversation begins, one does not want it ever to stop.

Tony Brown, 1984

What have I personally learned in my association with Friends over the years? It has taught me that there is something of God within each person, even those in whom it seems impossible to find it. In fact, this Divine Presence is in all creation. I cannot claim that I always remember that it is so – in fact, I forget more often than I remember. But when I do remember it changes my life, and the world around me. These changes are usually not dramatic, but subtle, and at its best this has enabled me to '. . . know an inward stillness, even amid the activities of daily life' (*Advices & Queries* 3).

This Divine Presence takes many forms. Some *see* it as the Inward Light. Others *hear* it as the Still Small Voice. Whether you see or hear depends upon your temperament. Within the practice of yoga, it is recognised that there are different types of human beings. Some are devotional, others are more intellectual, while a third group is more practical. There are different types of spiritual practice for each type. I have observed this among Friends, but the Quaker way of worship in the silence eventually transcends these differences and brings us to Oneness. The Inward Light and the Still Small Voice are One, and in the end it is the Oneness that really matters.

I have discovered that we can all contact the Spirit within us. We do not need the external aid of special ministers or special rituals. Through this Spirit, ordinary people have the potential to become extraordinary. Through It, I have come to realise that ordinary people are extraordinary. Because, in the words of Tennyson, this Spirit is 'Closer . . . than breathing, nearer than hands and feet'. It is there whether we acknowledge it or not, but when we do recognise it, and in the silence provide a space for it to act within our consciousness, It can transform our lives, and the lives of all around us.

In the preceding paragraphs I have referred to the Divine as It, but the Christian teaching, on which Quakerism is based, teaches us that God is personal, and can be experienced as a loving and forgiving Presence. It can be experienced as male or female, though for most Friends it equates with the presence of God or Christ. (Mother Julian of Norwich said that Christ is also our Mother, and some Quakers would confirm that experience.) I have come to know this Divine Power through the deep silence of the gathered group in Quaker worship, and discovered that the power of the group is greater than the sum of the individuals present. I have also found it through meditation.

And I have learned that if I make the intention – even if I often fail to live up to it – to live my life as if it is so, then I can experience that Presence and Power in a very real way at any time. All this, for me, has been a powerful and life-changing message.

Jim Pym, 1999

The Peace Testimony, silent worship and avoiding outward observation of sacraments are the most obviously distinctive features of traditional Quakerism, though there are others. From the outside they might look like historical accidents, each with its particular justi-fication and reason to be. However, that is not their true character. They are not held independently in a rounded Quakerism, but take their strength from being integrally related to the whole.

Indeed, that is why Friends maintain them, for they are part of the reply Quakers would give to the scepticism and disorder of the modern world and the influence they would wish to exert in the church as it struggles to find its own larger response. Part of the common faith is to bear witness to one's understanding of apostolic Christianity within the fellowship. Another is to accept and learn from the diversity of witness that will arise. This can only be done if one accepts that there can be diverse insights into the common faith and that a comprehensive understanding of Christianity will be better able to meet the demands of the future than a collection of narrow sectarian ones.

It is on the issue of sacraments that these things are put to the test. Friends neither baptize with water nor observe the Lord's Supper. This mystifies many other Christians. How can that possibly be? Is not the New Testament explicit about these things? Are they not the marks of Christianity? The issue is likely to generate considerable heat; we are not dealing here with rarified heights of doctrine but with the common experience of millions of people.

To make sense, Christianity has to speak about God. If the God question can be put in such a way that Christianity has nothing to say, its God is false and its worship meaningless. Quaker silence is therefore related intimately to an understanding of the nature of the divine. There are Friends who do not accept the Christian understanding of God, and for them the question of the sacraments is irrelevant. The majority, however, do, and it is their conception of the way God works that causes them not to baptize or celebrate communion.

It will be generally agreed that God is the divine principle of creation and meaning. Beauty and love are expressions of the divine energy and consciousness, and we tend to use the word 'truth' to encompass everything we know about the divine. Another useful word is 'ultimate'. It indicates the limits of our understanding and powers, and beyond which we are unable to go. The word 'God' means all these things, but if it is to be taken in a Christian sense, it must additionally mean that God communicates with us – that there is a divine revelation.

Friends believe the Bible to teach that this revelation comes directly to every single human being, without exception. Not everybody responds to revelation; we are free to ignore it or disobey it as we wish. It states, but does not compel. It can show us meaning but needs no interpretation in itself; we know inwardly that this revelation is the truth, and it guides us and lays burdens upon us when we embrace it as the source of spiritual life. It draws us into the company of others and redeems us out of the world. This is the work of the Holy Spirit, what Friends call the Light of Christ within.

John Punshon, 1987

'I believe in God' or 'I do not believe', 'There is a God' or 'There is no God' – these are verbal statements the one in the end as good as the other to indicate the thing that really matters: moral power, faith, hope, love. So I would say: whenever you feel that abandoning a formula will weaken a part of your moral strength, preserve it as one keeps the scaffolding standing until the keystone of the arch is in position or the ferro-concrete has set firm. And with equal emphasis: whenever you feel that by retaining a formula you are impeding and weakening your moral strength, destroy it without compunction.

Therefore don't be timid. Remember that all your words, all your expressions of belief are mere approximations and eternally inadequate. The crime is to want to nail everything down in a final way with the authority of the Church or the Bible. Men have to get used to seeing the scaffolding of their faith becoming ever more lofty and sublime. There is no avoiding a move in the direction of agnosticism when reaching out for greater moral power. We have to test the scaffolding now and again to see if the time has come to remove another support so that the structure is free to rise to loftier and nobler heights.

Pierre Ceresole, published 1954

Our understanding of the Divine, of God, is the foundation of our actions and our thinking, of the way we choose to live and to worship. Even if we don't consciously formulate our understanding, it is there as a motive, as the basis, the root of our lives. Each of us has our own understanding of God, created consciously or not out of our own experiences, starting before our birth, and out of our own emotional and intellectual history. We share some elements of it with others, while other elements are unique to us.

Our understanding of God is like a big house in which we have been born and which we explore as we grow. We make ideas and pictures with the materials we find in it, we bring lots of things in from outside, we find some interesting things in its library, we cook other things up for ourselves in its kitchen, and we make our own music and pictures. Sometimes things in the cellar burst through and surprise us, sometimes we rummage in the attic and find an old concept which we re-make into something useful. Meeting for worship is one place where we turn over the pictures, re-play the video clips and connect the ideas. Talking with others is another chance to look at our understandings together and to learn from each other. Living by our ideas is where we really test them out in practice. What happens if I follow this leading? Is there that of God in everyone? Does nonviolence work?

It's useful to be aware of the imagery and metaphor which is often hidden in the words we use and which other Friends use. We Quakers love the picture language of metaphor – our classic two are the slightly abstract metaphor of Light, and the more organic one of Seed and growth. Listen to ministry in meeting for worship and see how often it is given in a variety of metaphorical forms. Our concern for truth asks us to appreciate and enjoy the metaphors but also to look behind them, grasping what is being said and perhaps recasting it in our own picture language, often a language or a way into experience which is personal to us as individuals.

Beth Allen, 2007

The God I know does not ask us to conform to some abstract norm for the ideal self. God asks us only to honour our created nature, which means our limits as well as potentials. When we fail to do so, reality happens – God happens – and the way closes behind us.

The God I was told about in church, and still hear about from time to time, runs about like an anxious schoolmaster measuring people's behaviour with a moral yardstick. But the God I know is the source of reality rather than morality, the source of what is rather than what ought to be. This does not mean that God has nothing to do with morality: morality and its consequences are built into the God-given structure of reality itself. Moral norms are not something we have to stretch for, and moral consequences are not something we have to wait for: they are right here, right now, waiting for us to honour, or violate, the nature of self, other, world. . . .

The God whom I know dwells quietly in the root system of the very nature of things. This is the God who, when asked by Moses for a name, responded, 'I Am who I Am' (Exodus 3:14), an answer that has less to do with the moral rules for which Moses made God famous than with elemental 'isness' and selfhood. If, as I believe, we are all made in God's image, we could all give the same answer when asked who we are: 'I Am who I Am'. One dwells with God by being faithful to one's nature. One crosses God by trying to be something one is not. Reality – including one's own – is divine, to be not defied but honoured.

Parker J. Palmer, 2000

This chapter closes with two prayers and a poem. It is unusual for Quakers to publish prayers. The first was intended only for the use of its author and was found in his notebooks after he died. The second is the work of a Japanese Quaker who was one of the founders of The League of Nations and who left a huge body of written work (his *Complete Works* run to twenty-five volumes) of which this fragment is a minuscule part. Finally, the poem by John Greenleaf Whittier has achieved lasting recognition through its transformation into a hymn (sung to a tune from an unconnected oratorio by Hubert Parry) which is in constant use by Christian denominations across the world.

ETERNAL, be thou our guide and our inspiration; thy will be done.

Strengthen our hands for the work that lies before us so that we may complete it without pride or self-centredness, cowardice or sloth.

Grant us strength to resist temptation and to forgive others as freely as we ourselves would wish to be forgiven.

Grant that we may repay injuries solely by redoubling our efforts never to cause injury to others.

Eternal, we resolve to listen for thy summons, that through obedience we may hear thy voice ever more clearly.

Grant us the honesty to examine our own thoughts and actions just as scrupulously and severely as those of others.

Deliver us from the fanaticism and pride which hinder us from welcoming the truth of other people's teaching and experience.

Grant us the quiet conviction that thou canst reveal thy truth and justice directly to others, just as we believe thou hast in a measure revealed them to us.

Teach us how to work together wholeheartedly, without self-seeking, petty vanity or ambition, in the common quest for truth.

Teach us how to pity, and how to bring real comfort to those who suffer.

Grant us the quiet courage necessary in all circumstances and natural to those who have dedicated their lives to thee.

On the highest pinnacle of living, where man and woman meet, may there be above all else a passionate respect for the true values of life; may thy truth and thy love come first.

May no defeat or failure or backsliding ever separate us from thee; in the midst of all our tribulations, hold us fast in thy love and lift us little by little up to thee.

Pierre Ceresole, published 1954

I ask for daily bread, but not for wealth, lest I forget the poor.
I ask for strength, but not for power, lest I despise the meek.
I ask for wisdom, but not for learning, lest I scorn the simple.
I ask for a clean name, but not for fame, lest I condemn the lowly.
I ask for peace of mind, but not for idle hours, lest I fail to hearken to the call of duty.
For these and much more, O Father, do I crave, knocking at thy door;
And, if I dare not enter, yet Thou canst dole out the crumbs fallen from Thy table.

Inazo Nitobe, 1936

Dear Lord and Father of mankind
Forgive our foolish ways!
Reclothe us in our rightful mind,
In purer lives thy service find,
In deeper reverence, praise.

In simple trust like theirs who heard
Beside the Syrian sea
The gracious calling of the Lord,
Let us, like them, without a word,
Rise up and follow thee.

O Sabbath rest by Galilee!
O calm of hills above,
Where Jesus knelt to share with thee

The silence of eternity
Interpreted by love!

With that deep hush subduing all
Our words and works that drown
The tender whisper of thy call,
As noiseless let thy blessing fall
As fell thy manna down.

Drop thy still dews of quietness,
Till all our strivings cease;
Take from our souls the strain and stress,
And let our ordered lives confess
The beauty of thy peace.

Breathe through the heats of our desire
Thy coolness and thy balm;
Let sense be dumb, let flesh retire;
Speak through the earthquake, wind, and fire,
O still, small voice of calm!

                                John Greenleaf Whittier, 1872

QUAKER JOURNALS 2:
MARY PENINGTON

Mary Penington (1625–1682) wrote her journal (variously called *Experiences in the Life of Mary Penington* and *Some Account of the Circumstances in the Life of Mary Penington*) about five years after she became a Quaker and a full twenty years before she died. It is entirely unlike the journal of George Fox in that she had no interest in proclaiming her Quakerism to the world. Nor did she want to chronicle the important events of her life. She wrote it just for her friends and family to explain to them the spiritual journey that brought her to the Quakers – and we assume they already knew the story after that. It is a tale that begins in spiritual doubt, in 'darkness and distress about religion', and has clear resonances today in the alienation and ennui felt by many people confronted by traditional spiritual teaching.

Born Mary Proude, she was orphaned at a young age and raised by the Springetts, relations of hers who lived in Kent. One of the sons of the family, Sir William Springett, with whom she had already spent much of her childhood, became her husband when she was eighteen. They lived happily together and Mary gave birth to a son. A little over two years into their marriage, however, a series of catastrophes overtook Mary's life which would have surely dominated any conventional journal devoted to family history.

In 1645, William contracted a fever while on active service with the Parliamentary army and suddenly died. Mary was pregnant again when the disaster happened, and she embarked on a life of single motherhood in which she was greatly helped by the devoted assistance of William's mother. In due course she gave birth to a second child, Gulielma. Reading her journal, we learn of her wish not to have her daughter baptised – an important and difficult religious decision for anyone in the 1640s – but the subsequent death of her little boy, and also within two years the fatal illness of her mother-in-law, are not mentioned.

So Mary was a widow with a nine-year-old daughter when, in 1654, she met and married Isaac Penington. He too went on to become a Quaker and there are examples of his outstanding spiritual writing elsewhere in this book. At the time of his marriage to Mary, however, they both shared a deep scepticism about religion in general and about the Quakers in particular. In *Experiences in the Life of Mary Penington*, she explains how she came to change her mind. They went to their first Friends' meeting in 1657 (by which time they had two more children) and seem to have begun to identify themselves as Quakers by the middle of the following year.

The first scripture I remember to have taken notice of was, 'Blessed are they that hunger and thirst after righteousness, for they shall be filled'. This I heard taken for a text when I was about eight years of age, and under the care of people who were a kind of loose Protestants, that minded no more about religion than to go to their worship-house on first days, to hear a canonical priest preach in the morning, and read common prayers in the afternoon. They used common prayers in the family, and observed superstitious customs and times, days of feasting and fasting, Christmas, (so called), Good Friday, Lent, &c. About this time I was afraid, in the night, of such things as run in my mind by day, of spirits, thieves, &c. When alone in the fields, and possessed with fears, I accounted prayers my help and safety; so would often say (as I had been taught) the Lord's Prayer, hoping thereby to be delivered from the things I feared.

After some time I went to live with some that appeared to be more religious. They would not admit of sports on first days, calling first day the Sabbath. They went to hear two sermons a day, from a priest that was not loose in his conversation: he used a form of prayer before his sermon, and read the common prayer after it. I was now about ten or eleven years of age. A maidservant that waited on me and the rest of the children was very zealous in their way: she used to read Smith's and Preston's sermons on first days, between the sermon times. I diligently heard her read, and at length liked not to use the Lord's Prayer alone, but got a prayer-book, and read prayers mornings and evenings; and that scripture of 'howling on their beds', was much on my mind: by it I was checked from saying prayers in my bed.

About this time I began to be very serious about religion. One day, after we came from the place of public worship, the maid before mentioned read one of Preston's sermons, the text was: 'Pray continually'. In this sermon much was said respecting prayer: amongst other things, of the excellency of prayer, that it distinguished a saint from a sinner; that in many things the hypocrite could imitate the saint, but in this he could not. This thing wrought much on my mind. I found that I knew not what true prayer was; for what I used for prayer, an ungodly person could use as well as I, which was to read one out of a book; and this could not be the prayer he meant, which distinguished a saint from a wicked one. My mind was deeply exercised about this thing. When she had done reading, and all were gone out of the chamber, I shut the door, and in great distress I flung myself on the bed, and oppressedly cried out: 'Lord, what is prayer!'

This exercise continued so on my mind, that at night, when I used to read a prayer out of a book, I could only weep, and remain in trouble. At this time I had never heard of any people that prayed any other way than by reading prayers out of a book, or composing themselves. I remember one morning it came into my mind that I would write a prayer of my own composing, and use it in the morning as soon as I was out of bed; which I did, though I could then scarcely join my letters, I had learnt so little a time to write. The prayer I wrote was something after this manner: 'Lord, thou commandest the Israelites to offer a morning sacrifice, so I offer up the sacrifice of prayer, and desire to be preserved this day'. The use of this prayer for a little while gave me some ease. I soon quite left my prayer-books, and used to write prayers according to my several occasions. The second that I wrote was for the assurance of the pardon of my sins. I had heard one preach, 'that God of his free grace pardoned David's sins'. I was much affected by it, and, as I came from the worship place, I thought it would be a happy thing to be assured that one's past sins were pardoned. I wrote a pretty long prayer on that subject, and felt, that as pardon came through grace, I might receive it, though very unworthy of it. In said prayer I used many earnest expressions.

A little time after this, several persons spoke to me about the great-ness of my memory, and praised me for it. I felt a fear of being puffed up, and wrote a prayer of thanks for that gift, and desired to be enabled to use it for the Lord, and that it might be sanctified to me.

These three prayers I used with some ease of mind, but not long, for I began again to question whether I prayed aright or not. I was much troubled about it, not knowing that any did pray extempore; but it sprung up in my mind, that to use words descriptive of the state I was in, was prayer, which I attempted to do, but could not. Sometimes I kneeled down a long time, and had not a word to say, which wrought great trouble in me. I had none to reveal my distress unto, or advise with; so, secretly bore a great burden a long time.

One day as I was sitting at work in the parlour, one called a gentleman (who was against the superstitions of the times) came in, and looking sadly, said 'it was a sad day: that Prynne, Bastwick, and Burton, were sentenced to have their ears cut, and to be banished'. This news sunk deep into my mind, and strong cries were raised in me for them, and the rest of the innocent people in the nation. I was unable to sit at my work, but was strongly inclined to go into a private room, which I did, and shutting the door, kneeled down and poured out my soul to the Lord in a very vehement manner. I was wonderfully melted and eased, and felt peace and acceptance with the Lord; and that this was true prayer, which I had never before been acquainted with.

Not long after this an account was brought to the house, that a neighbouring minister, who had been suspended by the bishops for not being subject to their canons, was returned to his flock again, and that he was to preach at the place where he did three years before, (being suspended so long). I expressed a desire to go thither, but was reproved by those that had the care of my education, they saying that it was not fit to leave my parish church. I could not be easy without going, so I went. When I came there, he prayed fervently (he was one called a Puritan) and with great power. Then I felt that was true prayer, and what my mind pressed after, but could not come at in my own will, and had but just tasted of it the time before mentioned. And now I knew that this alone was prayer, I mourned solely because I kneeled down morning after morning, and night after night, and had not a word to say. My distress was so great, that I feared I should perish in the night, because I had not prayed; and I thought that by day my food would not nourish me, because I could not pray.

I was thus exercised a great while, and could not join in the common prayer that was read in the family every night; neither could I kneel down when I came to the worship-house, as I had been taught to do; and this scripture was much in my mind: 'Be more ready to hear, than to offer the sacrifice of fools'. I could only read the Bible, or some other book, whilst the priest read the common prayer. At last I could neither kneel nor stand up to join with the priest in his prayer before the sermon; neither did I care to hear him preach, my mind being after the Nonconformist, the Puritan already mentioned.

By constraint I went with the family in the morning, but could not be kept from the Puritan preacher in the afternoon. I went through much suffering on this account, being forced to go on foot between two and three miles, and no one permitted to go with me; except sometimes a servant, out of compassion, would run after me, lest I should be frightened going alone. Though I was very young, I was so zealous that all the tried reasonings and threatenings could not keep me back. In a short time I refused to hear the priest of our parish at all, but went constantly, all weathers, to the other place. In the family I used to hear the Scripture read; but if I happened to go in before they had done their prayers, I would sit down though they were kneeling.

These things wrought me much trouble in the family, and there was none to take my part; yet at length two of the maid-servants were inclined to mind what I said against their prayers, and so refused to join them, at which the governors of the family were much disturbed, and made me the subject of their discourse in company, saying that I would pray with the spirit, and rejected godly men's prayers; that I was proud and schismatic; and that I went to those places to meet young men, and such like. At this time I suffered, not only from those persons to whose care I was committed by my parents, (who both died when I was not above three years of age), but also from my companions and kindred; yet, notwithstanding, in this zeal I grew much, and sequestered myself from my former vain company, and refused playing at cards, &c. I zealously kept the Sabbath, not daring to eat or be clothed with such things as occasioned much trouble, or took up much time on that day, which I believed ought to be devoted to hearing, reading, and praying. I disregarded those matches proposed to me by vain persons, having desired of the Lord, that if I married at all, it might be a man that feared him. I had a belief, that though I then knew of none of my outward rank that was such a one, yet that the Lord would provide such a one for me.

Possessed of this belief, I regarded not their reproaches, that would say to me, that no gentleman was of this way, and that I should marry some mean person or other. But they were disappointed, for the Lord touched the heart of him that was afterwards my husband, and my heart cleaved to him for the Lord's sake. He was of a good under-standing, and had cast off those dead superstitions; which, that they were dead, was more clearly made manifest to him in that day, than any other person that I knew of, of his rank and years. He was but young, compared to the knowledge he had attained in the things of God. He was about twenty years old. We pressed much after the knowledge of the Lord, and walked in his fear; and though both very young, were joined together in the Lord; refusing the use of a ring, and such like things then used, and not denied by any that we knew of.

We lived together about two years and a month. We were zealously affected, and daily exercised in what we believed to be the service and worship of God. We scrupled many things then in use amongst those accounted honest people, viz. singing David's Psalms in metre. We tore out of our Bibles the common prayer, the form of prayer, and also the singing psalms, as being the inventions of vain poets, not being written for that use. We found that songs of praise must spring from the same source as prayers did; so we could not use anyone's songs or prayers. We were also brought off from the use of bread and wine, and water baptism. We looked into the Independent way, but saw death there, and that there was not the thing our souls sought after.

In this state my dear husband died, hoping in the promises afar off, not seeing or knowing him that is invisible to be so near him; and that it was he that showed unto him his thoughts, and made manifest the good and the evil. When he was taken from me I was with child of my dear daughter Gulielma Maria Springett. It was often with me that I should not be able to consent to the thing being done to my child, which I saw no fruit of, and knew to be but a custom which men were engaged in by tradition, not having the true knowledge of that scripture in the last of the Galatians, of circumcision or uncircumcision availing nothing, but a new creature. This was often in my mind, and I resolved that it should not be done to my child. When I was delivered of her, I refused to have her sprinkled, which brought great reproach upon me; so I became a by-word and a hissing among the people of my own rank in the world; and a strange thing it was thought to be, among my relations and acquaintance. Such as were esteemed able ministers, (and I formerly delighted to hear), were sent to persuade me; but I could not consent and be clear. My answer to them was: 'He that doubteth is damned'.

After some time I waded through this difficulty, but soon after I unhappily went from the simplicity into notions, and changed my ways often, and ran from one notion into another, not finding satisfaction nor assurance that I should obtain what my soul desired, in the several ways and notions which I sought satisfaction in. I was weary of prayers, and such like exercises, finding no peace therefrom; nor could I lift up my hands without doubting, nor call God father. In this state, and for this cause, I gave over all manner of religious exercises in my family and in private, with much grief, for my delight was in being exercised about religion. I left not those things in a loose mind, as some judged that kept in them; for had I found I performed thereby what the Lord required of me, and was well pleased with, I could gladly have continued in the practice of them; I being zealously affected about the several things that were accounted duties; a zealous Sabbath-keeper, and fasting often; praying in private, rarely less than three times a day, many times oftener; a hearer of sermons on all occasions, both lectures, fasts, and thanksgiving. Most of the day was used to be spent in reading the scriptures or praying, or such like. I dared not go to bed till I had prayed, nor pray till I had read scripture, and felt my heart warmed thereby, or by meditation. I had so great a zeal and delight in the exercise of religious duties, that when I questioned not but it was right, I have often in the day sought remote places to pray in, such as the fields, gardens, or out-houses, when I could not be private in the house. I was so vehement in prayer that I thought no place too private to pray in, for I could not but be loud in the earnest pouring out of my soul. Oh! This was not parted with but because I found it polluted, and my rest must not be there.

I now had my conversation among a people that had no religion, being ashamed to be thought religious, or do anything that was called so, not finding my heart with the appearance. And now I loathed whatever profession any one made, and thought the professors of every sort worse than the profane, they boasted so much of what I knew they had not attained to; I having been zealous in all things which they pretended to, and could not find the purging of the heart, or answer of acceptation from the Lord.

In this restless state I entertained every sort of notion that arose in that day, and for a time applied myself to get out of them whatever I could; but still sorrow and trouble was the end of all, and I began to conclude that the Lord and his truth was, but that it was not made known to any upon earth; and I determined no more to enquire after Him or it, for it was in vain to seek Him, being not to be found. For some time, pursuant to my resolution, I thought nothing about religion, but minded recreations as they are called, and ran into many excesses and vanities; as foolish mirth, carding, dancing, singing, and frequenting of music meetings; and made many vain visits at jovial eatings and drinkings, to satisfy the extravagant appetite, and please the vain mind with curiosities; gratifying the lust of the eye, the lust of the flesh, and the pride of life. I also frequented other places of pleasure, where vain people resorted to show themselves, and to see others in the like excess of folly in apparel; riding about from place to place, in the airy mind. But in the midst of all this my heart was constantly sad, and pained beyond expression; and after a pretty long indulgence in such follies, I retired for several days, and was in great trouble and anguish.

To all this excess and folly I was not hurried by being captivated with such things, but sought in them relief from the discontent of my mind; not having found what I sought after, and longed for, in the practice of religious duties. I would often say to myself, What is all this to me? I could easily leave it all, for my heart is not satisfied therewith. I do these things because I am weary, and know not what else to do: it is not my delight; it hath not power over me. I had rather serve the Lord, if I knew how acceptably.

In this restless, distressed state, I often retired into the country, without any company but my daughter and her maid; and there I spent many hours each day in bemoaning myself, and desiring the knowledge of the truth; but was still deceived, and fell in with some delusive notions or other, that wounded me, and left me without any clearness or certainty. One night, in this retired place, I went to bed very disconsolately and sad, through the great and afflicting exercise of my mind. I dreamed that night that I saw a book of hieroglyphics of religion, of things to come in the church, or a religious state. I thought I took no delight in them, nor felt any closing in my mind with them, though magnified by those that showed them. I turned from them greatly oppressed, and it being evening, went out from the company into a field, sorrowing, and lifting up my eyes to heaven, cried: 'Lord, suffer me no more to fall in with any wrong way, but show me the truth'. Immediately I thought the sky opened, and a bright light, like fire, fell upon my hand, which so frightened me that I awoke, and cried out so that my daughter's servant, who was in the room, not gone to bed, came to my bedside to know what was the matter with me. I trembled a long while after, yet knew not what to turn to; or rather believing there was nothing manifest since the apostles' days, that was true religion; for I knew nothing to be so certainly of God, that I could shed my blood in the defence of it.

One day, as I was going through London, from a country-house, I could not pass through the crowd, it being the day the Lord Mayor was sworn: I was obliged to go into a house till it was over. I, being burdened with the vanity of their show, said to a professor that stood by me: 'What benefit have we from all this bloodshed, and Charles being kept out of the nation, seeing all these follies are again allowed?' He answered: 'None, that he knew of, except the enjoyment of true religion.' I replied 'that it is a benefit to you that have a religion to be protected in the exercise of, but it is none to me.'

But here I must mention a state that I then knew, notwithstanding all my darkness and distress about religion, which was in nothing to be careful, but in all cases to let my requests be known to the Lord in sighs and groans; and help he was graciously pleased to afford me in the most confused disquieted estate I ever knew; even in the day when I had no religion I could call true. Wonderful is the remembrance of his kindness! If I wanted to hire a servant, or remove to any place, or do any other thing that concerned my condition in this world, I always retired and waited upon the Lord, to see what the day would bring forth; and as things presented to me I would embrace them, without making much enquiry after accommodations of that kind; but was in all things else in a dissatisfied, hurried condition; for I thought the beloved of my soul was neither night nor day with me. Yet in the anguish of my soul I would cry to Him, and beseech that if I might not come to Him as a child, not having the spirit of sonship, yet, as he was my creator, I might approach him as the beasts that have their food from him: 'For, Lord, thou knowest I cannot move or breathe as thy creature, without thee: help is only in thee. If thou art inaccessible in thy own glory, yet I can only have help where it is to be had, and thou only hast power to help me'.

O, the distress I felt at this time! Having never dared to kneel down to pray for years, because I could not in truth call God father, and dared not mock or be formal in the thing. Sometimes I should be melted into tears, and feel inexpressible tenderness; and then, not knowing from whence it proceeded, and being ready to judge all religion, I thought it was some influence from the planets that governed the body, and so accounted for my being sometimes hard, and sometimes tender, as being under such or such a planet; but dared not to own anything in me to be of God, or that I felt any influence of his good spirit upon my heart; but I was like the parched heath, and the hunted hart for water, so great was my thirst after that which I did not believe was near me.

My mind being thus almost continually exercised, I dreamed that I was sitting alone, retired and sad; and as I was sitting, I heard a very loud, confused noise: some shrieking, yelling, and roaring in a piteous, doleful manner; others casting up their caps, and hallooing in a way of triumph and joy. I listened to find out what the matter was, it was manifested to me that Christ was come; and the different noises I heard were expressive of the different states the people were in at his coming – some in joy, some in extreme sorrow and amazement. I waited in much dread to see the issue; at length I found that neither the joying nor sorrowing part of the multitude were they that truly knew of his coming, but were agitated by a false rumour. So I abode still in the room solitary, and found I was not to join with either party, but to be still, and not affected with the thing at all, nor go forth to enquire about it. Sitting thus a while, all was silent. Remaining still in the same place, cool and low in my mind, all this distracted noise being over, one came in, and speaking in a low voice said: 'Christ is come indeed, and is in the next room; and with him is the bride, the Lamb's wife'. At this my heart secretly leaped within me, and I was ready to get up and go and express my love to him, and joy at his coming; but something within me stopped me, and bade me not to be hasty, but patiently, coolly, softly, and soberly go into the next room, which I did, and stood just within the entrance of a spacious hall, trembling and rejoicing, but dared not to go near to him, for it was said unto me: 'Stay and see whether he will own thee, or take thee to be such an one as thou lookest upon thyself to be'. So I stood still at a great distance, at the lower end of the hall, and Christ was at the upper end, whose appearance was that of a fresh, lovely youth, clad in grey cloth, very plain and neat, (at this time I had never heard of the Quakers or their habit), of a sweet, affable, and courteous carriage. I saw him embrace several poor, old, simple people, whose appearance was very contemptible and mean, without wisdom or beauty. I seeing this, concluded within myself, that though he appeared young, his discretion and wisdom were great; for he must behold some hidden worth in these people, who to me seem so mean, so unlovely and simple. At last he beckoned to me to come near him, of which I was very glad. I went tremblingly and lowly; not lifted up, but in great weightiness and dread.

After a little while it was said: 'The Lamb's wife is also come'; at which I beheld a beautiful young woman, slender, modest, and grave, in plain garments, becoming and graceful. Her image was fully answering his, as a brother and sister. After I had beheld all this, and joyed in it, I spoke to Thomas Zachary, (whom I then knew to be a seeker after the Lord, though tossed, like myself, in the many ways, yet pressing after life), saying: 'Seeing Christ is come indeed, and few know it; and those that in the confusion mourned or rejoiced, know it not, but Christ is hid from them; let us take the king's house at Greenwich, and let us dwell with and enjoy him there, from those that look for him and cannot find him'. Without receiving any reply, I awoke.

Several years after this, I had another dream about Friends in their present state, which I shall relate in the close.

In the situation I mentioned, of being wearied in seeking and not finding, I married my dear husband, Isaac Penington. My love was drawn towards him, because I found he saw the deceit of all nations, and lay as one that refused to be comforted by any appearance of religion, until he came to His temple, 'who is truth and no lie'. All things that appeared to be religion and were not so, were very manifest to him; so that, till then, he was sick and weary of all appearances. My heart became united to him, and I desired to be made serviceable to him in his disconsolate condition; for he was as one alone and miserable in this world. I gave up much to be a companion to him in his suffering state. And oh! the groans and cries in secret that were raised in me, that I might be visited of the Lord, and come to the knowledge of his way; and that my feet might be turned into that way, before I went hence, if I never walked one step in it, to my joy or peace; yet that I might know myself in it, or turned to it, though all my time was spent in sorrow and exercise.

I resolved never to go back to those things I had left, having discovered death and darkness to be in them; but would rather be without a religion, until the Lord taught me one. Many times, when alone, did I reason thus: 'Why should I not know the way of life? For if the Lord would give me all in this world, it would not satisfy me'. Nay, I would cry out: 'I care not for a portion in this life: give it to those who care for it. I am miserable with it: it is acceptance with thee I desire, and that alone can satisfy me'.

Whilst I was in this state I heard of a new people, called Quakers. I resolved not to enquire after them, nor what principles they held. For a year or more after I heard of them in the north, I heard nothing of their way, except that they used *thee* and *thou*; and I saw a book written in the plain language, by George Fox. I remember that I thought it very ridiculous, so minded neither the people nor the book, except that it was to scoff at them and it. Though I thus despised this people, I had sometimes a desire to go to one of their meetings, if I could, unknown, and to hear them pray, for I was quite weary of doctrines; but I believed if I was with them when they prayed, I should be able to feel whether they were of the Lord or not. I endeavoured to stifle this desire, not knowing how to get to one of their meetings unknown;

and if it should be known, I thought it would be reported that I was one of them.

One day, as my husband and I were walking in a park, a man, that for a little time had frequented the Quakers' meetings, saw us as he rode by, in our gay, vain apparel. He cried out to us against our pride, &c. at which I scoffed, and said he was a public preacher indeed, who preached in the highways. He turned back again, saying he had a love for my husband, seeing grace in his looks. He drew nigh to the pales, and spoke of the light and grace, which had appeared to all men. My husband and he engaged in discourse. The man of the house coming up, invited the stranger in: he was but young, and my husband too hard for him in the fleshly wisdom. He told my husband he would bring a man to him the next day, that should answer all his questions, or objections, who, as I afterwards understood, was George Fox. He came again the next day and left word that the friend he intended to bring could not well come; but some others, he believed, would be with us about the second hour; at which time came Thomas Curtis and William Simpson.

My mind was somewhat affected by the man who had discoursed with us the night before; and though I thought him weak in managing the arguments he endeavoured to support, yet many scriptures which he mentioned stuck with me very weightily: they were such as showed to me the vanity of many practices I was in; which made me very serious, and soberly inclined to hear what these men had to say. Their solid and weighty carriage struck a dread over me. I now knew that they came in the power and authority of the Lord, to visit us, and that the Lord was with them. All in the room were sensible of the Lord's power manifest in them. Thomas Curtis repeated this scripture: 'He that will know my doctrine, must do my commands'. Immediately it arose in my mind, that if I would know whether that was truth they had spoken or not, I must do what I knew to be the Lord's will. What was contrary to it was now set before me, as to be removed; and I must come into a state of entire obedience, before I could be in a capacity to perceive or discover what it was which they laid down for their principles. This wrought mightily in me. Things which I had slighted much, now seemed to have power over me. Terrible was the Lord against the vain and evil inclinations in me, which made me, night and day, to cry out; and if I did but cease a little, then I grieved for fear I should again be reconciled to the things, which I felt under judgment, and had a just detestation of. Oh! how I did beg not to be left secure or quiet till the evil was done away. How often did this run through my mind: 'Ye will not come to me, that ye may have life'. 'It is true I am undone if I come not to thee, but I cannot come, unless I leave that which cleaveth close unto me, and I cannot part with it'.

I saw the Lord would be just in casting me off, and not giving me life; for I would not come from my beloved lusts, to him, for life. Oh! the pain I felt still. The wrath of God was more than I could bear. Oh! in what bitterness and distress was I involved! A little time after the friends' visit before mentioned, one night on my bed it was said unto me: 'Be not hasty to join these people called Quakers'. I never had peace or quiet from a sore exercise for many months, till I was, by the stroke of judgment, brought off from all those things, which I found the light made manifest to be deceit, bondage, and vanity, the spirit of the world, &c. and I given up to be a fool and a reproach, and to take up the cross to my honour and reputation in the world. The contemplation of those things cost me many tears, doleful nights and days; not now disputing against the doctrine preached by the Friends, but exercised against taking up the cross to the language, fashions, customs, titles, honour, and esteem in the world.

My relations made this cross very heavy; but as at length I happily gave up, divested of reasonings, not consulting how to provide for the flesh, I received strength to attend the meetings of these despised people, which I never intended to meddle with, but found truly of the Lord, and my heart owned them. I longed to be one of them, and minded not the cost or pain; but judged it would be well worth my utmost cost and pain to witness such a change as I saw in them – such power over their corruptions. I had heard objected against them, that they wrought not miracles; but I said that they did great miracles, in that they turned them that were in the world and the fellowship of it, from all such things. Thus, by taking up the cross, I received strength against many things which I had thought impossible to deny; but many tears did I shed, and bitterness of soul did I experience, before I came thither; and often cried out: 'I shall one day fall by the overpowering of the enemy'. But oh! the joy that filled my soul in the first meeting ever held in our house at Chalfont. To this day I have a fresh remembrance of it. It was then the Lord enabled me to worship him in that which was undoubtedly his own, and give up my whole strength, yea, to swim in the life which overcame me that day. Oh! long had I desired to worship him with acceptance, and lift up my hands without doubting, which I witnessed that day in that assembly. I acknowledged his great mercy and wonderful kindness; for I could say, 'This is it which I have longed and waited for, and feared I never should have experienced'.

Many trials have I been exercised with since, but they were all from the Lord, who strengthened my life in them. Yet, after all this, I suffered my mind to run out into prejudice against some particular Friends. This was a sore hurt unto me: but after a time of deep, secret sorrow, the Lord removed the wrong thing from me, blessing me with a large portion of his light, and the love and acceptance of his beloved ones. And he hath many times refreshed my soul in his presence, and given me assurance that I knew that estate in which he will never leave me, nor suffer me to be drawn from all which he has graciously fulfilled; for though various infirmities and temptations beset me, yet my heart cleaveth unto the Lord, in the everlasting bonds that can never be broken. In his light do I see those temptations and infirmities: there do I bemoan myself unto him, and feel faith and strength, which give the victory. Though it keeps me low in the sense of my own weakness, yet it quickens in me a lively hope of seeing Satan trodden down under foot by his all-sufficient grace. I feel and know when I have slipped in word, deed, or thought; and also know where my help lieth, who is my advocate, and have recourse to him who pardons and heals, and gives me to overcome, setting me on my watch-tower: and though the enemy is suffered to prove me, in order more and more to wean me from any dependence but upon the mighty, Jehovah, I believe he will never be able to prevail against me. Oh! that I may keep on my watch continually: knowing, the Lord only can make war with this dragon. Oh! that I may, by discovering my own weakness, ever be tender of the tempted; watching and praying, lest I also be tempted. Sweet is this state, though low; for in it I receive my daily bread, and enjoy that which he handeth forth continually; and live not, but as he breatheth the breath of life upon me every moment.

POSTSCRIPT

After I had written the foregoing, it lay by me a considerable time. One day it came into my mind to leave it with Elizabeth Walmsby, to keep it till after my decease, and desire her then to show it to such as had a love for me. So one day I desired her to meet me at John Mannock's, at Giles-Chalfont. There I spoke to her about it, read it to her, and desired she would write it out, (intended to leave it with her), but it afterwards went out of mind. It was in the year 1668 that I made this proposal; it is now almost 1672, when I found it among some other writings, and reading it over, found it was a true, though brief account, of many passages from my childhood to the time it was written. I am now willing to have it written over fair, for the use of my children, and some few particular friends who know and feel me in that which hungereth and thirsteth after righteousness, and many times being livingly satisfied in God my life.

FOUR TESTIMONIES

Conscientious objection is not a total repudiation of force; it is a refusal to surrender moral responsibility for one's action.

Kenneth C. Barnes, 1987

Love the truth more than all.

George Fox, undated epistle

I ask no favours for my sex. All I ask of our brethren is, that they will take their feet from off our necks and permit us to stand upright on the ground which God designed us to occupy.

Sarah Grimke, 1837

So great is the hurry in the spirit of this world that in aiming to do business quick and to gain wealth, the creation at this day doth loudly groan!

John Woolman, published 1772

In the first of the *Advices and Queries* (see page 42) we are asked to 'take heed to the promptings of love and truth' in our hearts and 'trust them as the leadings of God'. Such promptings and leadings cause Quakers to tread entirely different paths from one another. The sheer range of Friends' interests – from prison reform to the conquering of disease, from conflict resolution to radical journalism – can be quite startling; and the number of fields of work they are involved with at a local level is no less remarkable. The actions of Quakers, whether at a national, local or personal level, have in common certain key principles and aspirations which derive from their religious experience. Friends call them testimonies, because they bear witness to the way Quakers live their lives. They are born not of compulsion, nor of a desire to be good – they come simply from the Quaker advice to 'do what love requires of you'.

The direct encounter with the mystery of the divine at the heart of Quaker faith demands not only the response of worship and continued expectant waiting but an active demonstration of the insights God gives us. In other words, we are not given guidance that is private only to us either in its scope or in its application. Faith is about action in the world.

Ben Pink Dandelion, 2009

There is no definitive roster of testimonies that can be said to have applied to all Quakers through history. Most have been initiated in a spirit of protest. Some no longer resonate with Friends. The seventeenth-century testimony against 'hat honour', for example – the refusal to bow or remove one's hat to a social superior – clearly no longer applies. The testimony to times and seasons, involving as it did the use of the expressions 'First Day' or 'First Month' to replace 'Monday', 'January', and so on, has largely fallen out of use in the detail, though not in its spirit: no Quaker, for example, would celebrate a religious festival or suggest that Sunday was a holier day than any other.

Four testimonies are of crucial importance to Quakers today: those to equality, peace, simplicity and truth. The list is not definitive or exclusive. Some call their truth testimony 'the testimony to truth and integrity'. Others talk of a testimony to community. And there has been a strong feeling among Quakers for some years that they should formalise and give more attention to a testimony to the earth.

One thing is certain. All these testimonies derive from an urge to create, preserve and celebrate equality. Quakers' total commitment to that essential human right leads logically to the rest of their testimonies: to their refusal to kill another human being, to their insistence on the need – as they often say – to 'speak truth to power', to the importance of living simply and sharing the earth's resources. Yet it is a mistake to look at these testimonies just at their face value. In a speech to Quakers in 1993, Mary Lou Leavitt made their richness eminently clear.

There is [. . .] a cluster [of testimonies] round equality. If there is something of God in each of us, then we are all of equal worth in God's sight, and we can't doff caps (hat honour) or call each other 'sir' or 'you' (plain speech). Eventually we see that we can't own one another either (slavery) or punish by separating and degrading the wrongdoer (penal reform). From this same cluster comes, in more recent times, Friends' use of inclusive language and [our] statement of intent on racism.

There is another cluster round truth. If we let our yea be yea and our nay, nay, then we can't swear at all (oaths), and we must be honest in our business dealings (integrity in business). A recent development from within this cluster is the concern for truth and integrity in public affairs [. . .]

Then there is another cluster round peace, which gives rise in time to Friends' testimonies on capital punishment and conscription, but also to our witness in relief of suffering. A more recent development here is the concern on taxation for military purposes.

[. . .] Very important in other strands of Quaker tradition is a fourth cluster around doctrine – the matter of Friends' theological understanding. The testimony we're familiar with here is that on tithes – if we believe that God's spirit is accessible to all without inter-mediary, then we can't pay tithes for the upkeep of an established church and a hireling priesthood. This was the war tax issue of its day – and, with oaths, one of the two key testimonies for early Friends (peace ran a poor third). Hundreds of Friends were jailed and their goods distrained because of the challenge this testimony presented to the authority of the state. In this same theological cluster comes our refusal of outward sacraments: water baptism, the eucharist, and our peculiar habit of worshipping – and even marrying one another – without benefit of clergy.

The final cluster of testimonies is around simplicity: plain language belongs here, too, along with plain dress. Here also is the testimony on times and seasons: seeing every day as holy as Sunday [...], every day as full of new life coming into the world as Christmas or Easter. I suppose you could say that 'temperance and moderation' come in this cluster, too, and perhaps even 'betting and gambling', i.e. being content with what we have, not coveting more than is needful.

Mary Lou Leavitt, 1993

Testimonies are accepted by Quakers through osmosis rather than as a result of outside direction. There is no rule book. The testimonies derive from the lives of Quakers who find that they are simply unable to live in any other way.

Testimony must not be seen as an oppressive body of regulations to which we have to conform. It is nothing of the sort. It is of the utmost importance that we understand that, that although testimony derives from corporate discernment, each individual Friend has to interpret it and find ways of making it true for her or himself. What we then need is to know how our individual path sets off from the corporate highway and constantly rejoins it; to know how our path relates to the path taken by Friends in my community and how, together, our paths relate to the common highway of the testimonies.

Jonathan Dale, 2000

Newcomers to the Society are often attracted by our values and practices, like peace work, simplicity of life and the pursuit of integrity. They are soon told that these are testimonies. They then find that there is no authoritative statement of what the testimonies are, only hallowed examples of their implications in particular circumstances.

They find that Friends debate the demands which the clearly recognised testimonies make on people, and also what new testimonies there ought to be. Thus, they find that the testimonies are what Quakers stand for. They are religious, ethical, collective, demanding, developing – and vague.

In fact, the area of imprecision with which they are surrounded is the greatest strength of the testimonies. It enables them to be flexible as circumstances in the world change, and provides individual Friends with a constant challenge to work out for themselves what God is asking of them. It would be a mistake to interpret them as granting license, however, for they have a strong corporate dimension, and theologically reflect the freedom of the gospel against the literalism of the law. Newcomers need to understand that the testimonies are not pragmatic responses to the spirit of the age, being neither political principles nor programmes, but the outcome of Quaker religious tradition, the greater whole against which they have to be valued and practised.

John Punshon, 1990

I wish I might emphasize how a life becomes simplified when dominated by faithfulness to a few concerns. Too many of us have too many irons in the fire. We get distracted by the intellectual claim to our interest in a thousand and one good things, and before we know it we are pulled and hauled breathlessly along by an over-burdened programme of good committees and good undertakings. I am persuaded that this fevered life of church workers is not wholesome. Undertakings get plastered on from the outside because we can't turn down a friend. Acceptance of service on a weighty committee should really depend upon an answering imperative within us, not merely upon a rational calculation of the factors involved. The concern-oriented life is ordered and organised from within. And we learn to say *No* as well as *Yes* by attending to the guidance of inner responsibility. Quaker simplicity needs to be expressed not merely in dress and architecture and the height of tombstones but also in the structure of a relatively simplified and co-ordinated life-programme of social responsibilities. And I am persuaded that concerns introduce that simplification, and along with it that intensification which we need in opposition to the hurried, superficial tendencies of our age.

We have tried to discover the grounds of the social responsibility and the social sensitivity of Friends. It is not in mere humanitarianism. It is not in mere pity. It is not in mere obedience to Bible commands. It is not in anything earthly. The social concern of Friends is grounded in an experience – an experience of the Love of God and of the impulse to saviourhood inherent in the fresh quickenings of that Life. Social concern is the dynamic Life of God at work in the world, made special and emphatic and unique, particularized in each individual or group who is sensitive and tender in the leading-strings of love. A concern is God-initiated, often surprising, always holy, for the Life of God is breaking through into the world. Its execution is in peace and power and astounding faith and joy, for in unhurried serenity the Eternal is at work in the midst of time, triumphantly bringing all things up unto Himself.

Thomas R. Kelly, 1941

Ever since I first came among Friends, I was attracted to the Testimonies as an ideal. I wanted to belong to a church which made the rejection of warfare a collective commitment and not just a personal option. I admired a simplicity, a devotion to equality, and a respect for others which reflected what I already knew of Christ. In a deceitful world I warmed to those who did not swear oaths and strove to tell the truth in all circumstances. But this was a beginning in the spiritual life. The seed that was sown in my mind and my politics germinated and struck root in my soul and my faith.

The choice of the word 'Testimony' is instructive. The Testimonies are ways of behaving but are not ethical rules. They are matters of practice but imply doctrines. They refer to human society but are about God. Though often talked about, they lack an authoritative formulation. Though they are not a matter of words, it is through them that the unprogrammed branch of Quakerism does most of its preaching and that the distinctive Quakerism of the programmed tradition is demonstrated.

A 'testimony' is a declaration of truth or fact. Specifically, it is the story a witness tells in court, for the word comes from the Latin word for 'witness'. It is also a particular form of speaking in the churches of the Reformation in which people get up and tell (bear testimony) to what God has done in their lives. Thus, it is not an ejaculation, a way of letting off steam or baring one's soul. It has a purpose, and that is to get other people to change, to turn to God. Such an enterprise, be it in words or by conduct and example, is in essence prophetic and evangelical.

So it is a serious business to adopt the Testimonies. The seriousness comes not through any outward act or sign of adoption visible to other people, but in the implications. On the definition I have suggested, the Testimonies are not just moral challenges or statements about what people may find wise, expedient, agreeable or politically desirable in this world. They carry with them an implication that they are definitive, because they express what God wants. I did not make these things my own until they had been fired in an experience of the world made intelligible by deep reflection and leading in the meeting for worship.

John Punshon, 1987

These testimonies are about deeds, not creeds. They involve work, change and the following of one's conscience. Sometimes the shift can be painful. In the following extract, Luke Cock, a butcher from North East Yorkshire, charts his spiritual journey.

Necessity, Friends, outstrips the law: necessity has made many people go by the Weeping Cross [. . .] I remember I was yonce travelling through Shrewsbury, and my Guide said to me: 'I'll show thee the Weeping Cross.' 'Nay', said I, 'thou need not; I have borne it a great while'. Now this place that he showed me was four lane ends.

I remember when I first met with my Guide. He led me into a very large and cross [place], where I was to speak the truth from my heart – and before I used to swear and lie too for gain. 'Nay, then,' said I to my Guide, 'I mun leave Thee here: if Thou leads me up that lane, I can never follow: I'se be ruined of this butchering trade, if I mun't lie for a gain.' Here I left my Guide, and was filled with sorrow, and went back to the Weeping Cross: and I said, if I could find my good Guide again, I'll follow Him, lead me whither He will. So here I found my Guide again, and began to follow Him up this lane and tell the truth from my heart. I had been nought but beggary and poverty before; and now I began to thrive at my trade, and got to the end of this lane, though with some difficulty.

But now my Guide began to lead me up another lane, harder than the first, which was to bear my testimony in using the plain language. This was very hard; yet I said to my Guide, 'Take my feeble pace, and I'll follow Thee as fast as I can. Don't outstretch me, I pray Thee.' So by degrees I got up here.

But now I was led up the third lane: it was harder still, to bear my testimony against tithes – my wife not being convinced. I said to my Guide, 'Nay, I doubt I never can follow up here: but don't leave me: take my pace, I pray Thee, for I mun rest me.' So I tarried here a great while, till my wife cried, 'We'se all be ruined: what is thee ganging stark mad to follow t'silly Quakers?' Here I struggled and cried, and begged of my Guide to stay and take my pace: and presently my wife was convinced. 'Well,' says she, 'now follow thy Guide, let come what will. The Lord hath done abundance for us: we will trust in Him.' Nay, now, I thought, I'll to my Guide again, now go on, I'll follow Thee truly; so I got to the end of this lane cheerfully [. . .].

My Guide led me up another lane, more difficult than any of the former, which was to bear testimony to that Hand that had done all this for me. This was a hard one: I thought I must never have seen the end of it. I was eleven years all but one month in it. Here I began to go on my knees and to creep under the hedges, a trade I never forgot since, nor I hope never shall. I would fain think it is unpossible for me to fall now, but let him that thinks he stands take heed lest he fall.

I thought to have had a watering: but ye struggle so I cannot get you together. We mun have no watering tonight, I mun leave you every yan to his own Guide.

Luke Cock, 1721

Quakers have chosen to follow their moral and religious instincts in this way for three and a half centuries. Their conscientious objection has not just been to violence, nor has their commitment to simplicity and truth been only about dress, life-style or a disinclination to lie. The following selection attempts to highlight some of the origins of some of their concerns. Broadly, the headings here are equality, truth, peace and simplicity, but to try to draw lines between them is futile. Indeed, it is important that we are clear about just how blurred the boundaries can be between one testimony and another.

For conscience' sake to God, we are bound by his just law in our hearts to yield obedience to [authority] in all matters and cases actively or passively; that is to say, in all just and good commands of the king and the good laws of the land relating to our outward man, we must be obedient by doing [...] but [...] if anything be commanded of us by the present authority, which is not according to equity, justice and a good conscience towards God [...] we must in such cases obey God only and deny active obedience for conscience' sake, and patiently suffer what is inflicted upon us for such our disobedience to men.

Edward Burrough, 1661

The arguments of the Christian, like the religion from which they are derived, are plain and simple, but they are in themselves invincible. The gospel of our Lord Jesus Christ is a system of peace, of love, of mercy, and of goodwill. The slave trade is a system of fraud and rapine, of

violence and cruelty. [. . .] That which is morally wrong cannot be politically right.

Yearly Meeting, 1822

When William Penn was convinced of the principles of Friends, and
became a frequent attendant at their meetings, he did not immediately relinquish his gay apparel; it is even said that he wore a sword, as
was then customary among men of rank and fashion. Being one day in
company with George Fox, he asked his advice concerning it, saying
that he might, perhaps, appear singular among Friends, but his sword
had once been the means of saving his life without injuring his antagonist, and moreover, that Christ had said, 'He that hath no sword, let
him sell his garment and buy one'. George Fox answered, 'I advise
thee to wear it as long as thou canst'. Not long after this they met
again, when William had no sword, and George said to him, 'William,
where is thy sword?' 'Oh'! said he, 'I have taken thy advice; I wore it
as long as I could'.

Samuel L. Janney, 1852

God, who made all, pours out of his spirit upon all men and women
[. . .] upon whites and blacks, Moors and Turks, and Indians,
Christians, Jews and Gentiles.

George Fox, undated epistle

They that offered in the Jews' temple were to wear the holy garments. So
are you to do that are the true Christians, and are called a royal priesthood. What! Are all true Christians priests? Yes, What! Are women
priests? Yes, women priests. And can men and woman offer sacrifices
without they wear the holy garments? No. What are the holy garments
men and women must wear? The fine linen and they must go in white.
What! Is this the priest's surplice? Nay [. . .] it is the righteousness of
Christ, which is the righteousness of the saints, this is the royal garment
of the royal priesthood, which everyone must put on, men and women.

George Fox, undated epistle

Everyone is equal in the human condition. Or, if you prefer, we are all equal before the Divine: unique, precious, children of God. We are all born. We all experience suffering and pain; most know joy and love, and perhaps the presence of God. We all die. Naked came I out of my mother's womb, and naked shall I return thither. In death there are no distinctions of class, race, gender or wealth. As my auntie used to say: there are no pockets in shrouds.

This acceptance of equality is an obvious truth to Quakers. Although we have no creeds, no set form of words to abide by, there are certain truths at which we do all arrive when we worship together, when, in stillness, we open ourselves to the eternal Divine. These we call testimonies, and they inform the way we try to live our lives, and how we treat other people. Equality is one of these testimonies, and perhaps the most basic of them.

There are many facets to the testimony to equality, but it was gender equality among Quakers that was one of the first to impress me personally. I had grown up in a church in which the clergy was entirely male, from the bishops down to the pastors of the smallest churches. In addition to this hierarchical, male, structure there was a congregational element, and some decisions affecting the individual church were decided by a vote of its members. Its male members, that is. As a thirteen-year-old girl I was told that I would have influence in the church rather than a vote. This influence would be exercised through my father, my husband (for such there would surely be) and my brothers. My brothers! Surely this was some sort of joke.

It was a joke from which I did not recover. When I had left that church far behind and discovered Quakers, in my early twenties, one of the things I most valued was the equal status of men and women in the organisation. I was delighted to find that I was wholly accepted as a woman, and there was no aspect of church affairs from which I would be excluded because of my sex. I was accepted in my own right, my successes and failures were due to me as a person, not as a woman.

And this had been the case from the earliest days of the Quaker movement, in the mid-seventeenth century, when women ministered, and travelled in the ministry, in the same way as men. Although there were separate men and women's business meetings, women were never treated as spiritually second rate. And although it is true that in present-day Quaker meetings catering committees tend to have more female members than do finance committees, there is no office in the Society from which a woman is debarred. Men and women play an equal part in our Meetings for Worship, with no hierarchical structure of any sort. We are equal in our business meetings, and in our witness in the world. No one's talents are lost because of gender requirements for specific positions.

Although the repression of women in religious bodies has always been a reflection of their role in society at large, there have, of course, always been theological bases put forward to justify it. Traditionally, it had been found in the misogynist statements of Paul in the New Testament epistles, especially, famously, his injunction in Corinthians to women to keep silent in the church. (Might this not be a plea to women to stop gossiping during the service, sometimes to be found in the present-day Greek church?) Less frequently quoted is the passage in Paul's letter to the Galatians: 'There is neither Jew nor Greek, there is neither bond nor free, there is neither male nor female: for you are all one in Christ Jesus'. Scripture can indeed be made to support arguments on either side of most given issues.

As abuses of women in the world go, just failing to be given a voice or a role in a religious body may seem slight. Many women live in cultures where their basic freedoms are severely curtailed. They may be imprisoned in their homes; deprived of education and health care; raped, beaten, and even killed with impunity.

Women are not a minority and yet have long suffered repression and discrimination in all cultures, being vulnerable as the bearers and carers of infants. For me, it is one thing to have this be the case in society at large. To have it as a judgement on my ability to experience the Divine, my relationship with God, is another, intolerable thing. And as a Quaker woman, I don't have to put up with it.

Unnamed Quaker, 2007

Take heed of giving people oaths to swear, for Christ our Lord and master saith, 'Swear not at all, but let your communications be yea, yea, and nay, nay, for whatsoever is more than these cometh of evil'. And if a man was to suffer death, it must be by the hand of two or three witnesses; and the hands of the witnesses were to be put first upon him to put him to death. And the Apostle James saith, 'My brethren, above all things swear not, neither by heaven, nor by earth, nor by any other oath, lest ye fall into condemnation'. Now you may see, those that swear fall into condemnation, and are out of Christ's and the Apostle's doctrine. Therefore, every one of you having a light from Christ, who saith, 'I am the light of the world', and doth enlighten every man that cometh into the world; who also saith, 'Learn of me', whose doctrine is not to swear; and the Apostle's doctrine is not to swear; but 'Let your yea be yea, and your nay be nay, in all your communications; for whatsoever is more, cometh of evil'. So then they that go into more than yea and nay, go into evil, and are out of the doctrine of Christ.

George Fox, published 1694

Many gay people actually see the media and the churches as enemies and I have much sympathy with them. This hostility has made it very difficult for me both as a Jew and as a gay man to understand for example Christian fundamentalism and Roman Catholicism, as both of these are almost enemies by instinct to my way of looking at the world. (Though I admit I have a much greater sympathy now for the latter than for the former, however much I try to understand both of them.) One of the things I have always known about the Quaker Peace Testimony is that it is very important to my faith not because it comes easily, but precisely because I find it so terribly difficult to put into practice. Anger and resentment are two emotions I have still to come to terms with. And yet at the same time there is a great joy in being alive and in the fact that so many have refused to be browbeaten in spite of the pressure upon them to conform to what are for them false ways of living.

Harvey Gillman, 1988

An understanding of identity that is based on difference – between insiders and outsiders, men and women, haves and have-nots – produces fearfulness and disrespect, and overrides compassion. It nurtures, serves and is perpetuated by the culture and structures of domination that give rise to war. Paradoxically, constructions of identity that are focused on difference also involve 'lumping' people together. We identify ourselves (or are identified by others) with a particular generalised group – often extremely diverse and including people we might dislike or disagree with on many issues. We achieve this identification by seeing ourselves as separate from other groups that are probably equally diverse and include many people with whom we would have a great deal in common.

In this approach to identity our notion of who we *are* is defined in terms of who we are *not*. When the sense of our own identity is weak or under threat we shore it up by sharpening our focus on the otherness of the other, generating enemy images, hostility, fear, and the desire to control, exclude or dominate. On the basis of this notion of separateness, of us and them, it is possible for one group or 'nation' to go to war against another.

Diana Francis, 2004

As a family we were also 'special' in less comfortable ways. I was five when my father was diagnosed as a schizophrenic, and my world changed. After those five golden years, the uncertainty, embarrassment, responsibility, of my father's illness – as he obeyed his voices, talked to himself, accosted people in the street, emptied a suitcase full of banknotes into the gutter – took over the lives of my mother and myself. Friends and family deserted him; my mother – a Russian, a Jew, and never really accepted by my father's family – was a stranger in a foreign land. And I felt an outsider, never knowing where I fitted in. As a defence I accepted the status of being 'special', took a pride in being different.

It's only as I've grown older that I have realised that many people feel that they don't belong, and maybe bolster themselves, as we did, by feeling superior to those who are more visibly 'different'. I have come to recognise that the way society excludes some groups of people is not only a fear of the difference of others, it's a fear of their own difference. So, for me, working with the 'outsiders' in society has been closer to home than others would know.

For the more I hear the stories of homeless people, of refugees or of prisoners, the more I know that it could have been my father, had my mother not looked after him for forty years. It could have been my alcoholic ex-husband. It could have been me. I now understand how completely we are one in our human predicament. *There is no other.*

But if we recognise the potential for disintegration in ourselves, the obverse is also true – and more important. The generosity shown by people who have least, the dignity of many suffering pain or injustice, show that no matter in what condition people live, no matter what misfortune has descended, or what mistakes have been made, the potential for achievement, for a good life, is there in everyone.

Equality does not mean I am not special. It means we all are.

Unnamed Quaker, 2007

Truth is then neither a philosophical notion nor a matter of ethical principles – even ones as worthy as the Quaker testimonies. Such codifying of behaviour is actually the very opposite of the experience to which Quakerism points us, which is obedience to something alive and dependable within, a source of revelation available to all beyond any system of religious belief. This is surely what Penn meant by the 'one religion' of the humble, just and meek – this was not prescriptive, how we should live, but descriptive, how we will live when we are 'dwelling in the light'.

Alex Wildwood, 1999

All of us [...] are diminished and dishonoured when we do not meet each other half way. How can we in truth and lovingly help one another in this? Because we must remember that truth without love is violence. And love without truth is sentimentality. We do need both.

Muriel Bishop, 1990

Friends take seriously some of the hard sayings of Jesus, but not all of them. Few of us refrain from taking thought for the morrow; most of us have, in a modest way, laid up treasure on earth. I know of no Friends who have sold *all* that they have and given the proceeds to the poor.

Much that Jesus told his followers can be found in the moral teaching of his contemporaries; in the main Jewish sects (Pharisees, Sadducees, Essenes), in the Qumran community, in Greek philosophy, in Roman law. But it seems to me that in two respects the teaching of Jesus was unique. First, his stress on the primacy of unconditional love: love of God, love of neighbour, love for tax collectors and prostitutes, even love of enemy. Second, his insistence that all human beings are of equal worth, so that there are to be no barriers derived from gender, national origin, skin colour, social status, political allegiance, sexual orientation, or other arbitrary distinction.

The follower of Jesus is to discover and then promote the Kingdom of God. That Kingdom has two tenses: it is already here, in each one of us; and it is still to come, when God's goodness becomes a universal norm. We are to live now 'as if' the Kingdom of God were already fulfilled.

Sydney D. Bailey, 1993

I have sometimes been asked what were my reasons for deciding on that refusal to register for war duties that sent me to Holloway Jail 22 years ago. I can only answer that my reason told me that I was a fool, that I was risking my job and my career, that an isolated example could do no good, that it was a futile gesture since even if I did register my three small children would exempt me. But reason was fighting a losing battle. I had wrestled in prayer and I knew beyond all doubt that I must refuse to register, that those who believed that was the wrong way to fight evil must stand out against it however much they stood alone, and that I and mine must take the consequences. The 'and mine' made it more difficult, but I question whether children ever really suffer loss in the long run through having parents who are willing to stand by principles; many a soldier had to leave his family and thought it his duty to do so. When you have to make a vital decision about behaviour, you cannot sit on the fence. To decide to do nothing is still a decision, and it means that you remain on the station platform or the airstrip when the train or plane has left.

Kathleen Lonsdale, 1964

Violence is what happens when God has been treated with such contempt that he is no longer able to intervene. To prepare for violence is to prepare for the moment when God can no longer intervene.

Violence is, in a sense, God's collective punishment, falling on good and bad alike; it is God's punishment in the sense of his withdrawal, his disappearance, his absence.

Pierre Ceresole, published 1954

Through violence, a conflict is reduced to purely physical terms. The practitioner of violence is saying to his opponent: 'No matter what your metaphysical or moral rights and merits, my physical superiority obliges you to yield to me. We are removing this conflict to a different plane. You must abandon your will to mine'.

He who resorts to violence is thus renouncing the use of reason, persuasion or prayer and putting his antagonist in a lower category than himself. He may feel he has been driven to it, that the other man began it all, and that he himself is acting reluctantly and in self-defence. But invariably the other side is described as 'unreasonable'. Words no longer meet the case. The other man has ignored or rejected the arguments and misread the signals. No other course is left but violence – which would here almost certainly be termed force.

If we really felt that our enemy, our victim, was like ourselves – having the same feelings, hopes, rights and dependents – empathised with him, loving our neighbour as ourselves and putting ourselves in his place, we could not do to him what we would not choose to have done to us. Some of us retain that ability in spite of everything, a point worth recalling when faced with the claim that Man is inherently vicious. But almost every outbreak of hostilities between nations, every campaign of repression against a minority or act of individual violence, is accompanied by a conviction that the opposing party is a lower form of life – 'dirty Jews', 'pigsty Pakkies', 'slant-eyed Gooks'.

Gerald Priestland, 1974

I speak not this against any magistrates' or people's defending themselves against foreign invasions, or making use of the sword to suppress the violent and evil-doers within their borders [. . .] but yet there is a better state, which the Lord hath already brought some into, and which nations are to expect and travel towards. Yea, it is far better to know the Lord to be the defender, and to wait on him daily, and see the need of his strength, wisdom, and preservation, than to be ever so strong and skilful in weapons of war.

Isaac Penington, 1661

The word 'pacifist' has an old-fashioned ring and is associated by most people with irrelevant idealism. Often, indeed, it is used as a derogatory term. While some regard pacifists as worthy souls, to be respected if not taken seriously, others see them as self-indulgent and dishonest, refusing to face the harsh realities of the world we inhabit. Because they resist war as a system, it is inferred that they are unconcerned with the real circumstances of particular wars.

Yet if we refuse to reconsider the fundamental assumptions that underlie the justification and acceptance of war, we shall remain caught in a dynamic of cruelty and destruction that will know no end, that undermines all that makes for human happiness, decency and meaning and that could lead to our destruction as a species.

Saying no to war, on the other hand, could be the first step to saying yes to a very different future. Why does it seem so impossible?

Precisely because war is an integral part of a historic and pervasive system within which we are all enmeshed, because we have always seen it as inevitable, and because recent events make it seem even more so.

[. . .] I have come to see more clearly than ever that to protest in an *ad hoc* way against individual wars is not enough. The military machine is far too powerful and integral to global economic domination to be stopped by anti-war movements that fade once a particular war is over and struggle to get under way again as the next calamity looms and peak too late to prevent it. And, as things stand, it seems there are too many vested interests and too much inertia within the current system for particular wars to be stopped – even when a majority opposes them. Our 'democracies' have proved themselves unresponsive to their people.

What is needed is a massive and sustained movement against war *as such*, and towards constructive approaches to collective human relationships. This will entail a fundamental change in the way the world is organised and in prevailing approaches to power. This is indeed an ambitious project, but vital nonetheless. War must be seen for what it is: a human catastrophe, a violation of humanity. It must 'cease to be an admissible human institution' (Professor Sir Joseph Rotblat).

It must cease to be an admissible human institution because people matter. They matter more than wealth or power or convenience, and they matter unconditionally. As human beings, we owe each other, without question, respect for the dignity and needs that are inherent in our humanity.

Diana Francis, 2004

Our principle is, and our practices have always been, to seek peace, and ensue it, and to follow after righteousness and the knowledge of God, seeking the good and welfare, and doing that which tends to the peace of all. All bloody principles and practices we do utterly deny, with all outward wars, and strife, and fightings with outward weapons, for any end, or under any pretence whatsoever, and this is our testimony to the whole world. That spirit of Christ by which we are guided is not change-able, so as once to command us from a thing as evil, and again to move unto it; and we do certainly know, and so testify to the world, that the spirit of Christ which leads us into all Truth will never move us to fight and war against any man with outward weapons, neither for the kingdom of Christ, nor for the kingdoms of this world.

And as for the kingdoms of this world, we cannot covet them, much less can we fight for them, but we do earnestly desire and wait, that by the word of God's power and its effectual operation in the hearts of men the kingdoms of this world may become the kingdoms of the Lord and of his Christ, that he might rule and reign in men by his spirit and truth, that thereby all people, out of all different judg-ments and professions might be brought into love and unity with God and one with another, and that they might all come to witness the prophet's words, who said, 'Nation shall not lift up sword against nation, neither shall they learn war any more'.

Quaker declaration to Charles II, 1660

I told [the Commonwealth Commissioners] I lived in the virtue of that life and power that took away the occasion of all wars [. . .]. I told them I was come into the covenant of peace which was before wars and strife were.

George Fox, published 1694

May we look upon our treasures, and the furniture of our houses, and the garments in which we array ourselves, and try whether the seeds of war have nourishment in these our possessions.

John Woolman, 1763

The originating Spirit, our Source, was utter simplicity, pregnant with all possibility. Humanity's quest to make meaning of life has been a series of experiments to resonate with that Power. The finding of many is that the simpler the way the deeper the experience. There is a common thread between the silence and stillness of meditation, contemplation, inward prayer, Quaker worship and the enlighten- ment practices of mystic and guru. Deeper than reason and thought is the inner heart of feeling, locus of divine transformation from matter to mind, source of our creativity, wisdom and healing. The more over- laid our reaching out to that ultimate reality is with ritual, words, music and image, the more it is masked by human reality: perform- ance appreciated for itself, not as a pointer to the Other.

These were the discoveries of early Quakers in the crucible of seventeenth-century religious turmoil and civil war. It is impossible for us fully to appreciate their breath-taking spiritual daredevilry in breaking with liturgies, priesthood and patriarchy, to stand as equals together in a simple silence. That way of worship changed my life when I encountered it in my late twenties. I know it could change the dis-ease of the world, bound by clamour and conflict. For the simplicity of worship and meeting house leads us to question the wastage of fashion, domestic cumber, ambition and lifestyle in order to focus on the essence of a Spirit-led life [. . .].

For simplicity has two dangers. The Spirit is essentially creative; its expression is celebration and exuberance, variety and beauty, awe and wonder, joy and laughter. Life denial and asceticism have so often led to narrow-mindedness, ugliness, uniformity and spiritual pride. Simplicity then becomes its own idol. Let there be beauty in our simplicity and a life fulfilled in creativity, sensuality and wholeness. Killjoy drabness and meanness as well as consumerism and materi- alism are evidence of an impoverishment within.

The other danger is simple-mindedness, seeing life as if it were simple when its reality is an evolved profound complexity. Originating energy, atoms, galaxies, even stars are relatively simple compared with the intricate interdependencies of the systems of weather, economics and human health. Human problems can only have multiple solutions. Beware any occupant of the White House or Downing Street who is simple-minded enough to see a multi-hued moral issue as only black and white. For ourselves, the demands of time and focus as a teenager or senior citizen are vastly different from how they are in middle age as we juggle with work, family, religion and leisure. It's a matter of times and seasons.

Waiting in the simplicity of stillness is to wait in reverence. This is the heart of simplicity as it is of all the Quaker testimonies. Our first reverence is to Truth, the divine Cause and its irradiation throughout the entire creation. If all beings are sacred then we are impelled to revere all human life, neither killing in war nor neglecting in need, treating everyone with equal dignity. In terms of animal life, our generation is being called to re-evaluate our determination to eat meat. Today's threat of catastrophic climate change reawakens our need for reverence for planet earth itself: foul our habitat and we destroy humanity. On our one world, all living beings are one inter-connected family. The call for a simpler lifestyle is now urgent; the tipping point has happened. Those who experienced the Second World War will remember that under rationing came a fair distribu-tion, better health and no obesity. We now have the basic needs of the world's entire population to take into account. A war on pollution is a spiritual war on the selfishness, greed and unawareness that lie behind it: our cause may be sustainability but our watch-cry is reverence – the essence of simplicity.

Unnamed Quaker, 2006

Simplicity clears the springs of life and permits wholesome mirth and gladness to bubble up; it cleans the windows of life and lets joys radiate.

Philadelphia Yearly Meeting, 1955

We do face a planetary crisis. It is fundamentally a spiritual crisis with practical consequences. Human society's beliefs created the exploita-tive behaviour which so threatens the stability of Earth's evolving life systems and climate at present. We Quakers stand in the heart of the culture whose global spread has caused much of the mess, and maybe that gives us a responsibility to search for the spiritual and ethical keys to change. Relationship with the earth is the key to many 'peak' spiritual experiences. Yet we as a culture tend to isolate and romanticise these experiences, refusing them a social content, and not experiencing them as a spur to a radical questioning of our attitude and actions towards the natural world. If we look into ourselves more deeply, and relate more deeply to the Earth's sacredness, not denying the real teaching of our experience of the natural world, we may find as a Society a transformed and inspirational relationship with the Earth.

Suzanne Finch, 1999

The Creator of the earth is the owner of it. He gave us being thereon, and our nature requires nourishment, which is the produce of it. As he is kind and merciful, we as his creatures, while we live answerable to the design of our creation, are so far entitled to a convenient subsistence that no man may justly deprive us of it. By the agreements and contracts of our fathers and predecessors, and by doings and proceedings of our own, some claim a much greater share of this world than others: and whilst those possessions are faithfully improved to the good of the whole, it consists with equity. But he who, with a view to self-exaltation, causeth some with their domestic animals to labour immoderately, and with the monies arising to him therefrom, employs others in the luxuries of life, acts contrary to the gracious design of him [the Creator] who is the true owner of the earth; nor can any possessions, either acquired or derived from ancestors, justify such conduct.

John Woolman, 1763

Our planet is seriously ill and we can feel the pain. We have been reminded of the many ways in which the future health of the earth is under threat as a result of our selfishness, ignorance and greed. Our earth needs attention, respect, love, care and prayer.

In comfortable Britain we are largely insulated from the effects of the environmental crisis. It is the poor of the world who suffer first.

As a Religious Society of Friends we see the stewardship of God's creation as a major concern. The environmental crisis is at root a spiritual and religious crisis; we are called to look again at the real purpose of being on this earth, which is to till it and keep it so as to reveal the glory of God for generations to come.

It is a stony road ahead but our faith will uphold us; the power to act is God's power which is mediated through each of us as we give and receive support one from another. We can all listen if we will to the sounds of the earth, tuning into it with joy.

London Yearly Meeting, 1988

The liberal Quaker tradition usually thinks of the testimonies as principles of activity rather than the means of evangelism, or claims as to the true nature of Christian faith. Thus, it tends to concentrate on matters of social and political importance to which particular Quaker values are seen to have a major relevance. These values are often not peculiar to Quakerism and are held by many people who have no particular feelings about religion. This causes the testimonies to be seen in a secular light, and sometimes occasions difficulty when Friends seek to be consistent over them, and are drawn to adopt positions which reveal their religious basis – the stop in the mind is an important part of Quaker spirituality.

John Punshon, 1990

Perhaps the most neglected of all the advices is that we should live adventurously. If there is one wish I would pray the Spirit to put into our Christmas stockings, it is warmth, openness, passion, a bit of emotion that doesn't mind making a fool of itself occasionally.

Gerald Priestland, 1981

PEACEMAKING

Peace begins within ourselves. It is to be implemented within the family, in our Meetings, in our work and leisure, in our own localities, and internationally. The task will never be done. Peace is a process to engage in, not a goal to be reached.

Sydney D. Bailey, 1993

And you, in that state, are to pray for the enemies that put you there; and if they curse and hate you, you are to bless them, and to do good to them, and you are to pray for them that despitefully use you, and persecute you, and love your enemies, that you may be children of your Father which is in heaven.

George Fox, 1684

Peace making, as I have tried to define and describe it, consists of manifesting the truth and applying it to disordered relationships, relationships that are disordered specifically because they are not nurtured by the truth. Thus peacemaking is not merely the removal of what is sick or ignorant, smoothing out the crinkles of misunderstanding, but the stimulation of growth and the unfolding of all our God-given capacities.

Adam Curle, 1981

No exposition of the Quaker way can ignore the heritage of skill and expertise – to say nothing of resourcefulness – which Friends draw on in their role as peacemakers and resolvers of conflict. A cursory glance at the list of four Quaker testimonies might prompt a casual observer simply to put 'peacemaking' into the pigeonhole marked 'peace', and leave it at that. But equality, simplicity and truth (as clearly shown in Adam Curle's paragraph above) are all part of the process and excite the endeavours of Quakers to be of value.

The Alternatives to Violence Project, to take just one example of many, began in 1975 in Green Haven Prison, New York, in collaboration with the Quaker Project on Community Conflict. It has developed into a world-wide association of volunteer groups offering experiential workshops in conflict resolution, responses to violence, and personal growth. The training provided helps people from all walks of life to handle conflict well. 'Conflict is part of daily life, but violence doesn't have to be', is the strap-line of the British branch of the organisation, stating clearly one of the most important lessons learnt in all aspects of peacemaking – that conflict is a fact of human existence and enriches our lives as well as having the capacity to devastate them. When the damage has been done, however, the work of the peacemakers is invariably arduous and demanding.

I should make it clear [. . .] that in presenting ideas about the practice of peace making, I am not suggesting that it is at all easy or that there is any set of gimmicks or magical solutions. On the contrary, it is very hard. The process of peace making is hardly ever simple and is seldom brought to a complete conclusion. The more complex the situation, and the greater the number of interlocking elements – economic, political, historical and so on – the more difficult it is to achieve peace. It is unusual, moreover, for everyone involved to agree to the terms of a settlement. An angry, dissenting minority that feels its interests to have been improperly represented may easily bring again to boiling point the cauldron of strife. There is, moreover, a more fundamental difficulty. Human affairs are most intricately inter-connected, and there are few isolated conflicts. It is impossible to separate them neatly from each other, resolving their problems piecemeal. Yet this is not necessarily bad, for although the unpeacefulness of one situation may flow over into another, so may the peacefulness.

Whatever the difficulties of peace making, however, it is an integral human activity. It is taken to restore harmony in one corner of a universe whose very existence perfectly demonstrates balance and harmony. Frequently a particular peace making effort seems to have been completely unsuccessful or at least to have had no ascertainable effect, but we must act in faith. No one can assess the impact of genuine peace making, undertaken with love. The ripples may spread throughout eternity.

Adam Curle, 1981

In place of a process which trusts technology and mistrusts humanity, we must learn and live out a process that builds trust between people and their institutions. [. . .] From the earliest days of Friends, we have known that safety cannot be defended in our own strength, but only in God's. [. . .] And we don't have to do it with tools of our own fashioning, ever more elaborate technological juggling acts, ever more devastatingly destructive bombs. [. . .] [We can] learn to lay down carnal weapons, practising with weapons of the spirit: love, truth-saying, nonviolence, the good news of God's birth and rebirth among us, imagination, vision, and laughter.

No one ever said it would be easy, no one promised it wouldn't hurt. This way of life, this trusting one another and trusting God, is no impermeable shield, guaranteed to protect us by cutting us off, building barriers, keeping the bad things and the bad people out. It's messy, muddly and sometimes painful – but the other way, the search for some kind of mechanical invulnerability, for some kind of scientific guarantee against physical death, that way I am sure lies the death of the Spirit. We know the choice – we've known it all along – and we make it every day.

Mary Lou Leavitt, 1987

It is the resistance that matters more than the effect of the resistance. By this I mean exactly what I say. That non-violent resistance can no more guarantee a short-term victory over evil than violent resistance can; but that evil must be resisted, victory or no victory.

Kathleen Lonsdale, 1957

We should not think that peace making will bring popularity. If peace making means, and is based upon, the truth of our nature as beings made in the image and likeness of God, enshrining a particle of His nature, it will arouse hostility among many. A large proportion of humanity have been misled into believing that their happiness depends upon their possessions, position, power, prosperity and all the other adjuncts of material well-being – and even if they do not have them, they believe this and strive for them. Some, faced with a truth that proclaims something diametrically different, will abandon their illusions. Others, however, will cling to them; and the more they are threatened by reality, the more desperately they will cling. Often they will attempt to evade the threat to their precariously ill-founded sense of security by attacking the peace maker. For this reason, throughout history, many have been slain.

Adam Curle, 1981

The author of the last extract, Adam Curle (1916–2006), was a Quaker who served in the British army during World War Two and became a lecturer in Psychology and Education at various institutions of further education during the 1950s and 1960s. He was a mediator in both the Nigerian civil war in the late 1960s and the Indo-Pakistan war of 1971. In 1975, partly as a consequence of his experience in conflict resolution, he was invited to become the first Professor of Peace Studies at Bradford University. The new department was the brainchild of a small group of Quakers and has gone on to be the largest academic centre for the study of peace and conflict in the world. Adam Curle was a superb communicator of the temperament and techniques required for conflict resolution.

The absolute necessity for attentive listening was borne in on me very early in my experience of peacemaking. I became aware that what my friends and I were trying to say was often not heard, especially at the start of a meeting or if the situation were particularly tense. A question or observation would, it is true, be answered, but not responded to in any meaningful way. It was as though our words were filtered through a compound of anger, fear, resentment and preconception that radically changed their meaning. It was to this new meaning that the people we were talking with responded, often angrily and usually irrelevantly. Because of the general circumstances, what we said was often perceived as having a threatening or insulting meaning, or a perfectly straightforward question would be taken as a criticism. During the Nigerian civil war, for example, the federal government was extraordinarily sensitive to the harsh judgements of the world's press, and the most innocent enquiry about some aspect of the war would be seen as hostile. We, in fact, were not being listened to, but if we had responded with irritation, it would mean that we, too, had not been listening. We assumed without question that the way to overcome these difficulties of communication was to say very little, certainly not to argue, re-explain or contradict, but to be inwardly still and as receptive as possible. This would usually enable the storm of emotion, so natural in men under great pressure, to blow itself out. Listening, however, does not come easily to us. We are obsessed by the noise of our own thoughts and can hardly wait until the other person has stopped talking before making our own little speech – which we have been too busy composing to hear what the other said. Recall almost any party or committee meeting.

Adam Curle, 1981

Quakers have a clear understanding that restorative measures are an inevitable part of conflict resolution. Quakers are not idealists. They work with what they have.

Changing the hardened heart is not achieved by military force or by buying people, it is not achieved by intellectually persuading people; it is achieved by touching them as humans through treating them as valuable. It is achieved particularly by sacrifice on behalf of others, as exemplified in the life and work of Martin Luther King, Mahatma Gandhi, Desmond Tutu.

The attitude of deep ethics is not that you are *always* self-sacrificing on behalf of others, it is that you are prepared to do so if and when it will make a strategic difference. That is a different thing. There are times when it is the only thing which will make a real difference. [. . .] Changing enemies into friends is the basis of true security.

George Ellis, 2004

Restorative justice is based on the premise that the appropriate response to a crime requires much more than the delivery of a 'just measure of pain' to individual offenders. [. . .] Restorative justice is more concerned with the preservation and restoration of relationships both at an individual level and at a community level. [. . .] Restorative justice views crime primarily as injury (rather than lawbreaking) and the purpose of justice as healing (rather than as punishment alone). It emphasises the accountability of offenders to make amends for their actions and focuses on providing assistance and services to victims. Its objective is the successful reintegration of both victim and offender as productive members of safe communities.

Tim Newell, 2000

People matter. In the end human rights are about people being treated and feeling like people who matter. We are reminded graphically of violations of human rights far away and near at hand. In ignorance or knowingly we all violate human rights. We are all involved in the exercise of power and the abuse of power.

The multitude and complexity of the problems of oppression and injustice often seem to overwhelm us. We can do something. Friends are already working in a variety of ways: through international bodies, through voluntary organisations and by personal witness. Those who can give something of their lives to human rights require our support and we can look for opportunities to help those in need around us.

At the international level we affirm our support of Friends World Committee for Consultation and other bodies in ensuring that the standards and ideals of the UN Universal Declaration of Human Rights are attained, that the world does not slip backwards.

Above all we must take risks for God: look around us to the people who need help; listen to those who experience oppression; engage in the mutual process of liberation.

London Yearly Meeting 1986

As the last extract makes clear, Quakers regard peace and peacemaking as a religious issue as much as a practical and ethical one. Although conscientious objection is by no means a necessary part of Quakerism, the fact is that, for most Friends, it would be incompatible with their faith to adopt any other stance. As far as they are concerned there is no dilemma: there may be many just causes, but it simply does not follow that there can be a just war.

The just war advocate cannot escape the fact that within an under-standing of peace as the integrity of relationships, it is not possible to choose to harm another person (or fight a war) without violating those we harm and kill. This is self-evident but still needs saying while violent acts continue to be framed in humanitarian terms. Typically, to wage war is to elect others to suffer and die for purposes that we, not they, have chosen, when few of us would be willing to bear that suffering ourselves for the same ends. This is to treat human beings on a large scale as means, rather than ends, and in this respect is a massive violation of relationship.

David Gee, 2005

Quakers will continue to stand for a world without weapons. We take this position ultimately out of our faith: because it is right rather than because it works. We are prepared to pay the price of this commitment if need be. In the course of this witness a major role of the Society is to point up the 'myth' that violence works (as we have seen earlier).

Not only do we work for a world without weapons. We also work for, and believe in, the possibility of a world without violence of any kind, without domination. A world in which there is no abuse or beating, no rape or battering, no assertion of power through gender, race, age, sexual orientation or physical abilities. A world in which humankind does not abuse the planet, but cares for and enhances the life-giving biosphere.

Another dimension of this witness consists in exposing for the wider public the real horrors of war. Most Nation states that engage in wars today try hard to conduct them out of the gaze of the general public, who are fed highly censored stories and images. Despite, or perhaps because of, the presence of 700 journalists 'embedded' in US and British military formations during the most recent Gulf War, much of the misery and devastation was overlooked. The perspective taken was often (with some notable exceptions) one of 'us' and 'them', with a tacit or more overt viewpoint that 'we' are justified and 'they' are either criminals or hapless victims. Casualties on 'our' side were often described (but the true reality not seen), while Iraqi deaths were largely invisible, and numbers unknown. When Al Jazeera, the Arabic television station, carried pictures of Iraqi civilian bodies mutilated by a purported strike from US forces, the cry of 'unfair play' was loud from British and American officialdom. The palpable fear was that if the public really saw the horrors being perpetrated in their name, they would no longer agree to support the war.

Simon Fisher, 2004

War can topple regimes but it cannot make peace, being a contradiction of its values and ethics, which demand mutual respect and the wholehearted acknowledgement of human equality, rights and responsibilities. Any war is a crime against humanity. Yet the myth of war's inevitability and effectiveness has provided a context in which elites have pursued their own agendas with relatively little challenge. While the argument of 'last resort' is often used, it is seldom – if ever – justified, since leaders' attempts to find alternatives are more often than not derisory. There *are* alternatives to war as a means of addressing violence and injustice – achieving just ends. The power of the few cannot be maintained without the acquiescence of the many. The last century saw not only a terrible number of cruel wars but also some staggering examples of the effectiveness of nonviolent civilian action. It overthrew tyrants and changed the face of international relations. Yet such is the strength of the myth of war and the old beliefs in militarism that we have scarcely digested that reality.

Although human beings have undoubted capacities for aggression and cruelty, they are not doomed to continue killing each other and squandering their resources in elaborate systems for doing so. Intergroup violence is a relatively recent phenomenon in the history of humanity. Though for the last few thousand years we have developed hierarchical systems and cultures that sanction and glorify violence, that is not the best of which we are capable. Though we may be influenced and shaped by our context, we also have the power to change it.

If we are to relegate war to the history books – as we can and must – we will need to draw on and develop the constructive means of addressing conflict that are commonplace in all our cultures but are all too rarely tried and never exhausted in international relations. We must take nonviolent methods as seriously – and if necessary fund them as generously – as we currently do our military methods (though since nonviolence destroys nothing and requires no hardware, its costs can never be so great). We must develop the attitudes, skills and capabilities necessary for preventing violence and resolving conflict, and the methods of civil resistance and intervention for situations where conflict prevention and resolution have failed and violence is ongoing. We must support and harness the goodwill and energy of ordinary people in acting for change and building genuine peace. We must think globally and act locally. Putting our own house in order will have a huge impact on the possibilities of making others' more habitable.

Diana Francis, 2004

It requires great self-denial and resignation of ourselves to God, to attain that state wherein we can freely cease from fighting when wrongfully invaded, if, by our fighting, there were a probability of over-coming the invaders. Whoever rightly attains to it does in some degree feel that spirit in which our Redeemer gave his life for us; and through Divine goodness many of our predecessors, and many now living, have learned this blessed lesson; but many others, having their religion chiefly by education, and not being enough acquainted with that cross which crucifies to the world, do manifest a temper distinguishable from that of an entire trust in God. In calmly considering these things, it hath not appeared strange to me that an exercise hath now fallen upon some, which, with respect to the outward means, is different from what was known to many of those who went before us.

John Woolman, published 1772

In the process of being transformed by the power and truth of God, we enter a deeper, mutual relationship with both God and the world. In the Judaeo-Christian tradition, this relationship is often called a 'covenant', which signifies the bond or partnership between humanity and God that is at the heart of religious faith and practice. It makes a claim upon our lives, such that within the meaning of an authentic life of faith, we are not only loyal to ourselves and to the wider body of life to which we belong, but also to our covenants with God, whatever we conceive God to be.

When we express this loyalty through the way we live and relate to the world, we *testify* to our covenant (relationship) with God. Quakers' founder George Fox explained that his commitment to peace arose out of the covenant with God, saying that the reason he would not bear arms was because he 'was come into the covenant of peace which was before wars and strife were'. The covenant comes first and the life committed to peace arises out of it; without the covenant, there is no *testimony* in the sense that Quakers use the word. In being rooted in a covenant with God as Quakers experience it, the Quaker peace and social testimonies are the discernment of God's will for the Quaker community and provide a vision of authentic society: one of peace and nonviolence; equality and community; truth and integrity, and simplicity and mindfulness.

Fox pioneered the view, which Penn and others would later reflect, that Christ, as an eternal and active principle present to each of us, calls us into a renewal of the covenant with God, which is in peace. He urged his fellow Quakers: 'Live in the peace [wholeness and integrity] of God, and not in the lusts from whence wars arise'. By *lust*, Fox means attachment to what does not really matter or does not belong in a truly abundant life. Such attachment leads us into betraying God, ourselves and one another. He thought that violence takes place when we reject the covenant of God, and so is not only problematic in secular moral terms but blasphemous also. Within this view, violence is a form of idolatry because it involves placing faith in something that does not offer the real potential of redemption.

David Gee, 2005

When people in Britain reminisce about World War II, they are often nostalgic about the sense of solidarity that it evokes: the way in which people 'did their bit' and 'pulled together'. They compare this sadly with what they see as today's selfish, atomised society. Civilian-based defence requires both a sense of individual responsibility and the feeling – and reality – of 'pulling together'. Personal commitment and collective action are two sides of the same coin. The central idea of nonviolent or civilian defence is to make a people self-reliant in the face of tyranny – able to resist it not by countering it in kind but by withholding co-operation and exercising the right to autonomy. This power of refusal is complemented by the power of communication and persuasion. The goal is not conquest but the overcoming of violence and enmity.

Nonviolence has nothing to do with inaction or passivity. The fact that it does not kill people or destroy the earth is, in itself, certainly an enormous advantage. But it offers, positively, both a means of combating violence and injustice and, at the same time, of upholding and strengthening the values and practices of peace. Nonviolence is peace and democracy in action, while war is the opposite. War is the exercise of lethal power by a certain section of society at the behest of a few powerful people, who take decisions behind closed doors. The power of nonviolence comes from a broad base, from the 'weak' as well as the 'strong'. It is founded in popular participation, both in decision-making and in action. It relies on all kinds of qualities – analysis, imagination, courage, persistence and the power to communicate. It can use all kinds and all levels of contribution.

Essentially, nonviolence depends on the will of individual human beings to take up their own power and responsibility to act with others for the things they believe in – just as organised violence depends on the participation of individual human beings. Both can call for great courage – but that is one of the positive values celebrated in war. In Idi Amin's Uganda, while some people were following the dictator's orders to kill their fellow citizens in their homes, others were giving neighbours shelter and refusing entry to those who would murder them. In Israel today, an increasing number of young men and women refuse to do their military service and act in solidarity with Palestinians who are under attack. There is always a choice.

But peace is more than the absence of war and tyranny. 'Positive peace' requires a continuous process of building and maintenance, which, if it were carried out, would remove the causes of war. The turbulence and violence that followed the collapse of Communism in Europe and Eurasia are a sad demonstration of the fact that removing dictatorships, even nonviolently, is far easier than building peace. Those who had put their all into ending a system had apparently not thought out, conceptually or strategically, the alternative that should replace it. The countries that have experienced the least difficulty in that regard have been those at the periphery of the former Soviet empire, later additions to it, that had stronger democratic traditions and where the change from opposition to government – however dramatic – was part of an ongoing process for those involved.

Achieving genuine and lasting peace means transforming societies. It involves addressing not only immediate behaviour and attitudes but the whole context in which people think and act, including the prevailing culture, social patterns, and political and economic systems. Preventing or stopping a war or removing a tyrant is one step on a long road, and even societies that face no such dramatic challenge may nonetheless need to be transformed. 'Reality' is confined to what happens in the big arena, the national stage. It is also what is done in a particular home or school, factory or village.

And even where people's action seems to fail, with hindsight they can be seen to have sown the seeds of peace.

Our participation, then, is necessary to peace and fundamental to nonviolent options. Peace is not something that is bestowed on us, still less imposed on us – or on anyone else – from outside. It is something we create and work on where we live. It is the job of all people in all countries. We need to develop the will and the skills that are necessary for peacebuilding work, at whatever stage and of whatever kind: resistance, advocacy of all kinds, bridge-building, mediation, education, building movements or 'constituencies' for peace, participating in peace processes and negotiations, institution-building, and more general social and political participation.

Diana Francis, 2004

This chapter closes with two eloquent and passionate public statements by Quakers agitating for peace, followed by a greatly loved and often quoted affirmation by William Penn: 'Let us then try what love will do.'

We totally oppose all wars, all preparation for war, all use of weapons and coercion by force, and all military alliances; no end could ever justify such means.

We equally and actively oppose all that leads to violence among people and nations, and violence to other species and to our planet. This has been our testimony to the whole world for over three centuries.

We are not naive or ignorant about the complexity of our modern world and the impact of sophisticated technologies – but we see no reason whatsoever to change or weaken our vision of the peace that everyone needs in order to survive and flourish on a healthy, abundant earth.

The primary reason for this stand is our conviction that there is that of God in every one which makes each person too precious to damage or destroy.

While someone lives there is always the hope of reaching that of God within them: such hope motivates our search to find non-violent resolution of conflict.

Peacemakers are also empowered by that of God in them. Our individual human skills, courage, endurance, and wisdom are vastly augmented by the power of the loving Spirit that connects all people.

Refusal to fight with weapons is not surrender. We are not passive when threatened by the greedy, the cruel, the tyrant, the unjust.

We will struggle to remove the causes of impasse and confrontation by every means of nonviolent resistance available. There is no guarantee that our resistance will be any more successful or any less risky than military tactics. At least our means will be suited to our end.

If we seemed to fail finally, we would still rather suffer and die than inflict evil in order to save ourselves and what we hold dear. If we succeed, there is no loser or winner, for the problem that led to conflict will have been resolved in a spirit of justice and tolerance.

Such a resolution is the only guarantee that there will be no further outbreak of war when each side has regained strength. The context in which we take this stand at this time is the increasing level of violence around us: child abuse; rape; wife battering; street assaults; riots; video and television sadism; silent economic and institutional violence; the prevalence of torture; the loss of freedoms; sexism;

racism and colonialism; the terrorism of both guerrillas and government soldiers; and the diversion of vast resources of funds and labour from food and welfare to military purposes.

But above and beyond all this, is the insane stockpiling of nuclear weapons which could in a matter of hours destroy everyone and everything that we value on our planet.

To contemplate such horror can leave us feeling despairing or apathetic, hardened or blasé.

We urge all New Zealanders to have the courage to face up to the mess humans are making of our world and to have the faith and diligence to cleanse it and restore the order intended by God. We must start with our own hearts and minds. Wars will stop only when each of us is convinced that war is never the way.

The places to begin acquiring the skills and maturity and generosity to avoid or to resolve conflicts are in our own homes, our personal relationships, our schools, our workplaces, and wherever decisions are made.

We must relinquish the desire to own other people, to have power over them, and to force our views on them. We must own up to our own negative side and not look for scapegoats to blame, punish, or exclude. We must resist the urge towards waste and the accumulation of possessions.

Conflicts are inevitable and must not be repressed or ignored but worked through painfully and carefully. We must develop the skills of being sensitive to oppression and grievances, sharing power in decision-making, creating consensus, and making reparation.

In speaking out, we acknowledge that we ourselves are as limited and as erring as anyone else. When put to the test, we each may fall short.

We do not have a blueprint for peace that spells out every stepping stone towards the goal that we share. In any particular situation, a variety of personal decisions could be made with integrity.

We may disagree with the views and actions of the politician or the soldier who opts for a military solution, but we still respect and cherish the person.

What we call for in this statement is a commitment to make the building of peace a priority and to make opposition to war absolute.

What we advocate is not uniquely Quaker but human and, we believe, the will of God. Our stand does not belong to Friends alone – it is yours by birthright.

We challenge New Zealanders to stand up and be counted on what is no less than the affirmation of life and the destiny of humankind.

Together, let us reject the clamour of fear and listen to the whisperings of hope.

Public statement of the Yearly Meeting of
Aotearoa/New Zealand,
Te Haahi Tuuhauwiri, 1987

If we would know peace, it is clear that our thinking has to change. For we have had set before us life and good, and death and evil, and people have constantly chosen evil and given its fruits status in our nations. This has inevitably been accompanied by those companions: deceit, distrust, despair, with their associates fear and hatred, insecurity and helplessness. Evil brings with it death in all its forms. However, we have failed to realise that the power of evil is nothing more than the power of our cooperation with it.

If, then, we would have peace, we must turn our lives around, and alter that fundamental choice:

Peace requires embracing life – in all its forms, in all its aspects.

Peace means casting out fear with love, and through love, finding our way to other hearts at a point in them beyond weakness and strength. Peace is loving our enemies, and thereby changing the relationship.

Peace is honouring truth, upholding it, speaking it.

Peacemakers use truth to overcome lies, and love to overcome hatred – even to the point of sacrifice and suffering.

Peace involves love and care of the earth, its waters, its atmosphere.

Peacemakers stand in the authority of the Spirit and dare to think with one another in terms of the whole planet.

They know that each of us is diminished by another's death, and will risk their part of the world that another might live.

They understand the difference between insecurity and vulnerability – the one with its roots in fear and distrust, the other a condition of life and growth.

They trust and build trust; they risk that faith in the other, both friend and adversary.

Peacemaking is listening – above the noise of our own thoughts.

It is being accountable for how our wealth is spent – remembering that wanting understanding also contributes to oppression.

Peace is living simply, that others may simply live.

Peacemakers will work to set at liberty the captive, to feed the hungry and relieve the oppressed.

They have knowingly chosen, that they and their children may live.

Peacemaking is a way of life: living in the Spirit, walking in the Spirit, and endeavouring to keep the unity of the Spirit.

I have set before you this day: Life and Death, and Peace is choosing Life.

Nancy Shelley, 1986

A good end cannot sanctify evil means; nor must we ever do evil, that good may come of it [. . .]. It is as great presumption to send our passions upon God's errands, as it is to palliate them with God's name [. . .]. We are too ready to retaliate, rather than forgive, or gain by love and information. And yet we could hurt no man that we believe loves us. Let us then try what Love will do: for if men did once see we love them, we should soon find they would not harm us. Force may subdue, but Love gains: and he that forgives first, wins the laurel.

William Penn, 1693

QUAKER JOURNALS 3:
JOHN WOOLMAN

John Woolman (1720–1772) was a Quaker from New Jersey, a unique personality who insisted on allowing himself to be led by the spirit in everything he did. He knew instinctively that, as he put it, 'conduct is more convincing than language' and he practised his Quakerism without compromise. In letting his life speak, he was an example to us all.

Three small illustrations will, I hope, hint at the detail and breadth of his vision. When he travelled to England by boat, he refused a cabin, preferring instead to live with the crew: 'I was now desirous to embrace every opportunity of being inwardly acquainted with the hardship and difficulties of my fellow creatures', he wrote. He had deep concerns over the welfare of animals, preferring to undertake his long journeys on foot, rather than using 'those coaches which run so fast as oft to oppress the horses'. And while early Friends sometimes thought nothing of denigrating other faiths, Woolman would have none of it: he 'found no narrowness respecting sects'.

He was, like many Quakers of the period, a successful business man. He began by retailing bakery products, but when he began to make money his conscience got the better of him. He felt 'a stop in my mind', realising that his thriving commercial enterprise was compromising his faithfulness to his vocation. So instead he decided to make his living as a tailor – a profession less likely to make large profits – and as a conveyancer and writer of wills. That allowed him to travel more freely and he devoted his life to long journeys as an itinerant Quaker minister.

He seemed a solitary figure, but he did not work alone. He almost always had travelling companions and he sought the backing of his Quaker

Meeting for everything he did. He would report his concerns to them and they would consider them carefully. If they agreed to what he was proposing, they would give him a certificate, endorsing his work and recommending him as a 'recorded minister' to other groups of Friends. 'Travelling in the ministry' is undertaken in a similar way by small numbers of Quakers today, and they still seek the backing of their Local Meeting to ensure that their actions are recognised as worthwhile before they set out. In the case of John Woolman, the work he undertook was of crucial importance.

He grasped earlier than most that the keeping of slaves was an abomination. It seems hard to believe now that there were Quakers in mid-eighteenth-century America who ignored their Society's testimony against slavery, but such was the case and Woolman made it his mission to persuade them of the evil which they were blindly perpetrating. Never confrontational, always quiet and conciliatory, he worked at a personal level to effect change. Woolman was no rabble-rouser.

He must have presented a somewhat bizarre picture as he travelled across America. He knew that the processes of dyeing fabric and leather involved the slave trade, so he only wore plain fabrics. In his white hat, undyed clothing and colourless leather boots, he could be an uncomfortable presence and his unshakable convictions sometimes caused considerable alarm. But his was a gentle, loving manner. He had a way of waiting quietly until the truth of his message hit home and he was effective in persuading slave-owning Quakers that they had to change.

His *Journal* is a testament to his scrupulousness, diligence and love. It was published posthumously in 1774 and is widely recognised as a classic of American literature. Its early champions included Charles Lamb ('Get the writings of John Woolman by heart') and Samuel Taylor Coleridge ('I should almost despair of that man who could peruse the life of John Woolman without an amelioration of heart'). But it is not only of historical interest: Woolman's ethical insights and sense of social responsibility speak as clearly to a twenty-first century audience as they did to readers in his own time.

I have chosen three episodes from the *Journal*. The first is a brief moment from his childhood which had an enduring effect on his character.

The second shows the growth of his concern about the slave trade and tells the story of Woolman's uncompromising attitude towards one slave-owner, combined with his quiet patience in negotiation. The third comes from a period in his life when he felt a compelling concern to build bridges with the Native American community, whose plight he understood at a profound level.

Woolman's *Journal* has never been out of print, but there are some bewildering differences in its various editions. These extracts are taken from a version of 1871 edited by John Greenleaf Whittier, whose hymn 'Dear Lord and Father of Mankind' appears on page 107 of this book.

I was born in Northampton, in Burlington County, West Jersey, in the year 1720. Before I was seven years old I began to be acquainted with the operations of divine love. Through the care of my parents, I was taught to read nearly as soon as I was capable of it; and as I went from school one day, I remember that while my companions were playing by the way, I went forward out of sight, and sitting down, I read the twenty-second chapter of Revelation: 'He showed me a pure river of water of life, clear as crystal, proceeding out of the throne of God and of the Lamb,' etc. In reading it, my mind was drawn to seek after that pure habitation which I then believed God had prepared for His servants. The place where I sat, and the sweetness that attended my mind, remain fresh in my memory. This, and the like gracious visitations, had such an effect upon me that when boys used ill language it troubled me; and, through the continued mercies of God, I was preserved from that evil. [. . .]

I may here mention a remarkable circumstance that occurred in my childhood. On going to a neighbour's house, I saw on the way a robin sitting on her nest, and as I came near she went off; but having young ones, she flew about, and with many cries expressed her concern for them. I stood and threw stones at her, and one striking her, she fell down dead. At first I was pleased with the exploit, but after a few minutes was seized with horror, at having, in a sportive way, killed an innocent creature while she was careful for her young. I beheld her lying dead, and thought those young ones, for which she was so careful, must now perish for want of their dam to nourish them. After some painful considerations on the subject, I climbed up the tree, took all the young birds, and killed them, supposing that better than to leave them to pine away and die miserably. In this case I believed that Scripture proverb was fulfilled, 'The tender mercies of the wicked are cruel.' I then went on my errand, and for some hours could think of little else but the cruelties I had committed, and was much troubled. Thus He whose tender mercies are over all His works hath placed a principle in the human mind, which incites to exercise goodness towards every living creature; and this being singly attended to, people become tender-hearted and sympathizing; but when frequently and totally rejected, the mind becomes shut up in a contrary disposition.

✦ ✦ ✦

Two things were remarkable to me in this journey: first, in regard to my entertainment. When I ate, drank, and lodged free-cost with people who lived in ease on the hard labour of their slaves, I felt uneasy; and as my mind was inward to the Lord, I found this uneasiness return upon me, at times, through the whole visit. Where the masters bore a good share of the burden, and lived frugally, so that their servants were well provided for, and their labour moderate, I felt more easy; but where they lived in a costly way, and laid heavy burdens on their slaves, my exercise was often great, and I frequently had conversation with them in private concerning it. Secondly, this trade of importing slaves from their native country being much encouraged amongst them, and the white people and their children so generally living without much labour, was frequently the subject of my serious thoughts. I saw in these southern provinces so many vices and corruptions, increased by this trade and this way of life, that it appeared to me as a dark gloominess hanging over the land; and though now many willingly run into it, yet in future the consequence will be grievous to posterity. I express it as it hath appeared to me, not once nor twice, but as a matter fixed on my mind. [. . .]

Finding a concern to visit Friends in the lower counties of Delaware, and on the eastern shore of Maryland, and having an opportunity to join with my well-beloved ancient friend, John Sykes, we obtained certificates, and set off the 7th of Eighth Month, 1748, were at the meetings of Friends in the lower counties, attended the Yearly Meeting at Little Creek, and made a visit to most of the meetings on the eastern shore, and so home by the way of Nottingham. We were abroad about six weeks, and rode, by computation, about five hundred and fifty miles.

Our exercise at times was heavy, but through the goodness of the Lord we were often refreshed, and I may say by experience, 'He is a stronghold in the day of trouble.' Though our Society in these parts appeared to me to be in a declining condition, yet I believe the Lord hath a people amongst them who labour to serve Him uprightly, but they have many difficulties to encounter.

About this time, believing it good for me to settle, and thinking seriously about a companion, my heart was turned to the Lord with desires that He would give me wisdom to proceed therein agreeably to His will, and He was pleased to give me a well-inclined damsel, Sarah Ellis, to whom I was married the 18th of Eighth Month, 1749.

In the fall of the year 1750 died my father, Samuel Woolman, of a fever, aged about sixty years. In his lifetime he manifested much care for us his children, that in our youth we might learn to fear the Lord; and often endeavoured to imprint in our minds the true principles of virtue, and particularly to cherish in us a spirit of tenderness, not only towards poor people, but also towards all creatures of which we had the command.

After my return from Carolina in 1746, I made some observations on keeping slaves which some time before his decease I showed to him; he perused the manuscript, proposed a few alterations, and appeared well satisfied that I found a concern on that account. In his last sickness, as I was watching with him one night, he being so far spent that there was no expectation of his recovery, though he had the perfect use of his understanding, he asked me concerning the manuscript, and whether I expected soon to proceed to take the advice of Friends in publishing it? After some further conversation thereon, he said, 'I have all along been deeply affected with the oppression of the poor negroes; and now, at last, my concern for them is as great as ever.'

By his direction I had written his will in a time of health, and that night he desired me to read it to him, which I did; and he said it was agreeable to his mind. He then made mention of his end, which he believed was near; and signified that, though he was sensible of many imperfections in the course of his life, yet his experience of the power of truth, and of the love and goodness of God from time to time, even till now, was such that he had no doubt that on leaving this life he should enter into one more happy.

The next day his sister Elizabeth came to see him, and told him of the decease of their sister Anne, who died a few days before; he then said, 'I reckon Sister Anne was free to leave this world?' Elizabeth said she was. He then said, 'I also am free to leave it'; and being in great weakness of body said, 'I hope I shall shortly go to rest.' He continued in a weighty frame of mind, and was sensible till near the last.

Second of Ninth Month, 1751 Feeling drawings in my mind to visit Friends at the Great Meadows, in the upper part of West Jersey, with the unity of our Monthly Meeting I went there, and had some searching laborious exercise amongst Friends in those parts, and found inward peace therein.

Ninth Month, 1753 In company with my well-esteemed friend, John Sykes, and with the unity of Friends, I travelled about two weeks, visiting Friends in Buck's County. We laboured in the love of the gospel, according to the measure received; and through the mercies of Him who is strength to the poor who trust in Him, we found satisfaction in our visit. In the next winter, way opening to visit Friends' families within the compass of our Monthly Meeting, partly by the labours of two Friends from Pennsylvania, I joined in some part of the work, having had a desire some time that it might go forward amongst us.

About this time, a person at some distance lying sick, his brother came to me to write his will. I knew he had slaves, and, asking his brother, was told he intended to leave them as slaves to his children. As writing is a profitable employ, and as offending sober people was disagreeable to my inclination, I was straitened in my mind; but as I looked to the Lord, he inclined my heart to His testimony. I told the man that I believed the practice of continuing slavery to this people was not right, and that I had a scruple in my mind against doing writings of that kind; that though many in our Society kept them as slaves, still I was not easy to be concerned in it, and desired to be excused from going to write the will. I spake to him in the fear of the Lord, and he made no reply to what I said, but went away; he also had some concerns in the practice, and I thought he was displeased with me. In this case I had fresh confirmation that acting contrary to present outward interest, from a motive of divine love and in regard to truth and righteousness, and thereby incurring the resentments of people, opens the way to a treasure better than silver, and to a friendship exceeding the friendship of men. [. . .]

Scrupling to do writings relative to keeping slaves has been a means of sundry small trials to me, in which I have so evidently felt my own will set aside, that I think it good to mention a few of them. Tradesmen and retailers of goods, who depend on their business for a living, are naturally inclined to keep the good-will of their customers; nor is it a pleasant thing for young men to be under any necessity to question the judgment or honesty of elderly men, and more especially of such as have a fair reputation. Deep-rooted customs, though wrong, are not easily altered; but it is the duty of all to be firm in that which they certainly know is right for them. A charitable, benevolent man, well acquainted with a negro, may, I believe, under some circumstances, keep him in his family as a servant, on no other motives than the negro's good; but man, as man, knows not what shall be after him, nor hath he any assurance that his children will attain to that perfection in wisdom and goodness necessary rightly to exercise such power; hence it is clear to me, that I ought not to be the scribe where wills are drawn in which some children are made sale-masters over others during life.

About this time an ancient man of good esteem in the neighbour-hood came to my house to get his will written. He had young negroes, and I asked him privately how he purposed to dispose of them. He told me. I then said, 'I cannot write thy will without breaking my own peace,' and respectfully gave him my reasons for it. He signified that he had a choice that I should have written it, but as I could not, consis-tently with my conscience, he did not desire it, and so he got it written by some other person. A few years after, there being great alterations in his family, he came again to get me to write his will. His negroes were yet young, and his son, to whom he intended to give them, was, since he first spoke to me, from a libertine become a sober young man, and he supposed that I would have been free on that account to write it. We had much friendly talk on the subject, and then deferred it. A few days after he came again and directed their freedom, and I then wrote his will.

Near the time that the last-mentioned Friend first spoke to me, a neighbour received a bad bruise in his body and sent for me to bleed him, which having done, he desired me to write his will. I took notes, and amongst other things he told me to which of his children he gave his young negro. I considered the pain and distress he was in, and knew not how it would end, so I wrote his will, save only that part concerning his slave, and carrying it to his bedside, read it to him. I then told him in a friendly way that I could not write any instruments by which my fellow-creatures were made slaves, without bringing trouble on my own mind. I let him know that I charged nothing for what I had done, and desired to be excused from doing the other part in the way he proposed. We then had a serious conference on the subject; at length, he agreeing to set her free, I finished his will.

✦ ✦ ✦

Having for many years felt love in my heart towards the natives of this land who dwell far back in the wilderness, whose ancestors were formerly the owners and possessors of the land where we dwell, and who for a small consideration assigned their inheritance to us, and being at Philadelphia in the Eighth Month, 1761, on a visit to some Friends who had slaves, I fell in company with some of those natives who lived on the east branch of the river Susquehanna, at an Indian town called Wehaloosing, two hundred miles from Philadelphia. In conversation with them by an interpreter, as also by observations on their countenances and conduct, I believed some of them were measurably acquainted with that divine power which subjects the rough and forward will of the creature. At times I felt inward drawings towards a visit to that place, which I mentioned to none except my dear wife until it came to some ripeness.

In the winter of 1762 I laid my prospects before my friends at our Monthly and Quarterly, and afterwards at our General Spring Meeting; and having the unity of Friends, and being thoughtful about an Indian pilot, there came a man and three women from a little beyond that town to Philadelphia on business. Being informed thereof by letter, I met them in town in the 5th Month, 1763; and after some conversation, finding they were sober people, I, with the concurrence of Friends in that place, agreed to join them as companions in their return. [. . .]

We met with an Indian trader lately come from Wyoming. In conversation with him, I perceived that many white people often sell rum to the Indians, which I believe is a great evil. In the first place, they are thereby deprived of the use of reason, and, their spirits being violently agitated, quarrels often arise which end in mischief, and the bitterness and resentment occasioned hereby are frequently of long continuance. Again, their skins and furs, gotten through much fatigue and hard travels in hunting, with which they intended to buy clothing, they often sell at a low rate for more rum, when they become intoxicated; and afterward, when they suffer for want of the necessaries of life, are angry with those who, for the sake of gain, took advantage of their weakness.

Their chiefs have often complained of this in their treaties with the English. Where cunning people pass counterfeits and impose on others that which is good for nothing, it is considered as wickedness; but for the sake of gain to sell that which we know does people harm, and which often works their ruin, manifests a hardened and corrupt heart, and is an evil which demands the care of all true lovers of virtue to suppress. While my mind this evening was thus employed, I also remembered that the people on the frontiers, among whom this evil is too common, are often poor; and that they venture to the outside of the colony in order to live more independently of the wealthy, who often set high rents on their land. I was renewedly confirmed in a belief, that, if all our inhabitants lived according to sound wisdom, labouring to promote universal love and righteousness, and ceased from every inordinate desire after wealth, and from all customs which are tinctured with luxury, the way would be easy for our inhabitants, though they might be much more numerous than at present, to live comfortably on honest employments, without the temptation they are so often under of being drawn into schemes to make settlements on lands which have not been purchased of the Indians, or of applying to that wicked practice of selling rum to them.

Tenth of Sixth Month We set out early this morning and crossed the western branch of Delaware, called the Great Lehie, near Fort Allen. The water being high, we went over in a canoe. Here we met an Indian, had friendly conversation with him, and gave him some biscuit; and he, having killed a deer, gave some of it to the Indians with us. After travelling some miles, we met several Indian men and women with a cow and horse, and some household goods, who were lately come from their dwelling at Wyoming, and were going to settle at another place. We made them some small presents, and, as some of them understood English, I told them my motive for coming into their country, with which they appeared satisfied. One of our guides talking awhile with an ancient woman concerning us, the poor old woman came to my companion and me, and took her leave of us with an appearance of sincere affection. We pitched our tent near the banks of the same river, having laboured hard in crossing some of those mountains called the Blue Ridge. The roughness of the stones and the cavities between them, with the steepness of the hills, made it appear dangerous. But we were preserved in safety, through the kindness of Him whose works in these mountainous deserts appeared awful, and towards whom my heart was turned during this day's travel.

Near our tent, on the sides of large trees peeled for that purpose, were various representations of men going to and returning from the wars, and of some being killed in battle. This was a path heretofore used by warriors, and as I walked about viewing those Indian histories, which were painted mostly in red or black, and thinking on the innumerable afflictions which the proud, fierce spirit produceth in the world, also on the toils and fatigues of warriors in travelling over mountains and deserts; on their miseries and distresses when far from home and wounded by their enemies; of their bruises and great weariness in chasing one another over the rocks and mountains; of the restless, unquiet state of mind of those who live in this spirit, and of the hatred which mutually grows up in the minds of their children, the desire to cherish the spirit of love and peace among these people arose very fresh in me.

This was the first night that we lodged in the woods, and being wet with travelling in the rain, as were also our blankets, the ground, our tent, and the bushes under which we purposed to lay, all looked discouraging; but I believed that it was the Lord who had thus far brought me forward, and that He would dispose of me as He saw good, and so I felt easy. We kindled a fire, with our tent open to it, then laid some bushes next the ground, and put our blankets upon them for our bed, and, lying down, got some sleep. In the morning, feeling a little unwell, I went into the river; the water was cold, but soon after I felt fresh and well. About eight o'clock we set forward and crossed a high mountain supposed to be upward of four miles over, the north side being the steepest. About noon we were overtaken by one of the Moravian brethren going to Wehaloosing, and an Indian man with him who could talk English; and we being together while our horses ate grass had some friendly conversation; but they, travelling faster than we, soon left us. This Moravian, I understood, has this spring spent some time at Wehaloosing, and was invited by some of the Indians to come again.

Twelfth of Sixth Month being the first of the week and rainy day, we continued in our tent, and I was led to think on the nature of the exercise which hath attended me. Love was the first motion, and thence a concern arose to spend some time with the Indians, that I might feel and understand their life and the spirit they live in, if haply I might receive some instruction from them, or they might be in any degree helped forward by my following the leadings of truth among them. [. . .]

The first Indian that we saw was a woman of a modest countenance, with a Bible, who spake first to our guide, and then with an harmonious voice expressed her gladness at seeing us, having before heard of our coming. By the direction of our guide we sat down on a log, while he went to the town to tell the people we were come. My companion and I, sitting thus together in a deep inward stillness, the poor woman came and sat near us; and, great awfulness coming over us, we rejoiced in a sense of God's love manifested to our poor souls. After a while we heard a conch-shell blow several times, and then came John Curtis and another Indian man, who kindly invited us into a house near the town, where we found about sixty people sitting in silence. After sitting with them a short time I stood up, and in some tenderness of spirit acquainted them, in a few short sentences, with the nature of my visit, and that a concern for their good had made me willing to come thus far to see them; which, some of them understanding, interpreted to the others, and there appeared gladness among them. I then showed them my certificate, which was explained to them; and the Moravian who overtook us on the way, being now here, bade me welcome.

But the Indians knowing that this Moravian and I were of different religious societies, and as some of their people had encouraged him to come and stay awhile with them, they were, I believe, concerned that there might be no jarring or discord in their meetings; and having, I suppose, conferred together, they acquainted me that the people, at my request, would at any time come together and hold meetings.

They also told me that they expected the Moravian would speak in their settled meetings, which are commonly held in the morning and near evening. So finding liberty in my heart to speak to the Moravian, I told him of the care I felt on my mind for the good of these people, and my belief that no ill effects would follow if I sometimes spake in their meetings when love engaged me thereto, without calling them together at times when they did not meet of course. He expressed his good-will towards my speaking at any time all that I found in my heart to say.

On the evening of the 18th I was at their meeting, where pure gospel love was felt, to the tendering of some of our hearts. The interpreters endeavoured to acquaint the people with what I said, in short sentences, but found some difficulty, as none of them were quite perfect in the English and Delaware tongues, so they helped one another, and we laboured along, divine love attending. Afterwards, feeling my mind covered with the spirit of prayer, I told the interpreters that I found it in my heart to pray to God, and believed, if I prayed aright He would hear me; and I expressed my willingness for them to omit interpreting; so our meeting ended with a degree of divine love. Before the people went out, I observed Papunehang (the man who had been zealous in labouring for a reformation in that town, being then very tender) speaking to one of the interpreters, and I was afterwards told that he said in substance as follows: 'I love to feel where words come from.'

Nineteenth of Sixth Month and first of the week This morning the Indian who came with the Moravian, being also a member of that society, prayed in the meeting, and then the Moravian spake a short time to the people. In the afternoon, my heart being filled with a heavenly care for their good, I spake to them awhile by interpreters; but none of them being perfect in the work, and I feeling the current of love run strong, told the interpreters that I believed some of the people would understand me, and so I proceeded without them; and I believe the Holy Ghost wrought on some hearts to edification where all the words were not understood. I looked upon it as a time of divine favour, and my heart was tendered and truly thankful before the Lord. After I sat down, one of the interpreters seemed spirited to give the Indians the substance of what I said.

Before our first meeting this morning, I was led to meditate on the manifold difficulties of these Indians who, by the permission of the Six Nations, dwell in these parts. A near sympathy with them was raised in me, and, my heart being enlarged in the love of Christ, I thought that the affectionate care of a good man for his only brother in affliction does not exceed what I then felt for that people. I came to this place through much trouble; and though through the mercies of God I believed that if I died in the journey it would be well with me, yet the thoughts of falling into the hands of Indian warriors were, in times of weakness, afflicting to me; and being of a tender constitution of body, the thoughts of captivity among them were also grievous; supposing that as they were strong and hardy they might demand service of me beyond what I could well bear. But the Lord alone was my keeper, and I believed that if I went into captivity it would be for some good end. Thus, from time to time, my mind was centred in resignation, in which I always found quietness. And this day, though I had the same dangerous wilderness between me and home, I was inwardly joyful that the Lord had strengthened me to come on this visit, and had manifested a fatherly care over me in my poor lowly condition, when in mine own eyes I appeared inferior to many among the Indians.

When the last-mentioned meeting was ended, it being night, Papunehang went to bed; and hearing him speak with an harmonious voice, I suppose for a minute or two, I asked the interpreter, who told me that he was expressing his thankfulness to God for the favours he had received that day, and prayed that He would continue to favour him with the same, which he had experienced in that meeting. Though Papunehang had before agreed to receive the Moravian and join with them, he still appeared kind and loving to us.

I was at two meetings on the 20th, and silent in them. The following morning, in meeting, my heart was enlarged in pure love among them, and in short plain sentences I expressed several things that rested upon me, which one of the interpreters gave the people pretty readily. The meeting ended in supplication, and I had cause humbly to acknowledge the loving-kindness of the Lord towards us; and then I believed that a door remained open for the faithful disciples of Jesus Christ to labour among these people. And now, feeling my mind at liberty to return, I took my leave of them in general at the conclusion of what I said in meeting, and we then prepared to go homeward. But some of their most active men told us that, when we were ready to move the people would choose to come and shake hands with us. Those who usually came to meeting did so; and from a secret draught in my mind I went among some who did not usually go to meeting, and took my leave of them also. The Moravian and his Indian interpreter appeared respectful to us at parting. This town, Wehaloosing, stands on the bank of the Susquehanna, and consists, I believe, of about forty houses, mostly compact together, some about thirty feet long and eighteen wide – some bigger, some less. They are built mostly of split plank, one end being set in the ground, and the other pinned to a plate on which rafters are laid, and then covered with bark. I understand a great flood last winter overflowed the greater part of the ground where the town stands, and some were now about moving their houses to higher ground.

We expected only two Indians to be of our company, but when we were ready to go we found many of them were going to Bethlehem with skins and furs, and chose to go in company with us. So they loaded two canoes, in which they desired us to go, telling us that the waters were so raised with the rains that the horses should be taken by such as were better acquainted with the fording-places. We, therefore, with several Indians, went in the canoes, and others went on horses, there being seven besides ours. We met with the horsemen once on the way by appointment, and at night we lodged a little below a branch called Tankhannah, and some of the young men, going out a little before dusk with their guns, brought in a deer.

Through diligence we reached Wyoming before night, the 22nd, and understood that the Indians were mostly gone from this place.

We went up a small creek into the woods with our canoes, and, pitching our tent, carried out our baggage, and before dark our horses came to us. Next morning, the horses being loaded and our baggage prepared, we set forward, being in all fourteen, and with diligent travelling were favoured to get near half-way to Fort Allen. The land on this road from Wyoming to our frontier being mostly poor, and good grass being scarce, the Indians chose a piece of low ground to lodge on, as the best for grazing. I had sweat much in travelling, and, being weary, slept soundly. In the night I perceived that I had taken cold, of which I was favoured soon to get better.

Twenty-fourth of Sixth Month This day we passed Fort Allen and lodged near it in the woods. We forded the westerly branch of the Delaware three times, which was a shorter way than going over the top of the Blue Mountains called the Second Ridge. In the second time of fording where the river cuts through the mountain, the waters being rapid and pretty deep, my companion's mare, being a tall, tractable animal, was sundry times driven back through the river, being laden with the burdens of some small horses which were thought unable to come through with their loads. The troubles eastward, and the difficulty for Indians to pass through our frontier, I apprehend, were one reason why so many came, expecting that our being in company would prevent the outside inhabitants being surprised. We reached Bethlehem on the 25th, taking care to keep foremost, and to acquaint people on and near the road who these Indians were. This we found very needful, for the frontier inhabitants were often alarmed at the report of the English being killed by Indians westward. Among our company were some whom I did not remember to have seen at meeting, and some of these at first were very reserved; but we being several days together, and behaving in a friendly manner towards them, and making them suitable return for the services they did us, they became more free and sociable.

Twenty-sixth of Sixth Month Having carefully endeavoured to settle all affairs with the Indians relative to our journey, we took leave of them, and I thought they generally parted from us affectionately. We went forward to Richland and had a very comfortable meeting among our friends, it being the first day of the week. Here I parted with my kind friend and companion Benjamin Parvin, and accompanied by my friend Samuel Foulk, we rode to John Cadwallader's, from whence I reached home the next day, and found my family tolerably well. They and my friends appeared glad to see me return from a journey which they apprehended would be dangerous; but my mind, while I was out, had been so employed in striving for perfect resignation, and had so often been confirmed in a belief that, whatever the Lord might be pleased to allot for me, it would work for good, that I was careful lest I should admit any degree of selfishness in being glad overmuch, and laboured to improve by those trials in such a manner as my gracious Father and Protector designed.

Between the English settlements and Wehaloosing we had only a narrow path, which in many places is much grown up with bushes, and interrupted by abundance of trees lying across it. These, together with the mountain swamps and rough stones, make it a difficult road to travel, and the more so because rattlesnakes abound here, of which we killed four. People who have never been in such places have but an imperfect idea of them; and I was not only taught patience, but also made thankful to God, who thus led about and instructed me, that I might have a quick and lively feeling of the afflictions of my fellow-creatures, whose situation in life is difficult.

COMMUNITY

Our life is love, and peace, and tenderness; and bearing one with another, and forgiving one another, and not laying accusations one against another; but praying for one another, and helping one another up with a tender hand.

Isaac Penington, 1667

I have become a good deal disillusioned over 'big' conferences and large gatherings. I pin my hopes to quiet processes and small circles, in which vital and transforming events take place.

Rufus M. Jones, 1937

You don't get converted into a Quaker; you gradually come to realise that you are one, usually because other Friends start treating you as one.

Gerald Priestland, 1978

A Quaker Meeting is just that: a meeting of bodies and souls. It is the people who worship there week after week; who take part in discussion groups, business meetings, weddings and funerals; who switch on the lights and lock up at the end; who do the announcements and make the tea; who just turn up once to see if they like it. Children are as valued as grown-ups, and as much part of the meeting as their parents. People who have joined The Religious Society of Friends are considered no more important than those who have not. No one is in charge.

Fundamentally we are a Society of Friends. Those who join us do not join 'the Society' as number so-and-so; they join a particular meeting (it might be Hampstead or Golders Green, Highgate, Edgware or Muswell Hill). It will probably be a small group of less than a hundred people, and it is to be hoped that these people really will become friends – perhaps people you will love and respect, to whom you can speak frankly, and whom you will not wish to offend unless compelled to by the truth. If you feel you simply do not care for these people as friends, then it may be that the Society is not for you at all. [. . .] It may surprise outsiders to learn that silence is used in business as well as worship meetings. Silent prayer, meditation, goes back far beyond George Fox, of course. But it was rare in the Anglican tradition, which liked to hear everyone saying the same thing at the same time.

Gerald Priestland, 1981

One of the unexpected things I have learnt in my life as a Quaker is that religion is basically about relationships between people. This was an unexpected discovery, because I had been brought up to believe that religion was essentially about our relationship with God.

If we are sensitive, we find that everything that happens to us, good or bad, can help us to build a vision of the meaning of life. We can be helped to be sensitive by reading the Bible and being open to experience of nature, music, books, painting, sport or whatever our particular interest may be. It is in and through all things that we hear God speaking to us. But I do not think I am alone in my certainty that it's in my relationships with people that the deepest religious truths are most vividly disclosed.

George Gorman, 1982

In a true community we will not choose our companions, for our choices are so often limited by self-serving motives. Instead, our companions will be given to us by grace. Often they will be persons who will upset our settled view of self and world. In fact, we might define true community as the place where the person you least want to live with always lives!

Parker J. Palmer, 1980

One of life's hardest lessons is that there is no justification for expecting that our neighbour is to traverse precisely the same path as that which we ourselves have followed. The varieties of religious experience are probably far greater than any of us suppose. The difficulty a man has in grasping this truth is increased in proportion as his own experience has been vivid and clearly defined. One who has been lifted out of the horrible pit, has had his feet set upon a rock, and a new song put into his mouth, finds it hard to believe that another who has arrived quietly and without crisis, with no strong consciousness of guilt and no corresponding ecstasy of deliverance can really be a disciple at all.

William Littleboy, 1916

Are there not different states, different degrees, different growths, different places? [. . .] Therefore, watch every one to feel and know his own place and service in the body, and to be sensible of the gifts, places, and services of others, that the Lord may be honoured in all, and every one owned and honoured in the Lord, and no otherwise.

Isaac Penington, 1667

It is often hard to accept that other people have their own valid relationship with God, their own specialness and insights. We are not just disciples – we are disciples together.

Our vision of the truth has to be big enough to include other people's truth as well as our own. We have to learn to love difficult unlovable people. Accepting each other, and each other's relationship with God, let us continue to hold together at our deepest level. We are a forgiven community. Part of the cost of discipleship is living with the other disciples.

Beth Allen, 1984

God comes to us in the midst of human need, and the most pressing needs of our time demand community in response.

How can I participate in a fairer distribution of resources unless I live in a community which makes it possible to consume less? How can I learn accountability unless I live in a community where my acts and their consequences are visible to all? How can I learn to share power unless I live in a community where hierarchy is unnatural? How can I take the risks which right action demands unless I belong to a community which gives support? How can I learn the sanctity of each life unless I live in a community where we can be persons, not roles, to one another?

Parker J. Palmer, 1980

Members and regular attenders of a Quaker Meeting are in frequent contact with one another. They are friends as well as Friends, living in the spirit together and sharing the experience. They run their meeting as a community. The Quaker life is not something that people dip into when they feel like it.

A meeting is more than simply a worshipping community. It is a group of people living in the world and facing the challenge of witnessing to it. Worship can lead far beyond what one does on Sunday. Meeting for worship can be more than just an occasion on which one's private religious needs are satisfied. Silent devotion should lead to an awareness that the meeting is less and less a place we choose ourselves, and more and more a place to which, out of love, God has called us. To understand this is to sense the meaning of those lovely phrases about the community of faith being the body of Christ.

Early Friends knew, practised and cherished this unity of spirit. They called it 'gospel order', for they felt the presence of the Lord among them, guiding and leading, so strongly that they dispensed with any human assistant or intermediary. But they were not the individualists of their detractors' imaginations. They had a close feeling of being together, irrevocably, for the nature of the light was to call people into fellowship.

The silence in which Friends assemble to worship, or which they uphold at the centre of their programmed devotions, is a sign of this community, and amid all the controversies and differences with which their history is littered, they know it. We have defined convincement and conversion in Quaker terms as the transcendence of self and a coming to wait upon the leadings of God in all things.

John Punshon, 1987

Decisions which affect the life of the Meeting are taken by the group at a Meeting for Worship for Business, where silence, ministry and stillness are no less important than in the regular Meeting for Worship.

[Business meetings] open with a period of quiet waiting in which a corporate journey can be made to the still centre from where alone true decisions can be made. Again the intention of the gathering affects its worship, for practical issues calling for unity in decision is the main reason for them. Quakers seek to reach their decisions without voting, for Quaker business meetings are theocratic rather than democratic, and they seek to achieve this by giving the freedom for all present to express their view if they feel drawn to do so. The way in which they do this will be similar to the way in which ministry arises in an ordinary meeting for worship. It will we hope not be an ill-thought-through contribution tossed lightly off the top of the mind, but one that arises from the deep centre of life. Of course, one must keep matters in proportion, for there are some decisions that can be quickly and easily reached without any profound exercise on the part of the meeting. But there will be others of such importance that they call for a most searching exploration in the depths of being, and even when this has been faithfully carried out it may not be possible for the meeting to achieve unity. On such occasions the wisdom and experience of the Society urge that no decision should be taken, it being better to delay action than to compromise in a judgement which does not represent a unity known and felt by all in the depth of the meeting's life. I have learnt by long experience that it is extremely unwise to make dogmatic statements about Quaker behaviour: however, I am perfectly prepared to be dogmatic about the fact that, if a decision overrides the sincere and strongly held convictions of a number of those present, then sooner or later it will be found to have been faulty.

George Gorman, 1973

In a Quaker meeting, for worship or for business, there is more than waiting and silence. There is also speaking for one's self and feeling the weight of the words of others. The quest for truth among Friends is meant to be corporate, not a private reverie. The leading of the gathered group is to be trusted, and when you or I speak we must be willing to test our truth against the truth received by others.

Here is where Friends can contribute to community by refusing to follow the religious individualism of our times. Behind these new movements lies the assumption that truth is totally subjective – one truth for you, another for me, and never mind the difference. But when we understand truth that way then the truth we are given will have no chance to transform society or ourselves. If we affirm community we must risk that our partial versions of truth will be enlarged or even made uncouth by the light given to others.

If true community is to flourish then the individual must flourish as well. Here, too, Friends have an important contribution to make. In a Quaker meeting for business there is not only the principle that the group must try to come together under its corporate leading. There is also the principle that the individual must never be overpowered, never put in the position of an outvoted and embittered minority. It is a remarkable fact that Friends for three hundred years have taken neither the path of religious authoritarianism nor the path of spiritual privatism. Instead, Friends have always accepted both the possibility of individual truth and the obligation of corporately testing that truth.

Parker J. Palmer, 1980

For the preservation of love, concord and a good decorum in this meeting, 'tis earnestly desired that all business that comes before it be managed with gravity and moderation, in much love and Amity, without reflections or retorting, which is but reasonable as well as comely, since we have no other obligation upon each other but love, which is the very bond of our society: and therein to serve the Truth and one another; having an eye single to it, ready to sacrifice every private interest to that of Truth, and the good of the whole community.

Wherefore let whatsoever is offered, be mildly proposed, and so left with some pause, that the meeting may have opportunity to weigh the matter, and have a right sense of it, that there may be a unanimity and joint concurrence of the whole. And if anything be controverted that it be in coolness of Spirit calmly debated, each offering their reasons and sense, their assent, or dissent, and so leave it without striving. And also that but one speak at once, and the rest hear. And that private debates and discourses be avoided, and all attend the present business of the Meeting. So will things be carried on sweetly as becomes us, to our comfort: and love and unity be increased: and we better serve Truth and our Society.

Wiltshire Quarterly Meeting, 1678

What is required is a willingness to listen to what others have to say rather than to persuade them that one's own point of view represents what is right and proper. It also requires restraint. The reiteration of one point by several Friends each in their own way lends no weight to the point. What the meeting must learn to discern is its rightness, not how many people support it.

This is why there are no votes and why a minority in a meeting can always frustrate the will of the majority. Friends are willing to sacrifice the despatch of business efficiently to the principle that the minority may be in the right, so that one of the best guides to the divine will is to wait patiently until the meeting is enabled to go forward in unity.

Moreover, in matters of great importance, it is often found that there is no way for a consensus view to be arrived at, even if it were sound in principle to attempt one. Where Friends are willing to adjust their views in matters of controversy, it is because they have loyalty to a higher truth, not because they wish to compromise for the sake of avoiding conflict. It would be easy to see these few brief remarks about how Friends do their business as quite a simple process of compromise dressed up in religious language and not really amounting to very much. People who think can be forgiven, but the proof comes in the practice.

John Punshon, 1987

In these solemn assemblies for the church's service, there is no one presides among them after the manner of the assemblies of other people; Christ only being their president, as he is pleased to appear in life and wisdom in any one or more of them; to whom, whatever be their capacity or degree, the rest adhere with a firm unity, not of authority, but conviction, which is the divine authority and way of Christ's power and spirit in his people: making good his blessed promise, that he would be in the midst of his, where and whenever they were met together in his name, even to the end of the world.

William Penn, 1694

When a person has been part of their Quaker Meeting for a few months or years, they may consider becoming a member of The Religious Society of Friends. They join their Area Meeting, which consists of a group of smaller Local Meetings. Applying for membership is a big decision, because it implies real commitment to the Quaker way and a desire to take the fullest possible part in its activities.

Our membership is never based upon worthiness. [...] We none of us are members because we have attained a certain standard of worthiness, but rather because, in this matter, we still are all humble learners in the school of Christ. Our membership is of no importance whatever unless it signifies that we are committed to something of far greater and more lasting significance than can adequately be conveyed by the closest association with any movement or organisation.

Edgar G. Dunstan, 1956

Becoming a Quaker is a simple procedure. It is also a tender one. People who wish to join are asked to talk confidentially about themselves and their spiritual journey to two sympathetic Friends. This, by mutual agreement, can take place on one or a number of occasions. The two Quakers ensure that the person is clear about what they are joining, and then write a short account which is prepared in collaboration with the applicant. That is presented to a Quaker Area Meeting which takes a decision either to admit the person or, very occasionally, to suggest that they wait a little longer. There is no expectation or requirement for applicants to put any of their experience into writing, but here are two who chose to do that.

I feel very strongly [. . .] that the spiritual life absolutely requires that we should not remain isolated. It is this deep need of getting out of a prolonged and dangerous relative isolation which urges me to ask now to be admitted among the Quakers. It is more and more clear to me that it is only in the bosom of a religious family, freely but very strongly constituted, that the individual can render to the world the services it sorely needs and which no politics, not based on a deep inspiration, can hope to organise.

Pierre Ceresole, 1936

I suppose the question to ask is not, why am I applying for membership, but, why not sooner than this? All I can say is that I am not a hasty person. I have been considering applying for at least four years. I have felt myself to be part of Friends for so long that it has shocked me, on occasions, to realise that I am not thought of as 'one of us' but rather 'one of them'. I have come to see that how I perceive myself in terms of commitment and belonging is not necessarily how I am perceived. At times this has made me sad. But I can see that I owe it to Friends to make my position clear. If the Society can be thought of as a ship, I would like to be one of the crew, not a passenger, and to be seen like this.

Jai Penna, 1989

In the following three extracts, Quakers reflect on their reasons for membership of The Religious Society of Friends.

What does being a Quaker mean to me? It means my work and my faith, my everyday life and my religious life, are all one. It means listening for God, waiting on him – not lecturing and pestering him, telling him what he already knows or what he ought to be doing for us. It means quietness (which is a blessing in a profession like mine). It means a constant searching after the truth; for surely God did not say his last word to Man with the final full stop of the Bible? It means active peacemaking and non-violence. It means a rather fascinating way of reaching group decisions, without scoring points or winning votes. It means real friendship; it means equality of sex and race; and it means having a tradition of many fine men and women behind you. Even if some of them did wear black hats.

Gerald Priestland, 1978

Why, I ask myself, did I go to worship with those rather small and not very distinguished groups of people? Surely it was that sitting among these quite ordinary people, to most of whom I remained a stranger and a foreigner for some months, I sensed an experience of belonging – of community. A true Friends' meeting for worship drawing individuals with varieties of temperament, talent and background always manages to engender a climate of belonging, of community which is infectious and creative. This experience of 'belonging' has remained with me over the years and it has grown both in intensity and universality. [. . .] The 'giving out' of such a sense of community is the natural witness of a Quaker meeting which has in it the seed of life and creative experience.

Ranjit M. Chetsingh, 1967

Why am I a Friend? Because Quakerism takes a whole view of life. Everyday living and religion are all of one piece, and we are including, not excluding, in our approach. [. . .] Over the years the Society has given me continuing friendship. To be human is to be a separate person and, therefore, to know the fact and the mystery of aloneness. Although I find I can make surface contact with people quite readily, I am often lonely and experience stretches of doubt and dryness. Then especially I need friends who will accept a quality of friendship which involves praying for me. By this I mean that they care enough to think of me, to ask themselves if there is any special need of mine they can meet, to commend what they don't know about me to God's wisdom, and when we meet to make me welcome.

Donald Court, 1965

The spiritual journeys of Quakers are not undertaken alone. Everything about Quakerism, from the local Meeting for Worship to work for conflict resolution, is achieved at a communal level. We close this chapter with extracts from the work of four Quakers who reflect on the different aspects of community.

To love one's neighbour is not simply a matter of understanding. Awareness is more than this. It is a compound of sensitivity and imagination. To be sensitive implies a readiness and an alertness to receive impressions as a photographic plate is quick to receive impressions of light. It means being quick (in the original sense of 'alive', as in 'the quick and the dead') to feel another's pain, as well as to understand another's point of view. But it also means being responsive to impressions that come from within as well as from without. This is well expressed in the Advice of Friends: 'Take heed, dear Friends, to the promptings of Love and Truth in your own hearts'.

William Oats, 1990

He receives some peaches in prison. I do not want to eat my peaches all alone . . . it is difficult to give them away, if I give only that, without giving anything else; I ought to exchange a few words, but there are all sorts of reasons against it; the principal one, perhaps – one too many in any case – is that I find it rather awkward. A difficult undertaking, to converse with the other prisoners, knowing nothing of their circumstances, from the standpoint of my own, which I do know. General conversation of a natural kind is too difficult and delicate and runs a great risk of being misleading, if one cannot at least speak to each one of them individually, and even then. . . .

I distribute my peaches among them with mathematical exactitude and in a spirit of mathematical fairness, as gracefully as I can, saying precisely four words: 'It makes a change'. I am not sure if 1 Corinthians 13 is absolutely satisfied thereby: I think St Paul would have added: 'And if you give away all your peaches, and have not love, it is absolutely nothing.'

But I feel, having acted in a mathematical spirit, at least a mathematical kind of satisfaction; that's perfectly all right, I ask nothing more. Casting one's bread and one's peaches on the water is always, in the end, even when we are no longer there, an excellent thing. And so I finished a good day which I almost spoilt by keeping my peaches – not through selfishness, but through shyness and, more precisely, fear of acting in a merely mathematical spirit. You have to do the best you can, as the Eternal made you, and as your conscience dictates; it is the first law, perhaps the only one.

Pierre Ceresole, published 1954

The real mind might be compared to a clear, deep pool. You can look down and down and never see the bottom. But the leaves of a nearby tree fall and cover the surface, so that only a pattern of leaves is visible (a different pattern of leaves for each person with their various 'identities', quirks, oddities, experiences, ideas, culture, notions, isms). You might never know, unless you had seen it earlier, that the pool was there at all. But sometimes a wind comes, a breath of reality, that disturbs the leaves and reveals part of the pool, and on very rare occasions the leaves are permanently blown away.

The leaves on the pool, those blobs on the mind, the frills, conceits, vanities and fears, have nothing to do with our true nature. But they obscure it, creating the mirage of illusions within which we so largely exist.

The most lethal of these illusions are false ideas of our own nature; that we are stupid, inadequate, wicked; or conversely that we are clever, charming, generous – which is just as bad so long as we think it is to our credit rather than God's.

Then we identify ourselves with our bodies. I am well. I am ill. I have a headache – which soon becomes I am a headache; the throbbing pain possesses me. But I am not my body. I am heir to all creation and my body is a temporary construction of celestial ideas for my habitation.

Yet again we identify ourselves with our work, or role, or function(s) in life. Most women, happily, have ceased to identify themselves as their husband's wife, but most would also still identify themselves as teacher, doctor, member of parliament, mother, housewife, or whatever. And I would have identified myself as professor, or whatever I was at the time. But although I worked in that capacity I was not a professor any more than I was a husband, ratepayer, owner of a driving licence, etc, etc.

No. We are not our roles. However important or splendid they may be, we are something more sublime: a self, described thus by Thomas Traherne in his poem *My Spirit*:

O wondrous Self! O Sphere of Light
O sphere of Joy most fair;
O Act, O Power infinit;
O Subtile and unbounded Air!
O living Orb of Light!
Thou which within me art, yet Me! Thou Ey,
And Temple of this whole Infinitie!

It stands to reason that we must also see others in the light of that of God within both them and us. As we view ourselves, so must we view them – indeed, as I have suggested, it may be easier to see in them the divine essence. If we are not to blame ourselves, we must be even more scrupulous about criticising others to whose inner struggles we cannot be privy. All we know is that they, as we, do have those struggles; they may be manifested differently, but they are basically the same – in criticising them we criticise ourselves and so do wrong to both. Most importantly, as we love ourselves, so we must love them. (I am told by a rabbinical scholar that the injunction to love our neighbours as ourselves means to love them because they are as, that is the same as, ourselves.)

By the same token, we cannot flatter our friends, telling them, for example, that they are cleverer, wiser, or kinder than so and so. We cannot give to an individual credit for something for which s/he is not responsible; this is taking from God what is properly his, and may be the inner meaning of the commandment concerning theft. What we can do, however, and seldom do sufficiently, is to praise in our friends the manifestation of divine qualities; love, intelligence, strength, courage, steadfastness, loyalty, sweetness, generosity, unselfishness. In a sense this is an act of worship in which divine and human love are wonderfully blended. It is also an act of service to our friends which helps them to recognise the nobility of their state and so to realise it more richly. The more we are able to treat people in this way, the more wealth of diversity shall we find in them. At each meeting we will discover something rare and wonderful, a new prism refracting the infinite radiance of eternity.

Adam Curle, 1981

When I am wrestling with an issue, I can take it to my Quaker friends, my Quaker network, my Quaker meeting. I can seek 'clearness' informally or formally. I can help others 'discern'. I can find help interpreting my sense of what God wants of me, and what that may mean in any particular situation. The well-known stories of Quaker action in the world, of reaction to the unforeseen, of resolve against the odds, of response to the dangerous and hostile, give me tools to mould and shape my own responses. I am both held by the community and am part of the holding – holding others as they discern, holding the tradition as we discern, holding the future of the Quaker way in a group that has no leaders but ourselves, no 'them' but us.

And I know that this desire to get my life right is a priority for me, but also is a shared priority. I know that others will listen to learn, and share what they already know so that I may learn. For all of us, these things matter enormously. We are friends as well as Friends, and we are friends with the shared purpose and desire to get our lives right.

This friendship transcends geography. It is wider than my immediate neighbourhood, stretches farther than my meeting's boundary, beyond the confines of any one yearly meeting and any one language. My Quaker belonging is about being part of a global network of those I have met, sat on committees with, worshipped with, discerned with. We have worked together and prayed together. We have washed pots, raked leaves, sat in meetings for hours or committees for days. We have known each other in the things which have felt eternal, as well as those things which truly are. We have slept on floors in meeting houses as Young Friends, stayed up all night talking excitedly, experimented with worship and had our hearts linked and broken along the way. We have travelled to visit each other, knowing that we will find a welcome and a like mind at the end of the journey. We have known that, as long as we stay within the Quaker fold, we will most likely meet again. It is a companionship of the greatest faith and trust. These are friendships 'for life' in every sense.

Ben Pink Dandelion, 2009

QUAKER JOURNALS 4:
PIERRE CERESOLE

Pierre Ceresole's journal is unlike the other three quoted at length in this book, because its author never imagined that it would be seen by anyone else. In its original form it consisted of more than a hundred small note-books — he always had one crammed into his back pocket — which were used for random jottings, scraps of arguments, prayers, discussions with God, descriptions of plants and flowers, explorations of his fears ('above all, fear of myself, fear of being inadequate') and philosophical enquiry. Key idioms, phrases and prayers often appear again and again over the thirty-six years he was writing ('The presence of the Spirit has always been very real to me', 'Grant us the honesty to examine our actions as we examine those of others') because he composed with no reader in mind. Yet when his wife decided to publish a selection from the notebooks after his death under the title *Vivre Sa Vérité* (*Living One's Truth*), she revealed a spiritual author of distinction and depth.

Pierre Ceresole lived from 1879 to 1945. He was a Swiss engineer, teacher and manual worker who became a Quaker quite late in life, when he was fifty-eight. He was one of ten children of a distinctly multi-cultural family. His father, originally from Italy, was a colonel in the Swiss army and a federal judge. His mother's family was French and he also had several relatives from Britain, including an English grandmother.

Pierre trained as a mechanical engineer in Zurich and went on to study maths and physics as a postgraduate in Göttingen and Munich. He was offered a teaching post at his Zurich college but declined it and thus began to live a restless existence in which he rarely stayed in one place for long. In 1908, he left for the USA, working first on a poultry farm in California, then in the oil fields of Santa Maria, and briefly as a grave-digger. He spent two years as a lecturer in French Literature at the University of Hawaii before leaving for Japan where he worked for eighteen months as an engineer. He went back to Switzerland in 1914.

All his life, he had a strong sense that he should give away all his surplus money. Before he left Hawaii, he decided not to keep the fifteen thousand dollars he had amassed as a private maths teacher to a member of the former royal family; they went to a local charity. On his arrival back in Switzerland, he wrote to the government saying that he wanted to donate his father's inheritance to the community, 'hoping that current events will be enough to explain my motive'. He meant, of course, the outbreak of war.

'I have the permanent constant feeling that we are enmeshed in an enormous lie', he wrote on his return to Switzerland. And the tone of his journal changed with the war: before 1914, his notebook entries were largely about his enthusiasm for a life lived in the Spirit, his profound distrust of the Church and his passionate personal relationship with what he called 'the Eternal'. When the war came, those radical impulses pushed him into a new religious commitment to work for peace. He had great regard for those refusing to fight (he himself was deemed to be medically unfit) and he declared his admiration for them in the journal through uncompromising expressions of pacifism and conscientious objection. 'Better to be outlawed by every party and everybody', he asserted, 'than to be their accomplice'.

He found work as an engineer again and then as a teacher, but his life was in his pacifism. He refused to pay military tax and thus had his first short taste of imprisonment, something that was to recur regularly during the ensuing years. When the war finally ended, he met Quakers for the first time through his appointment as Assistant Secretary of the newly founded International Movement for Reconciliation. And so began the work which was to occupy him for the rest of his life – the setting up of projects which would rebuild communities after the devastation of armed conflict.

In 1920, he founded *Service Civil International*, an organisation which still operates in forty-three branches world-wide. Their first initiative was to reconstruct the village of Esnes-en-Argonne, close to the battlefield of Verdun. Both French and German volunteers took part, building temporary dwellings and clearing farm land. Pierre loved manual labour and he at last found satisfaction in his work, recruiting like-minded people from nations which had only recently been at war with each other.

Between 1920 and 1937, Pierre worked on numerous projects with *Service Civil International* in Liechtenstein, France, Wales and India. His poor health was always a problem and between 1934 and 1937, when he helped with the reconstruction of seven Indian villages, he had to make regular return visits to Switzerland to recuperate. On one such occasion in 1937, he broke the journey home by attending a Friends' conference in the United States. He was deeply impressed by the Quaker experience of an unmediated relationship with the Divine – something he had been writing passionately about in his notebooks for nearly thirty years – and soon afterwards he joined The Religious Society of Friends.

In 1941, he married a distant cousin, Lise David, who shared his views and with whom he spent four more or less contented years in a house on the shore of Lake Geneva. What stopped them being idyllic were frequent spells in prison caused by his absolute compulsion to cross the Swiss-German border and speak to ordinary German people about the war. In the end, these periods of incarceration badly affected his already weak constitution and he died in his sleep on October 23rd 1945.

He is a fine example of a person who was already a Quaker in spirit before he came in contact with Friends. For many, there is a feeling of 'coming home' when they first encounter the Quaker way and that was clearly the case with Pierre Ceresole. All these pieces bear witness to the life of a committed Quaker, whether or not they were written after he joined The Religious Society of Friends.

Vivre Sa Vérité saw the light of day in 1950. A smaller selection of his writing was published in 1954 in an English translation by John W. Harvey and Christina Yates, under the title *For Peace and Truth*. The following extracts are from that volume and are taken from 1920 to 1933, the years when he was first setting up *Service Civil International*.

Nations commit crimes on the same principle as people who indulge in table-turning.

Everyone gives a push and each one thinks it is the voice of the 'Eternal'; and so on, not wishing to go counter to the spirit, they go on pushing harder and harder without realizing what they are doing and it all goes to confirm the 'manifest' presence of this 'Spirit'.

Let anyone who wants to pit his strength against the stuffing of men's minds with propaganda, experiment with table-turning and observe for himself the extent to which goodwill – simple goodwill, the desire not to be arrogant, not to oppose the manifestation of the spirit in a company one respects – may ultimately engender a collective illusion no less pathetic than absurd.

That is why the Kingdom of Heaven can only be for the *violent ones* – those who say: 'No. Sorry. Nothing doing!'

✦ ✦ ✦

The uselessness, the danger of saying hard truths by letter. Surgical operations are not carried out by long-range instruments. You need the straight glance with its greatest possible precision, and all the assurance that the surgeon's hand directly in contact with the patient can give.

✦ ✦ ✦

Old colonel of cavalry, with your cloak and your white beard and your red-rimmed eyes, wheezing and coughing, old colonel fearlessly saying your prayers in the station buffet in front of all the smart young officers: that is the kind of courage we need, Sir, – but turned in another direction.

✦ ✦ ✦

In the regions of the soul where the most important things happen, one is utterly alone. A great loneliness seizes you, no one but the Spirit is there.

✦ ✦ ✦

If you allow me to have Christ simply as a friend, he may become what you call God; if you force him on me as God, he cannot become a friend.

✦ ✦ ✦

Words hardly enable us to find fellowship any more. But true fellowship is renewed in action.

Actions unite men; words separate them. To express all we have on our minds with gentleness and without wounding, we must have love.

✦ ✦ ✦

To restore harmony in place of the chaotic confusion of men's wills, Buddhism proposes a passive self-forgetfulness, a suspension of desire; Christianity goes further and recommends active self-forgetfulness, service and love to the point of sacrifice.

✦ ✦ ✦

The best way of understanding and honouring Christ is not to be determined at all costs to reach God by way of Christ, but to do as he did and approach God directly.

✦ ✦ ✦

Useless to devote the least instant to an argument in favour of your truth so long as you have not lived it bravely.

The brave act, if you can do it – that is the argument, the only one. It's too simple otherwise and carries no weight. Christ had scarcely any other way of arguing.

✦ ✦ ✦

The conception of an outward Father, all-good and all-powerful, calls to mind a total picture which does not accord with what we see around us and within us. It jars on us, is self-contradictory. . . .

'Why hast thou forsaken me?' Christ's last words; the confession of disillusionment, of an error of logic; but not failure, not a denial of the sacrifice already made; the deed remained. The *Father* had abandoned him, has abandoned us, but what has not abandoned us and never will as long as life remains, is the *Spirit*, which is calling us to a higher state of unity and peace reached through and beyond sacrifice.

And so with his last cry of anguish it was still granted him to save us.

✦ ✦ ✦

Strange the satisfaction of belonging to a great machine; the attraction of a great machine; the delightful feeling of there being nothing to argue about.

✦ ✦ ✦

What is impressive is that whenever one word follows another the effect is weakened, while with each stroke of the pick the effect is strengthened. One becomes sick of words but not of a piece of work well done.

✦ ✦ ✦

Things as they should be have a much deeper and more essential reality than things as they are.

Things as they are, are purely temporary.

✦ ✦ ✦

It is cowardly to say: I have no right to examine, to question this or that. You have not only the right but the duty to question everything, with God's help, in all humility. And you will find that things do change.

✦ ✦ ✦

In the final analysis the only tolerable kind of obedience is to the Unseen.

✦ ✦ ✦

I feel myself definitely and thoroughly against every kind of formal worship, silence or prayer, as the essential, ordinary habitual expression of our deepest attitude of mind, our deepest relationship. Let those who wish, who like it, sing, pray and be silent as much as they like; but don't oblige everybody to follow the same road. For us, worship will be action – the highest, most generous, most disinterested that we can perform.

✦ ✦ ✦

Words today possess a quite remarkable faculty of causing misunderstandings, to such a degree that if you use them, even to disentangle a previous misunderstanding; you find that you have only made it worse (as well as making yourself a nuisance to everybody concerned).

✦ ✦ ✦

Pray the Eternal to keep your weather vane in good trim so that it readily responds to the true winds of the spirit and doesn't get jammed by the rust of tradition in a position unrelated to the truth or to the true currents of the spirit.

✦ ✦ ✦

If we are broken by calamity it is because, somewhere in the depths, we have cut our communications with the Eternal.

The deep grief we feel at the death of a brother or a friend is the measure of the flimsy, superficial, theoretical, accidental and unreal character of our acceptance of God, of our life in Him.

Obviously these words will be no consolation in themselves to those who have just been shaken to the depths. Words are nothing; it is the thing itself that matters.

✦ ✦ ✦

It is no good imagining that one will change anything at all; that is not our business, and to be preoccupied with this would be a waste of effort and ultimately lost illusion.

Each one must simply carry out, very scrupulously and exactly, and in all sincerity, the thing it is in him to do, developing a poetry of his own, according to the rhythm that is in him.

✦ ✦ ✦

If the name of Christian is to have any sort of meaning, it must never be one of exclusion or separation from anyone whatsoever but of understanding and inclusion even of tax-gatherers and prostitutes (and of churches too!) not excepting traitors, Judases and all.

✦ ✦ ✦

God: the supreme, universal instinct, the principle of integration.

God: the great mirror in which we must see ourselves quietly just as we are, with all our ugliness but with all our hopes.

God: the deep well of living water whence comes all strength, all purity; the thirst-quenching, refreshing out-flowing of the spirit, perpetually renewing itself and giving renewal; the living spring in which one can see and rediscover and cleanse oneself, in which one can rest and be raised up and depart a new man.

✦ ✦ ✦

I am determined to set my face resolutely against preaching sermons to others, on any pretext whatever.

And this includes a resolution not to preach sermons against sermon preaching.

No sermons, but confessions, humble if possible, and of experiences helpful to others.

There is strength in knowing how to keep silent.

✦ ✦ ✦

The relative importance of the virtues seems to vary according to the kind of individual we meet.

Very often, for instance, living in our moralising, Calvinistic circles, and still more amidst our prophets, major or minor, one feels irresistibly led to declare that of all the virtues far and away the foremost are graciousness and kindliness.

Each virtue in its perfection implies all the others, as an arc of a parabola if correctly drawn implies all the other arcs of the same perfect parabola. . . . It would seem that grace and kindliness are really the vertex of the parabola. In them are implied symmetry, elegance and equilibrium and also the promise of reaching the places stretching the most determinedly and rigidly towards infinity, the most completely and perfectly courageous.

Friends, friends, let us be gracious and kind to each other, from the bottom of our hearts; let us make each other's lives easier to bear. This is also a way of fulfilling the whole of the law and the prophets.

✦ ✦ ✦

God comes to us as a summons, an entreaty, an appeal, a behest, hence (if you like) as a will of an urge. To affirm that he is all-powerful has no meaning for us. What we can affirm is that he is all patient, all kind, all trusting and utterly serene; probably also that he suffers greatly and continually.

Hence it is understandable that men, to symbolise this, have asserted that the true God is not the almighty father, but the suffering Christ.

✦ ✦ ✦

Praying to God to cure an illness is like a call of my body praying to me to cure it. God apparently suffers when I am ill as much as I do myself.

What man, like the cells, has to do is to *let himself* be healed, to allow himself to be borne up by the central spirit, to entrust himself to it. Prayer for deliverance from illness is not a petition (which would be ridiculous) but a renewing of contact, an act of surrender.

Thy will be done. A centring down.

✦ ✦ ✦

God is not a personage who orders us to prostrate ourselves before him – a radically false position – but one who says: Stand up; here is my task for you; take it and get on with it.

✦ ✦ ✦

A lot of humbug: things treated as solemn which turn out to be *empty*; the Church; a certain State; the army; tremendous notions that are empty, totally empty.

✦ ✦ ✦

Consider that glorious but perfectly useless (!?) flower set in green velvet on some inaccessible ledge of the Alps where no one will ever see it.

✦ ✦ ✦

To seem, even for an instant, and in some respects only, the enemy of something very great – but imperfect from certain points of view – like the Christian tradition, for instance, is very painful. However, this is a pain I shall have to bear.

✦ ✦ ✦

You are not asked to be distinguished or pre-eminent in every respect; the only thing that is demanded of you is to provide, at just the right moment, a firm stepping-stone that will not give way when the eternal wants to pass over on it.

✦ ✦ ✦

God did not stop speaking two thousand years ago. He speaks to you personally today every time an inward voice asks you to do a kind or generous deed or to suffer for the sake of someone else. It is to you personally that God speaks at this moment, and it is *through you* that he speaks when he inspires you to do some service. Be brave enough to listen at first hand to what God says to you.

True courage consists in responding directly to God and in being willing to listen, not to be afraid of going up into the mountain.

✦ ✦ ✦

The fundamental condemnation of what is *called* faith is that it can be jeopardized by efforts towards sincerity. True faith is something that sincerity can only reinforce. For humble-minded sincerity, no matter what comes of it, is a manifestation of God.

✦ ✦ ✦

Let us remember that if we are a failure, others are successful; that if we suffer, others do achieve that rapturous joy which is the fruit of intimate communion with splendour; that if we are sinful and lonely others win through to the source of the spirit; the goal is reached . . . may that be our great consolation in all circumstances.

Let us remember that all things, directly or indirectly, work together for the triumph of truth – of God.

✦ ✦ ✦

I have never seen God – I've been shown him all too often, and the demonstrators all got in the light.

✦ ✦ ✦

Honesty prevents me from joining with you henceforward to worship Christ, live by Christ, etc., other than by *service* pure and simple.

We will sing and pray no more, we will do everything with our hearts turned towards God, receiving the power of God, but only in action, by serving, by patience, by loving the reflection, the real reflection of the light of God; and every time we remind each other to be patient and loving, it will be our way of speaking of God.

✦ ✦ ✦

One thing is certain – that if I prepare over a long period of time to meet a certain difficult situation with violence, I shall in fact have no other means of meeting it when it arises but by violence. If there is to be the slightest possibility of performing the miracle of a beneficent non-violent action, then it is essential not to concentrate on its direct opposite.

✦ ✦ ✦

Often one has a clear impression – in moments of dejection or sorrow – that one's physical body is nothing but a poor wavering unsubstantial shadow, merely a concrete indication of our intense longing for something more real and solid and harmonious.

Intense suffering is the protest of a shadow which knows itself to be in reality something far more than a mere shadow.

✦ ✦ ✦

Religious education as at present given prepares people for servility rather than for service.

✦ ✦ ✦

There is only one thing which equals the vastness and profundity of this war madness: and that is my determination to say *No* to it.

✦ ✦ ✦

Goodbye to my india-rubber. My little india-rubber, grown tiny in erasing so many thousand mistakes, existing only in the erasure of these mistakes, is now no bigger than one of those tiny bits of itself that is left behind each time it entered the fray. Brave little rubber – not one of that deceitful hard kind which dirties everything when you use it and, under pretext of erasing what is wrong, turns it into an irreparable catastrophe! My rubber only erases the fault by consenting to defile itself; it absorbs the faults of others, comes into intimate contact with them, puts them down to its own account, and then sets them aside and is free of them. A deep lesson here. You only succeed in correcting the fault of another if you begin by making it your own, that is to say, by showing that you have truly understood its cause, its fundamental nature – first the understanding and then, by the fact that your nature is able through its permanent communion with the eternal constantly to renew itself, you let the outward forms of action drop away like a skin and so finally get rid of the defilement.

✦ ✦ ✦

Blessed is he who, serene and content in the midst of outward difficulties, can spare some of his joy and good humour in generous charity for someone else who has an easier life.

✦ ✦ ✦

One man makes loaves, another steel; one is like oil, another like diamond; all these things are needed – this is God's will. That he still wants soldiers is possible; that he wants people who cannot and will not be soldiers any longer is certain.

✦ ✦ ✦

Never ask for easier circumstances . . . only for increasing strength; and accept with joy any rest and refreshment encountered on your way.

✦ ✦ ✦

Our attitude to suffering may in itself be a form of prayer. Suffering valiantly borne, not just endured with resignation but with faith, even when there is honestly and truly nothing to be done about it, such suffering *is* prayer.

Often, all that men are able to do for God, for the advancement of the spirit, is to suffer.

Thus it is perfectly true that those who suffer most are the best instruments of the Spirit. This is not so much on account of their 'moral' attitude, but lies rather in the very fact of their deep suffering and therefore of their continually and ardently turning the will towards something beyond.

Does anyone ever make a genuine and fervent act of will without the continual and incessant pressure of suffering?

I would venture to say: 'Woe unto those who have never known suffering'.

Thus it is that for many their sole, and for many others their best, prayer has been: 'Lord, Lord, I am so dreadfully troubled. . .'.

All these acts of injustice and stupidity, these wars and armies, all these closed minds and wills, my own weakness, my violence, my stupidity, oh, how they do afflict me!

✦ ✦ ✦

God is revealed in the essential fact that deep within us we are steered in a direction that does not in the least tally with the one we should constantly be taking if we simply followed our material interests within the physiological limits of our personality.

This call from God shows that we belong to something infinitely transcending our material bodies.

Prayer consists in establishing, as completely as possible, a free communication and an identification between our personal will and this higher will.

Certain personalities, like Jesus or St Francis, give the impression of having achieved this identification in a particularly complete and perfect fashion.

✦ ✦ ✦

In a garden near Paris. 1930. The first spring days are really here. Peach trees all covered with pink, white almond blossom, or some other perfume with white flowers; tiny red buds of Japanese quince; shining little faces of golden yellow. Daffodils and pink primroses among the grass; and the charming lilt of a French phrase floating towards me from somewhere on the morning breeze.

Well-grounded optimism of those who look facts in the face. We are going to love the marvels of this world of ours without allowing ourselves to be disturbed by the horrible atmosphere of impenetrable busy-ness which fills and poisons and pollutes this Paris air. Fundamentally, all that doesn't exist; it is an illusion. These folk have no idea what they are doing or what they are chasing after.

This pink peach tree is eternal, is the truth, and all this dazzling whiteness beginning to unfold.

A tree is spring; a confusion of tiny interlacing twigs among which one sees a few tiny buds thrusting up here and there, harbingers of a new season. A new grace, the grace of life renewed, of a flower – in a hard grey tangle of twigs.

I have seen something definite, something very good and enlightening – to stand fast, come what may! That is serving God.

✦ ✦ ✦

Not to be afraid of the depths: if one is in the region of great heights there must necessarily be great depths as well.

✦ ✦ ✦

It is good to remember that the vanity and pride of others shocks us chiefly – if not wholly – because of our own vanity and pride.

✦ ✦ ✦

How ardently we need to pray, if we are to escape the ravages of our own disillusioned, frustrated, dried-up egoism.

✦ ✦ ✦

'Let us study Religion'. By all means; but we must start from the very plain fact that the shark's jaw exists, continually called on to devour, quite indiscriminately, the leg or arm or head of some shipwrecked person.

Whether or not this fact be our starting point, it is only by acknowledging it definitely and heedfully that we may properly search after God, or rather prove him such as He is, likewise a very plain reality in certain places.

✦ ✦ ✦

What is God? The magnificent opposite of all the falsehoods, prejudices, fears of not being quite orthodox that have been gathered together under this name.

✦ ✦ ✦

When a man is faithful things begin to speak to him; they reveal their true and profound meaning.

✦ ✦ ✦

I am only an ordinary man, no better than anybody else; but I have seen one particular truth, one aspect of truth to which I must be faithful; feeling thus, I shall have the strength to do what must be done. I do not know what means most to Him, but I do know that for me the heart of the matter is to listen for, and to obey, that supreme voice, which is always there; and this is my whole significance, my existence, my life.

OPEN TO NEW LIGHT

And take heed of judging the measures of others, but every one mind your own; and there ye famish the busy minds and high conceits, and so peace springs up among you, and division is judged. And this know, that there are diversities of gifts, but one spirit, and unity therein to all who with it are guided. And though the way seems to thee diverse; yet judge not the way, lest thou judge the Lord, and knowest not that several ways (seeming to reason) hath God to bring his people out by; yet are all but one in the end. This is, that he may be looked to from all the 'ends of the earth, to be a guide and lawgiver'; and that none should judge before him. Deep is the mystery of godliness!

George Fox, undated epistle

In a permissive Quakerism, we decide what is appropriate, what is Quaker for us, how we interpret our Quaker faith in everyday life. We no longer look and sound different from the rest of the population, as the earlier Friends did with their Quaker grey and insistence on 'thee' and 'thou', numbering days and months instead of using their pagan names. The sense of difference between us and those whose behaviours we wish to challenge, as with our faith, is now an inward affair, and so equally, is the challenge, to live that difference inwardly, to 'know' it intimately and to live our lives in that spirit, still as co-agents with God.

Ben Pink Dandelion, 2009

Quakers try to be 'open to new light from whatever source it may come' (Advice 7 on page 43) and that principle causes Friends to differ widely in their beliefs. There are, as we have seen, both theist and nontheist Quakers. But there are also Quakers who are Buddhists, Hindus, Muslims and Jews. Some Quakers are Roman Catholics. And if that seems bewildering, it is important to recall that Friends have no creed; they offer a spiritual journey without religious certainties.

I personally believe that there is a quality in the bareness of Christian Quakerism, which may act as a bridge between the past and the future, allowing space for Friends to dare to search within. [. . .] To be a Quaker is by no means to say goodbye to myth, ritual and symbol, but rather to find myself set free to discover them as the very essence of the way I now experience. [. . .] Quakers are bridge people. I remain on that bridge, part of my roots reaching back into the Christian past and part stretching forward into the future where new symbols are being born.

Damaris Parker-Rhodes, 1985

The humble, meek, merciful, just, pious, and devout souls are everywhere of one religion; and when death has taken off the mask they will know one another, though the divers liveries they wear here makes them strangers. This world is a form; our bodies are forms; and no visible acts of devotion can be without forms. But yet the less form in religion the better, since God is a Spirit; for the more mental our worship, the more adequate to the nature of God; the more silent, the more suitable to the language of the Spirit.

William Penn, 1693

When I began, in my boyhood, to hear Christian sermons and read Christian books, including the Bible, I confess that they were not at all convincing to me. Only in Quakerism could I reconcile Christianity with Oriental thought. Let it be far from me to turn Quakerism into Oriental mysticism. Quakerism stays within the family of Christianity.

It professes to rest its structure on the person of Jesus Christ, whom it identifies with the Inner Light. It does not deny His incarnation and historicity, but it accepts His continued work of grace in each succeeding generation. Not only that, it believes His grace was retro-active, so that it was He who enlightened all the seers of old. He still dwells within us – in the least as in the greatest, even in the savage and the unlettered. [...] Curiously enough, the Cosmic sense, as described by those who attain it, is very much the same everywhere – whether it be by a Buddhist priest, a Shinto votary, a Mohammedan saint, a French mathematician, an American farmer, or a Jewish philosopher. Nothing confirms the identity of the human race better than this spiritual expansion. But I can speak only as a close observer of those who attain this high and lofty sense, and not as one who has himself attained it. [...] I believe Christianity has this advantage – not to call it a point of superiority – that it provides weak, ordinary mortals with a definite and concrete object upon which to focus their mind, thus facilitating their discovery of the Perfect Man. Acquaintance with Him makes us one with Him – at-one-ment. To follow Him is to be redeemed from a lower plane of life. To contemplate Him is to see God Himself and be saved.

Inazo Nitobe, 1927

It may appear to the casual observer that Friends practise a 'pick-and-mix' religion in which everyone believes just what they like. They do not. Quakerism has discipline. The individual religious path of each Quaker is of vital importance to the communal life of his or her Meeting, and the Meeting in turn offers guidance, oversight and clearness to each Quaker. So Friends work out their individual spiritual beliefs in practice: in fidelity to their community, and in the service of their faith.

In the early days of Quakerism, most spiritual experience was expressed in the language of the Bible. Quakers expanded the language of spiritual experience by using terms such as 'the Inward

Light', 'the Seed' or 'the Leaven'. Today, we have access to a great variety of spiritual language. There are many translations of the Bible, from the King James to the most modern versions. We have discovered lost scriptures that were a part of the Gnostic tradition and which were omitted from the canonical Bible. The majority of the scriptures of the world's religions have now been translated into English, and are also freely available to us. There are also the writings of mystics and poets, not only from the European traditions, but also from many other faiths and cultures. Likewise, the works of philosophers and scientists spanning more than a thousand years are also published in book form.

Quakerism is a religion of experience. Experience is best expressed in silence, but human beings also have a need to express it in words. The world's mystics – including Quakers – show us the silence that is behind the words, but they also felt the need to use language. Mystical experience inevitably leads to an expansion of the language that is used to express it. Quakers have always been interested in expanding the language of the spirit. It is no wonder that today many Friends have turned to the *Upanishads, Tao Teh Ching*, the *Qur'an*, the *Dhammapada* and other scriptures, to see if their language might be more helpful in describing the experience that is essentially beyond words, but which we find in a gathered Quaker Meeting and in contemplation of the Inward Light.

There is also another dimension that needs to be considered. Christianity is very good at describing and making real the presence of a Personal God. However, science increasingly shows us an expanding universe, and the media makes us aware of a world in which there are many problems such as suffering, war, hunger and natural disasters. The modern mind is no longer satisfied to see these as the will of God who is seen as fickle and discriminatory. Quakers, in our meetings for worship, experience the Presence of God as a living reality, but many find it hard to say whether this Presence was personal or impersonal. Whichever it is, we are mostly happy to affirm that we experience this presence as Love. So how do we reconcile this universal Love with the suffering and tragedies of a changing world? This is the dilemma facing Friends today, and, because the language of the Bible is mostly personal, it provides another reason to look elsewhere for suitable language to describe our experience.

None of this denies the Christian roots of the Quaker tradition. What it does do is to emphasise the special approach which sees the 'Inward Light' or 'That of God' as the final guide in spiritual matters. It is no wonder that many Friends feel in harmony with the Buddha, who, when he was speaking to the *Kalama* people in a discourse that has been called the first example of spiritual free enquiry, told them not to accept anything just because it has been said by a teacher, even the Buddha himself, or because it had been written in a holy book.

Jim Pym, 2000

The Christian Faith is not – as many outsiders take it to be – a system of unreasonable certainties, but one of reasonable uncertainties. By uncertainties I do not mean doubts, and by reasonable I do not mean logical. What I am talking about are beliefs – even convictions – that cannot be proved symbolically, like chemical or mathematical processes, yet which have a consistency which does not discredit the believer. As articulated by the believer they are clearly not the whole story – they are open-ended and liable to emendation or development; but the believer may claim of them that they check with experience – which others may confirm – and that above all, they make sense of life and make sense in life.

Gerald Priestland, 1982

If George Fox were to walk into a twenty-first century Quaker Meeting House, he would be hard pressed to recognise the Christian faith that he knew in the 1650s. He would find a complex mosaic of belief. He would encounter radical Christians of his stamp, but they would surely lack his exhaustive knowledge of the Bible and might find his brand of preaching distasteful. He would meet Quakers who thoughtfully declare themselves to be Christians but equally thoughtfully reject much of the theology that he embraced: many do not accept, to take just one example, that 'Jesus died to save us all'. He would find Christian Friends who acknowledge Jesus as a great religious teacher but reject much of what is done publicly in his name. And he would come across innumerable Quakers who love what Jesus said, but at the same time deny resolutely that they are Christians.

Fox would understand the reasons for the differences between his perceptions of Christianity and those of a present-day Quaker. They are experiential. When, in his journal, he talked about his spiritual awakening, he used five words that remain deeply significant for Friends: 'And that I know *experimentally*' – by which he meant *from experience*. Fox's journey, as he expressed it, was a progression through pain, anger and distress to a vision of hope: he sought spiritual help from religious people, and it never materialised; he became deeply depressed; and when his frustration was at its most agonisingly intense he had a moment of incandescent insight and understanding. Here is his account.

Now after I had received that opening from the Lord, that to be bred at Oxford or Cambridge, was not sufficient to fit a man to be a minister of Christ, I regarded the priests less, and looked more after the dissenting people. And among them I saw, there was some tenderness: and many of them came afterwards to be convinced; for they had some openings. But as I had forsaken all the priests, so I left the separate preachers also, and those called the most experienced people: for I saw, there was none among them all, that could speak to my condition. And when all my hopes in them, and in all men was gone, so that I had nothing outwardly to help me, nor could tell what to do; Then, O! then I heard a voice, which said, 'There is one, even Christ Jesus, that can speak to thy condition': and when I heard it, my heart did leap for joy. Then the Lord did let me see, why there was none upon the earth, that could speak to my condition, namely, that I might give him all the glory. For all are concluded under sin, and shut up in unbelief, as I had been; that Jesus Christ might have the pre-eminence; who enlightens, and gives grace, and faith, and power. Thus when God doth work, who shall let it? And this I knew experimentally.

George Fox, published 1694

George Fox's experience remains inspiring to Friends, but it is rare today to encounter such emotional Quaker writing. Here is another Friend, 350 years later, talking about Jesus in a way entirely unlike that of George Fox.

Once one sees Jesus not as a one-off but as an evolutionary fore-runner, a biological holotype, it is not so startling to discover many other individuals who shared with him the same kind of dual awareness of self. Indeed, the most ancient spiritual teaching of Hinduism, predating Jesus by a thousand years, is based on the principle of Advaita, or 'not-twoness', and is orthodox teaching today, but has on the whole become swamped with a popular polytheism. From the historical perspective, in preaching the vital importance of self-sacrifice Jesus was reinventing the wheel, and looking further, one can see that this particular wheel has been reinvented many times in many ages and in many societies. It is, in fact, so universal in religious culture that it is often referred to as the perennial philosophy, but the term is risky, since it implies a purely rational understanding, whereas self-sacrifice – when the stress is put on 'sacrifice' – is much more than a philosophical position.

It is clear from the quotations below that the authors are talking of something deeply emotional, but something disturbing and challenging as well as blissful. What is deeply significant is that, if one removes the cultural context (such as the Christian 'Father' and the Moslem 'Allah') the thoughts expressed could have come from within any theistic tradition.

The Father and I are one. Who sees me sees the Father.

(*Jesus, a Jew*)

I am He whom I love, and He whom I love is I. . . . If thou seest me, thou seest Him.

(*Al Hallaj, Moslem*)

This is your real Self, the Supreme Being. . . . Who does not look for liberation in the Divine Self is deluded and grasps at the unreal. Knowing reality is awakening to the unity of the Divine Self.

(*Shankara, Hindu*)

Where I am, there is God.

(*Meister Eckhart, Christian*)

Between Thou and me there stands an 'I'. O Allah, of thy mercy, take away this 'I'.

(*Abu Said, Moslem*)

The world teems with idols for us to break, but as long as you exist as a self, there is one more idol left to break.

(*Iqbal, Moslem*)

The true nature of all self-denial is to break down that which stands between God and us.

(*William Law, Christian*)

Such expressions can be found in thousands, if one cares to seek, but all are classified and routinely dismissed as 'mysticism' and thus not of central importance in religion, and again I return to the insistence of Jesus that in his perception of religion, this self-transformation is vitally important, for this is a statement of the crossroads at which religion in general now finds itself.

Frank Parkinson, 2009

Quakers acknowledge the Christian roots of their faith, but do not all feel that they are bound to them. Equally, interest in (and inspiration from) non-

Christian religions abounds within The Religious Society of Friends, while not necessarily implying membership of other faiths or even a commitment to them. Marjorie Sykes (1905–1995) was a Quaker who spent the best part of her life in India, working with, among many others, Rabindranath Tagore and Mahatma Gandhi. Her interest in the Hindu religion was an integral part of her Quaker faith, but she remained a Christian Friend all her life.

The living core of a religion is not to be sought in its outward observances, ceremonial, liturgy or festival (though it may be sought through them), nor yet in any intellectual world view which may emerge from its sacred writings; it is to be sought in the way it leads men, in the secret places of the heart, into the Presence of God. [. . .] All living religion begins with this awed recognition [. . .] of a Mystery and Power which is great beyond all comprehension, and yet is 'nearer than breathing and closer than hands and feet'. All living religion goes from this to a two-fold task: the human being is impelled to purify himself, to cleanse heart and mind and will, so that he may enter more and more fully into communion with that Reality and so fulfil the true purpose of his own life; at the same time he is impelled to share with other men his experience of the Mystery, and in so doing to use the words and symbols of his own age and country. Quakers also have a heritage of form and symbol, which was created to express a living truth of our experience; our very forms and symbols are a witness to the faith that God is beyond all forms and that the Free Spirit cannot be confined within any of its temporal symbols:

The One Breath enters the world, taking a myriad of forms,
Even so the One,
The innermost indwelling Life of all that is,
Taketh a myriad of form – Yet is that One beyond all forms.

(*Katha-Upanishad*)

[. . .] The flowers of unselfish living may be found growing in other men's gardens and rich fruits of the Spirit may be tasted from other men's trees. They spring from the same Holy Spirit of Truth, the same seed of God, whose power moves us through Christ. [. . .] We do not desire that all should take the name of Quaker or the outward name of Christ. We do desire that all should be guided by 'that Spirit which is pure and holy', and that God will speak to them in whatever language, and through whatever symbol, can best bring them to the True Centre of their lives.

Marjorie Sykes, 1957

Here is a description of an unusual wedding, both Quaker and Hindu.

Sarees glinted as they were draped over shoulders, every conceivable tone of skin colour glistened as conversations quietened and Friends and guests gathered for Meeting for Worship at our unusual wedding. Unusual in that our wedding was uniting two spiritual traditions: Christianity and Hinduism. The silence of the Meeting allowed these two traditions (including a strong Zoroastrian element) to meet on equal terms and share insights on this important day of our lives.

On the surface these two traditions may seem diametrically opposite. A traditional Hindu wedding is full of fanfare, ritual and colour. In comparison, a Quaker wedding can come over as rather restrained and austere. However, within Meeting for Worship, those superficial manifestations of separateness were soon dissolved making way for a deeper level of connection. In India, there are Meetings for Worship where Christians, Hindus, Muslims and Buddhists gather together under one roof. There is relative harmony of different spiritual traditions worshipping together within the silence. For those who practise meditation and yogi practices in India, Meeting for Worship is not an unusual encounter.

Ashok Jashapara, 2009

It is hardly surprising that many Quakers are influenced by Buddhism, because some aspects of the Buddhist religion, at least at a surface level, are similar to the Quaker way: both are at heart experiential; both embrace an attitude of tolerance; both are associated with a commitment to nonviolence; both use outwardly similar meditative techniques as part of their spiritual practice.

Enlightenment or awareness is an attractive concept. I suspect most of us have been striving at one stage or another in our lives. Awareness of ourselves, certainly, but even more awareness of the human condition, in relation to the universe and eternity. It is not surprising that this should be so amongst Quakers, as so many of us would define ourselves as seekers: seekers after Truth, insofar as anything so abstract can exist. In this way, life is a spiritual journey, along which one meets many ideas and many people, each offering an example to be pondered in tranquillity. Sometimes these ideas and individuals influence us, sometimes not. And in my own case, for a long time, it was Buddhism that has offered the most food for thought.

Jonathan Fryer, 2005

[. . .] If Jesus Christ and Gotama Buddha were to meet, there is no doubt in my mind that it would be in the deep silence, and that they would not waste words on idle discussion. They might laugh together, particularly at the ways in which learned commentators and committees have misunderstood their words. They might even weep together for the same reason. I am as certain as I can be, both from studying the teachings of both masters, and from what I have intuitively felt about them, that there would be a deep harmony between them. The scriptures of both Christianity and Buddhism are based on their dialogues with those they met, and I feel sure that both were able to discern the spiritual state of the questioners before they even opened their mouths, and that their teachings were given accordingly. Although we now have only the four short books of the life and teaching of Jesus, at one time there were many more, and the range of the teaching recorded extends from the deeply symbolic and esoteric – almost tantric – writings of a text such as *Pistis Sophia*, to the short pithy Zen-like sayings of the *Gospel of Thomas*. The full range of the gospels and other writings termed 'apocryphal' or 'Gnostic' compares very favourably with those of the Buddhist Scriptures, and many Friends are now investigating such of these writings as have survived.

Jim Pym, 2000

The Buddhist emphasis on right view and right thought I find beneficial in giving me an enhanced appreciation of the Bible amongst other sacred writings. What matters for me is how I perceive beneficially a passage from it, interpreted in the here and now for me personally. I do not have to neglect it as often happens nowadays as it gathers dust at Quaker Meeting Houses. In their books Thay and the Dalai Lama reveal their profound knowledge of the gospels and I too find them illuminating my spiritual journey. What is remarkable about the gospels is that they are remarkable. The sayings of Jesus and stories about him portrayed there are primarily the interpretations and perceptions of people profoundly influenced by the Christ within, and secondarily the very blurred memory of the man Jesus himself. Few of those sayings and stories are authentic accounts of Jesus himself as recent scholarship has shown, but what is miraculous is how the gospel writers and their sources wrote what they did. The gospels appear to have been written thirty to sixty years after Jesus' execution, and possibly the oral transmission over these decades was more accurate than the hundreds of years that elapsed between the death of Buddha and the first writings about him, and yet the oral transmission from monks to monks may have been more faithful than the transmission of the Jesus story as there was no need to show that Buddha fulfilled any prophecy.

Peter Jarman, 2005

The next two extracts are written by Friends with backgrounds in the Jewish religious tradition.

For Jews, at least three of [the Quaker] testimonies have been at the heart of their experience. God is seen as the God of Truth, to whom they have turned, on whom they have relied even when reason suggested they should do otherwise: for example, during the Crusades, the Inquisition or the Holocaust. The Psalms remind us that we praise God for truth: the truth of God and his love for all mankind is a reality for Jews, as is the equality of all people as part of God's creation. The vision of a time when that ideal will be realised in the world is a powerful incentive to work towards it. Since the earliest days, peace has been the eternal hope of the Jews. In one sense, the Sabbath represents a glimpse each week of that peace. During these awful years of conflict in the Middle East, it is hard to remember that throughout the millennia, Jews have prayed and acted constantly for peace. One of the most frequently recited prayers in the Jewish liturgy reflects just that: *May He who makes peace in the highest bring this peace upon us, upon all Israel, and upon the world.*

John Dunston, 2005

When I came across the very middle-class introverted Quakers there was quite a cultural problem. Not only that, there was a intellectual challenge. British Quakers, for all the variety of beliefs and outlooks, often assume that their corporate temperament is linked with their spirituality. Thus the Quaker way is seen to be introverted, quiet, not very passionate, highly articulate, and reserved. These are admirable qualities, no doubt; very useful in mediation and on peace demonstrations, but sometimes I wonder what I am doing with such a group of people. At least in the synagogue you get a whole range of types and social groups – though I suspect in a Roman Catholic church you would get a better social mix. My spirituality, wherever it is taking me, is passionate, often impatient, mystical yet not contemplative by nature, and argumentative with God (in the old Abrahamic manner). Not all Jews of course fit this mould, neither do all Quakers fit into the above stereotype. But the old stories of the mystical rabbis filled with passionate intensity, arguing with God, fill me with admiration. What old rabbi George Fox would have made of all this is quite beyond me – though he was a passionate soul; what rabbi Jesus would have said intrigues me, though it seems he did have a temper now and again; and whether king David leaping before the ark and with his various liaisons would have been admitted into Friends is a cause for speculation.

Perhaps there is a more profound membership beyond class and language, beyond formulation and psychology, where the human in all its forms encounters the divine in all its manifestations. To get there I suspect you have to work through the tradition(s) into which you are born, take from them those aspects which embrace the spirit, and leave behind what no longer speaks to your condition. The best journeys are undertaken with the fewest burdens. All that is required are eyes that can see, ears that remain open, arms capable of embracing unexpected miracles, and a willing heart.

Harvey Gillman, 2009

To list the religious sources and spiritual enthusiasms of Quakers would be a futile task. A faith based on personal experience is exactly that. Each community of Quakers is nourished by the variations of witness it contains and in its expression, both public and private. No two Quakers are alike: Friends are enriched by the differences among them.

At a recent Quaker retreat, I and about thirty other Quakers were asked to stand in the petals of a flower marked out on the floor of a large room. Each of the petals represented the sources of extra spiritual nourishment that we as individuals regularly draw on: the Christian tradition, Buddhist meditation, Eastern mysticism, the natural world, healing ministries such as Reiki, and so on, with the Quaker worshipping community as the flower's centre. Each person chose their appropriate petal. Some put their left foot in one petal and their right foot in another, and there were even acrobatics as Quakers put hands and feet in three or four different places.

This exercise acknowledged, in a visual and physical way, that our Quaker lives are fed by spiritual wisdom from outside the Quaker world. During the first three hundred years of Quakerism, this enrichment came from the Judaeo-Christian Bible and the accumulated wisdom of the Christian faith. During the last fifty years, historical and cultural changes have meant that we can draw on many other sources. The petals of our flower recognised this change and gave it a positive context of interest and sharing rather than a negative one of theological dispute.

                                                    Alison Leonard, 2005

This rainbow of faith traditions sometimes causes people – both newcomers and seasoned Quakers – to think that Friends have begun to ignore their Christian roots. It is worth remembering that there are many who continue to embrace Christianity in their witness, often as strongly and with as much commitment as did early Friends. Here, a Quaker writes of a new understanding.

Setting out again, I met two American Quaker ministers (some US meetings do have pastors). One had been in the very liberal wing of east coast Quakerism, the other from a strongly evangelical Quaker group on the west coast. Both had made radical shifts in their lives, and the message they carried was entirely new to me. They spoke of a Christ who had come to end all religion (including Christianity) by teaching people directly. They spoke of the risen Christ Jesus as a light within *all* people, revealing the things that separated them from true peace. This was something I craved and my ears pricked up. But the stick of dynamite that lifted me out of comfortable detachment was the message that Jesus Christ is as present to us today as he was to the disciples two thousand years ago. This really threw me and I now describe this as a 'shock of recognition'.

I started to make a connection between the pushings and pullings, joys and frustrations, highs and lows that had taken place with myself as I read of the historical person of Jesus in the Bible. What he was doing in Palestine he was doing in me: troubling my conscience, driving the money changers out of the temple, bringing the dead back to life, forgiving the unforgivable. With this connection I started to see that Jesus is not just a great teacher amongst many others. If *just* a teacher he is a confusing and poor one, simply because no human can go away with those teachings and hope to fulfil them on their own. About this time I had become interested in the lives of early Quakers and here I saw people doing exactly as Jesus had commanded: not returning violence with violence, receiving persecution as a blessing, treating all people equally, not acting deceitfully.

There seemed to be something superhuman in their behaviour, and it perplexed me until I started to see the divinity of Jesus Christ was being demonstrated in their own divinity. I started to pay some attention to the light within myself, and by obeying it I started to cease from some of my worst behaviours and attitudes. I felt I could speak with some conviction of Jesus' divinity, probably for the first time.

It was some time later that a much older Friend spoke to my still confused condition: 'People fret about the divinity of Jesus, but the thing they're really struggling with is the humanity of God.' I was once told by some Quakers, after a talk I gave about early Quakerism, that perfection is impossible. The cultural conditioning of our society strongly favours modesty and self-deprecation, but, at the end of the day, coming into God's kingdom and seeing it formed on earth is the very purpose of being a Quaker. We often say we are 'only human'. *Only* human?

Unnamed Quaker, 2007

This book closes as it began, with some words of George Fox. He reminds us of the light within all of us, which helps us to be open to new inspiration and witness, from whatever source it may come.

And dwelling in the light, there is no occasion at all of stumbling, for all things are discovered with the light: thou that lovest it, here is thy teacher; when thou art walking abroad, it is present with thee in thy bosom; thou needest not to say, lo here, or lo there: and as thou liest in thy bed it is present to teach thee, and judge thy wandering mind, which would wander abroad, and thy high thoughts and imaginations, and makes them subject; for following thy thoughts thou art quickly lost. But dwelling in this light, it will discover to thee the body of sin, and thy corruptions, and fallen estate, where thou art, and multitude of thoughts: in that light which shews thee all this, stand, neither go to the right hand, nor to the left: here is patience exercised, here is thy will subjected, here thou wilt see the mercies of God made manifest in death: here thou wilt see the drinking of the waters of Shiloah, which run softly, and the promises of God fulfilled, which are to the seed, which seed is Christ: here thou wilt find a saviour, and the election thou wilt come to know, and the reprobation, and what is cast from God, and what enters: he that can own me here, and receive my testimony into his heart, the immortal seed is born up, and his own will thrust forth, for it is not him that willeth, nor him that runneth, but the election obtaineth it, and God that shews mercy; for the first stop of peace is to stand still in the light (which discovers things contrary to it) for power and strength to stand against that nature which the light discovers: here grace grows, here is God alone glorified and exalted, and the unknown truth, unknown to the world, made manifest, which draws up that which lies in the prison, and refresheth it in time, up to God out of time, through time.

George Fox, 1653

SOURCE INDEX

page   QUAKER MEETING FOR WORSHIP

19   Fox, George: *Epistle 145. The Works of George Fox.* State College, PA: New Foundation Publications, 8 volumes, 1990 [1831]

19   Kelly, Thomas R: *The Gathered Meeting. Reality of the Spiritual World and The Gathered Meeting.* London: Quaker Home Service 1996 [1940]. Reproduced by permission of the publisher

19   Stephen, Caroline: *Quaker Strongholds.* London: Kegan, Paul, Trench, Trubner, 1890

19–20   Barclay, Robert: *An Apology for the True Christian Divinity.* Glenside PA: Quaker Heritage Press, 2002 [1678]

20–1   Penington, Isaac: *A Brief Account Concerning Silent Meetings*, published 1680. *The Works of Isaac Penington.* Glenside PA: Quaker Heritage Press, 4 volumes, 1996 [1863]

21–2   Stephen, Caroline: *Quaker Strongholds.* London: Kegan, Paul, Trench, Trubner, 1890

22–5   Gorman, George: *The Amazing Fact of Quaker Worship.* London: Quaker Books, 2nd edition, 2008 [1973]. Reproduced by permission of the publisher

25–6   Punshon, John: *Encounter with Silence.* Richmond, Indiana: Friends United Press, 1987. Reproduced by permission of the publisher

27   Jones, Rufus M: *The Faith and Practice of the Quakers.* Richmond, Indiana: Friends United Press, 3rd printing 2007 [1927]. Reproduced by permission of the publisher

27   McMullen, Marrianne: *Lessons in Ministry.* St Paul, Minnesota: *Friendly Woman*, Volume 8, No 1, 1987. Reproduced by permission of the author

27–8   Allen, Beth: *Ground and Spring.* London: Quaker Books, 2007. Reproduced by permission of the publisher

28   Langdale, Josiah: *A Quaker Spiritual Autobiography* (ed. Skidmore, Gil). Reading: Sowle Press, 1999. Reproduced by permission of the publisher

28–9   Kelly, Thomas R: *The Gathered Meeting. Reality of the Spiritual World and The Gathered Meeting.* London: Quaker Home Service 1996 [1940]. Reproduced by permission of the publisher

29   Taber, William: *The Four Doors to Meeting for Worship.* Wallingford, PA: Pendle Hill Pamphlet 306, 1992. Reproduced by permission of the publisher

29   Penington, Isaac: *Letter 16. The Works of Isaac Penington*. Glenside PA:
        Quaker Heritage Press, 4 volumes, 1996 [1863]
30   Stephen, Caroline: *Quaker Strongholds*. London: Kegan, Paul, Trench,
        Trubner, 1890
31   Southall, John Edward (attributed): *The Power of Stillness* (12th issue).
        Unnamed publisher, c.1900
31–2   Punshon, John: *Encounter with Silence*. Richmond, Indiana: Friends United
        Press, 1987. Reproduced by permission of the publisher
32   Bownas, Samuel: *A Description of the Qualifications Necessary to a Gospel
        Minister*. London: Luke Hinde, 1750
32   Fox, George: *Something Concerning Silent Meetings. The Works of George
        Fox*. State College, PA: New Foundation Publications, 8 volumes, 1990
        [1831]
33   Penington, Isaac: *Letter. The Works of Isaac Penington*. Glenside PA:
        Quaker Heritage Press, 4 volumes, 1996 [1863]
33–4   Kelly, Thomas R: *The Gathered Meeting. Reality of the Spiritual World and
        The Gathered Meeting*. London: Quaker Home Service 1996 [1940].
        Reproduced by permission of the publisher
34–5   Lampen, Diana: *Practical Issues* in *Seeing, Hearing, Knowing* (ed. Lampen,
        John). York: Sessions, 2008. Reproduced by permission of the author
35   Barclay, Robert: *An Apology for the True Christian Divinity*. Glenside PA:
        Quaker Heritage Press, 2002 [1678]
36   Smith, Mary F: *The Place of Prayer in Life* in *Studies in Quaker Thought and
        Practice, Part 2* (ed. Hibbert, G.K.). London: Friends Home Service
        Committee, 1936
36–7   Gillman, Harvey: *A Light that is Shining*, 1988. London: Quaker Books,
        2003. Reproduced by permission of the publisher
37   Woolman, John: *Journal* (ed. Whittier, J G). London: Andrew Melrose,
        1898 [1772]
38   Kelly, Thomas R: *The Eternal Promise*. Richmond, Indiana: Friends United
        Press, 1977 [1938]. Reproduced by permission of the publisher
38   Fox, George: Letter to Lady Claypole, quoted in *The Journal of George
        Fox* (ed. Nickalls, John). Cambridge: Cambridge University Press,
        1952. [1694]
38–9   Rack, Philip: *Quakerism in the 21st Century*. York: Sessions, 2002.
        Reproduced by permission of the copyright holder
39–40   Kelly, Thomas R: *The Gathered Meeting. Reality of the Spiritual World and
        The Gathered Meeting*. London: Quaker Home Service 1996 [1940].
        Reproduced by permission of the publisher
40   Fox, George: *Epistle 162. The Works of George Fox*. State College, PA: New
        Foundation Publications, 8 volumes, 1990 [1831]

ADVICES AND QUERIES

42–9   *Advices & Queries*. London: The Yearly Meeting of the Religious Society of
        Friends (Quakers) in Britain, 2007. Reproduced by permission of the
        publisher

QUAKER JOURNALS 1: GEORGE FOX

51–70   Fox, George: *An Autobiography* (ed. Jones, Rufus M). Philadelphia: Ferris and Leach, 1903 [1694]

FAITH IN ACTION

71   Palmer, Parker J: *Let your Life Speak*. San Francisco: Jossey-Bass, 2000. Reproduced by permission of the publisher

71   Penn, William: *No Cross, No Crown* (ed. Sellick, Ron). Richmond, Indiana: Friends United Press, 1981 [1693]. Reproduced by permission of the publisher

71   Woolman, John: *A Plea for the Poor*. Wallingford, PA: Pendle Hill Pamphlet 357, 2001 [1763]. Reproduced by permission of the publisher

72   Fox, Margaret: *The Testimony of Margaret Fox Concerning Her Late Husband*. Appendix to *The Journal of George Fox, Vol. 2*. London: Edward Hicks (Friends' Tract Association), 1891 [1694]

72   Fox, George: *The Journal of George Fox* (ed. Nickalls, John). Cambridge: Cambridge University Press, 1952 [1694]

73   Dale, Jonathan: *Quaker Social Testimony in our Personal and Corporate Life*. Wallingford PA: Pendle Hill Pamphlet 360, 2002. Reproduced by permission of the publisher

73–5   Rutter, Michael: *A Measure of our Values*. London: Quaker Home Service, 1983. Reproduced by permission of the publisher

75   Barratt Brown, A: *Wayside Sacraments*. London: Friends Book Centre, 1932

75   Stevenson, Elizabeth: *As the Seer Grows*. Quoted in *This We Can Say*. Armadale North, Australia Yearly Meeting of The Religious Society of Friends, 2003 [1993]. Reproduced by permission of the publisher

76   Ceresole, Pierre: *For Peace and Truth* (tr. Harvey, John W and Yates, Christina). London: Bannisdale Press, 1954

76–7   Penington, Isaac: *Letter. The Works of Isaac Penington*. Glenside PA: Quaker Heritage Press, 4 volumes, 1996 [1863]

77   Curle, Adam: *True Justice*. London: Quaker Books, 1981. Reproduced by permission of the publisher

77–8   Fox, George: *Epistle 200. The Works of George Fox*. State College, PA: New Foundation Publications, 8 volumes, 1990 [1831]

79   Scott, Janet: *On Being a Faithful People*. London: *The Friends Quarterly*, vol. 22, no. 12, October 1982. © *The Friends Quarterly*: reproduced with permission

79–80   Bearlin, Margaret: *Douglas Hobson Lecture*, 1984. Quoted in *This We Can Say*: Armadale North, Australia Yearly Meeting of The Religious Society of Friends, 2003. Reproduced by permission of the publisher

80–2   Palmer, Parker J: *The Active Life*. San Francisco: Jossey-Bass, 1990. Reproduced by permission of the publisher

82   Dewsbury, William, *The Faithful Testimony of that Antient Servant of the Lord*. London: Andrew Sowle, 1688

83–5   Fry, Elizabeth: Journal for 1817, quoted in Skidmore, Gil: *Elizabeth Fry: A Quaker Life*. Oxford: Altamira Press, 2005

85–6   Bailey, John, quoted in Smith, Lyn: *Pacifists in Action*. York: Sessions, 1998. Reproduced by permission of the publisher

86–7   Barber, Chris, quoted in Smith, Lyn: *Pacifists in Action*. York: Sessions, 1998. Reproduced by permission of the publisher

87   Swann, Donald, quoted in Smith, Lyn: *Pacifists in Action*. York: Sessions, 1998. Reproduced by permission of the publisher

88–9   Fox, George: *The Journal of George Fox* (ed. Nickalls, John). Cambridge: Cambridge University Press, 1952 [1694]

89   Penn, William: *Some Fruits of Solitude*. Richmond, Indiana: Friends United Press, 1978 [1693]. Reproduced by permission of the publisher

GOD, THE SPIRIT AND THE LIGHT WITHIN

90   Penington, Isaac: *Letter. The Works of Isaac Penington*. Glenside PA: Quaker Heritage Press, 4 volumes, 1996 [1863]

90   Penn, William: *A Key Opening a Way to Every Common Understanding*. Philadelphia: Friends Book Store, 1849 [1692]

90–1   Fox, George: *The Journal of George Fox* (ed. Nickalls, John). Cambridge: Cambridge University Press, 1952 [1694]

91–2   Alpern, Robin, writing In *Godless for God's Sake: Nontheism in Contemporary Quakerism* (ed. Boulton, David). Dent: Dales Historical Monographs, 2006. Reproduced by permission of the publisher

92   The Balby elders: postscript to an *Epistle*, 1656. Quoted in *Quaker Faith & Practice*. London: The Yearly Meeting of the Religious Society of Friends (Quakers) in Britain, 4th edition, 2009

93   Fox, George: *Epistle 10. The Works of George Fox*: State College, PA: New Foundation Publications, 8 volumes, 1990 [1831]

94   Fox, Margaret: *The Testimony of Margaret Fox Concerning Her Late Husband*. Appendix to *The Journal of George Fox, Vol. 2*. London: Edward Hicks (Friends' Tract Association), 1891 [1694]

94   Ambler, Rex: *Light to Live By*. London: Quaker Books, 3rd edition, 2008. Reproduced by permission of the publisher

95   Gorman, George: *Introducing Quakers*. London: Quaker Home Service, 1969. Reproduced by permission of the publisher

95–6   Gillman, Harvey: *A Minority of One*. London: Quaker Home Service, 1988. Reproduced by permission of the publisher

96   Lacout, Pierre: *God is Silence [Dieu est Silence]*. London: Quaker Books, 2001 [1969]. Reproduced by permission of the publisher

96–7   Hubbard, Geoffrey: *Quaker by Convincement*. London: Quaker Books, 2nd edition, 1985 [1974]. Reproduced by permission of the publisher

97–8   Canter, Bernard: *Editorial*. London: *The Friend*, vol. 120, no. 25, 1962. Reproduced by permission of the publisher

98–9   Penington, Isaac: *Concerning Love. The Works of Isaac Penington*: Glenside PA: Quaker Heritage Press, 4 volumes, 1996 [1863]

99–100   Nayler, James: *Testimony to Christ Jesus*. Fairnington: Quaker Heritage Press, 2009 [1660]

100   Brown, Tony: *Knock Knock, Who's There?* London: *The Friend*, vol. 142, no. 6, 1984. Reproduced by permission of the publisher

100–2   Pym, Jim: *Listening to the Light*. London: Rider Books, 1999. Reprinted by permission of The Random House Group Ltd

102–3   Punshon, John: *Encounter with Silence*. Richmond, Indiana: Friends United Press, 1987. Reproduced by permission of the publisher

103–4   Ceresole, Pierre: *For Peace and Truth* (tr. Harvey, John W and Yates, Christina). London: Bannisdale Press, 1954

104–5   Allen, Beth: *Ground and Spring*. London: Quaker Books, 2007. Reproduced by permission of the publisher

105   Palmer, Parker J: *Let your Life Speak*. San Francisco: Jossey-Bass, 2000. Reproduced by permission of the publisher

106–7   Ceresole, Pierre: *For Peace and Truth* (tr. Harvey, John W and Yates, Christina). London: Bannisdale Press, 1954

107   Nitobe, Inazo: *Selections from Inazo Nitobe's Writings*. Japan: Nitobe Memorial Fund, 1936

107–8   Whittier, John Greenleaf. *Poetical Works*. London: Frederick Warne & Co., 1892

QUAKER JOURNALS 2: MARY PENINGTON

110–25   Penington, Mary: *Experiences in the Life of Mary Penington*. London: Friends Historical Society, 1992 [1911]

FOUR TESTIMONIES

126   Barnes, Kenneth C: *The Sterility of Perfectionism*. London: *The Friend*, vol. 145, no. 44, 1987. Reproduced by permission of the publisher

126   Fox, George: *Epistle 65. The Works of George Fox*. State College, PA: New Foundation Publications, 8 volumes, 1990 [1831]

126   Grimke, Sarah. Quoted in *This We Can Say*. Armadale North, Australia Yearly Meeting of The Religious Society of Friends, 2003 [1837]. Reproduced by permission of the publisher

126   Woolman, John: *Journal* (ed. Whittier, J G). London: Andrew Melrose, 1898 [1772]

127   Dandelion, Ben Pink: *Celebrating the Quaker Way*. London: Quaker Books, 2009. Reproduced by permission of the publisher

128–9   Leavitt, Mary Lou: *Oaths, Hats and Outward Weapons*. Address to the Quaker Peace and Service Annual Conference, 1993. Reproduced by permission of the author

129   Dale, Jonathan: *Quaker Understanding of Testimony* in *Faith in Action: Quaker Social Testimony* (ed. Cave, Elizabeth and Morley, Ros). London: Quaker Books, 2000. Reproduced by permission of the publisher

129–30   Punshon, John: *Testimony and* Tradition. London, Quaker Home Service, Reproduced by permission of the publisher

130–1   Kelly, Thomas R: *A Testament of Devotion*. San Francisco: HarperCollins, 1992 [1941]. Copyright © 1941 by Harper & Row Publishers, Inc. Renewed 1969 by Lois Lael Kelly Stabler. New introduction Copyright © 1992 by HarperCollins Publishers, Inc. Reprinted by permission of HarperCollins Publishers

131–2   Punshon, John: *Encounter with Silence*. Richmond, Indiana: Friends United Press, 1987. Reproduced by permission of the publisher

132–4   Cock, Luke, extract from a sermon, 1721. Quoted in Braithwaite, William C: *The Second Period of Quakerism*. York: Sessions, 1979 [1919]

134   Burrough, Edward: *A Just and Righteous Plea Presented unto the King of England*. London: Wilson, 1661

134–5   Yearly Meeting, *An Address to the Inhabitants of Europe on the Iniquities of the Slave Trade*, 1822. Quoted in *Quaker Faith & Practice*. London: The Yearly Meeting of the Religious Society of Friends (Quakers) in Britain, 4th edition, 2009

135   Janney, Samuel L: *Life of William Penn*. Philadelphia: unnamed publisher, 1852

135   Fox, George, *Epistle 388. The Works of George Fox*. State College, PA: New Foundation Publications, 8 volumes, 1990 [1831]

135   Fox, George, *Epistle 249. The Works of George Fox*. State College, PA: New Foundation Publications, 8 volumes, 1990 [1831]

136–7   Unnamed Quaker: Article in *Twelve Quakers and Equality*. London: Quaker Quest, 2007. Reproduced by permission of the publisher. (Note: all contributors to this series remain anonymous)

138   Fox, George: *The Journal of George Fox* (ed. Nickalls, John). Cambridge: Cambridge University Press, 1952 [1694]

138   Gillman, Harvey: *A Minority of One*. London: Quaker Home Service, 1988. Reproduced by permission of the publisher

139   Francis, Diana: *Rethinking War and Peace*. London: Pluto Press, 2004. Reproduced by permission of the publisher

139–40   Unnamed Quaker: Article in *Twelve Quakers and Equality*. London: Quaker Quest, 2007. Reproduced by permission of the publisher. (Note: all contributors to this series remain anonymous)

140   Wildwood, Alex: *A Faith to Call our Own*. London: Quaker Books 1999. Reproduced by permission of the publisher

140–1   Bishop, Muriel: *Integrity*, 1990. Quoted in *Faith and Practice: The Book of Discipline of the New York Yearly Meeting of the Religious Society of Friends*. New York: New York Yearly Meeting of the Religious Society of Friends (Quakers), 2001. Reproduced by permission of the publisher

141   Bailey, Sydney D: *Peace is a Process*. London: Quaker Home Service, 1993. Reproduced by permission of the publisher

141–2   Lonsdale, Kathleen: *I Believe....* Cambridge: Cambridge University Press, 1964

142   Ceresole, Pierre: *For Peace and Truth* (tr. Harvey, John W and Yates, Christina). London: Bannisdale Press, 1954

142–3   Priestland, Gerald: *The Future of Violence*. London: Hamish Hamilton, 1974

143   Penington, Isaac: *Somewhat Spoken to a Weighty Question Concerning the Magistrate's Protection of the Innocent*, 1661. *The Works of Isaac Penington*. Glenside PA: Quaker Heritage Press, 4 volumes, 1996 [1863]

143–4   Francis, Diana: *Rethinking War and Peace*. London: Pluto Press, 2004. Reproduced by permission of the publisher

144–5   Quaker declaration to Charles II, 1660. Quoted in *Quaker Faith & Practice*. London: The Yearly Meeting of the Religious Society of Friends (Quakers) in Britain, 4th edition, 2009

PEACEMAKING

156   Gee, David: *Peace – A Philosophy of Relations* (Think Peace Pamphlet).
           London: Quaker Peace and Social Witness, 2005. Reproduced by
           permission of the publisher

156–7   Fisher, Simon: *Spirited Living*. London: Quaker Books, 2004. Reproduced
           by permission of the publisher

157–9   Francis, Diana: *Rethinking War and Peace*. London: Pluto Press, 2004.
           Reproduced by permission of the publisher

159   Woolman, John: *Journal*, 1772 (ed. Whittier, J G). London: Andrew
           Melrose, 1898

159–60   Gee, David: *Peace – A Leading of Faith* (Think Peace Pamphlet). London:
           Quaker Peace and Social Witness, 2005. Reproduced by permission of the
           publisher

160–2   Francis, Diana: *Rethinking War and Peace*. London: Pluto Press, 2004.
           Reproduced by permission of the publisher

162–5   Public statement of the Yearly Meeting of Aotearoa/New Zealand, Te
           Haahi Tuuhauwiri, 1987. Published online at http://www.quaker.org.nz/
           publications/statement-on-peace. Reproduced by permission of the
           publisher

165–6   Shelley, Nancy: *Peace: Who are the Peacemakers?* Address to Australian
           Association for Religious Education Conference, Brisbane, 1986. Quoted
           in *This We Can Say*. Armadale North, Australia Yearly Meeting of The
           Religious Society of Friends, 2003. Reproduced by permission of the
           publisher

166   Penn, William: *Some Fruits of Solitude*. Richmond, Indiana: Friends United
           Press, 1978 [1693]. Reproduced by permission of the publisher

QUAKER JOURNALS 3: JOHN WOOLMAN

169–83   Woolman, John: *Journal* (ed. Whittier, J G). London: Andrew Melrose,
           1898 [1772]

COMMUNITY

184   Penington, Isaac: *Letter. The Works of Isaac Penington*. Glenside PA:
           Quaker Heritage Press, 4 volumes, 1996 [1863]

184   Jones, Rufus M: letter. Quoted in *Quaker Faith & Practice*. London: The
           Yearly Meeting of the Religious Society of Friends (Quakers) in Britain,
           4th edition, 2009 [1937]

184   Priestland, Gerald: Introduction to *The Society of Friends* by George
           Gorman. Oxford: Pergamon Press, 1978. Reproduced by permission of
           the copyright holder

185   Priestland, Gerald: *Coming Home*, 1981. London: Quaker Books, 2003.
           Reproduced by permission of the publisher

185   Gorman, George: *Religion and Life*. London: *Quaker Monthly*, vol. 61,
           no. 3, 1982. Reproduced by permission of the publisher

185–6   Palmer, Parker J: *The Promise of Paradox: A Celebration of Contradictions in
           the Christian Life*. San Francisco: Jossey-Bass, 2008 [1980]. Reproduced by
           permission of the publisher

186   Littleboy, William: *The Appeal of Quakerism to the Non-Mystic*. London: Friends Home Service Committee, 1964 [1916]. Reproduced by permission of the publisher

186   Penington, Isaac: *Letter. The Works of Isaac Penington*. Glenside PA: Quaker Heritage Press, 4 volumes, 1996 [1863]

186   Allen, Beth: *The Cost of Discipleship*. London: *The Friends Quarterly*, vol. 23, no. 7, 1984. © *The Friends Quarterly*: reproduced with permission

187   Palmer, Parker J: *The Promise of Paradox: A Celebration of Contradictions in the Christian Life*. San Francisco: Jossey-Bass, 2008 [1980]. Reproduced by permission of the publisher

187–8   Punshon, John: *Encounter with Silence*. Richmond, Indiana: Friends United Press, 1987. Reproduced by permission of the publisher

188–9   Gorman, George: *The Amazing Fact of Quaker Worship*. London: Quaker Books, 2nd edition, 2008 [1973]. Reproduced by permission of the publisher

189   Palmer, Parker J: *The Promise of Paradox: A Celebration of Contradictions in the Christian Life*. San Francisco: Jossey-Bass, 2008 [1980]. Reproduced by permission of the publisher

190   Wiltshire Quarterly Meeting, 1678. Quoted in *Quaker Faith & Practice*. London: The Yearly Meeting of the Religious Society of Friends (Quakers) in Britain, 4th edition, 2009

190–1   Punshon, John: *Encounter with Silence*. Richmond, Indiana: Friends United Press, 1987. Reproduced by permission of the publisher

191   Penn, William, Preface to *The Journal of George Fox* (ed. Nickalls, John). Cambridge: Cambridge University Press, 1952 [1694].

191   Dunstan, Edgar G: *Quakers and the Religious Quest*. London: Allen and Unwin, 1956.

192   Ceresole, Pierre: *For Peace and Truth* (tr. Harvey, John W and Yates, Christina). London: Bannisdale Press, 1954

192   Penna, Jai, 1989. Quoted In *Quaker Faith & Practice*. London: The Yearly Meeting of the Religious Society of Friends (Quakers) in Britain, 4th edition, 2009. Reproduced by permission of the publisher

193   Priestland, Gerald: Introduction to *The Society of Friends* by George Gorman. Oxford: Pergamon Press, 1978. Reproduced by permission of the copyright holder

193   Chetsingh, Ranjit M: *Listening to God and Each Other* in *No Time but the Present*, 1967. Quoted in *Quaker Faith & Practice*. London: The Yearly Meeting of the Religious Society of Friends (Quakers) in Britain, 4th edition, 2009. Reproduced by permission of the publisher

193–4   Court, Donald: *A Scientific Age and a Declining Church*. London: *The Friend*, vol. 123, no. 39, 1965. Reproduced by permission of the publisher

194   Oats, William: *The Nurture of the Human Spirit*, Hobart 1990. Quoted in *This We Can Say*. Armadale North, Australia Yearly Meeting of The Religious Society of Friends, 2003. Reproduced by permission of the publisher

194–5   Ceresole, Pierre: *For Peace and Truth* (tr. Harvey, John W and Yates, Christina). London: Bannisdale Press, 1954

195–7   Curle, Adam: *True Justice*. London: Quaker Books, 1981. Reproduced by permission of the publisher

197–8   Dandelion, Ben Pink: *Celebrating the Quaker Way*. London: Quaker Books, 2009. Reproduced by permission of the publisher

QUAKER JOURNALS 4: PIERRE CERESOLE

201–14   Ceresole, Pierre: *For Peace and Truth* (tr. Harvey, John W and Yates, Christina). London: Bannisdale Press, 1954

OPEN TO NEW LIGHT

215   Fox, George: *Epistle 47. The Works of George Fox*. State College, PA: New Foundation Publications, 8 volumes, 1990 [1831]

215   Dandelion, Ben Pink: *Celebrating the Quaker Way*. London: Quaker Books, 2009. Reproduced by permission of the publisher

216   Parker-Rhodes, Damaris: *The Way Out is the Way In*. London: Quaker Home Service, 1985. Reproduced by permission of the publisher

216   Penn, William: *Some Fruits of Solitude*. Richmond, Indiana: Friends United Press, 1978 [1693]. Reproduced by permission of the publisher

216–17   Nitobe, Inazo: *A Japanese view of Quakerism*. London: Friends' Council for International Service, 1927

217–19   Pym, Jim: *The Pure Principle*. York: Sessions, 2000. Reproduced by permission of the author

219   Priestland, Gerald: *Reasonable Uncertainty*. London: Quaker Books, 1982. Reproduced by permission of the publisher

220–1   Fox, George: *The Journal of George Fox* (ed. Nickalls, John). Cambridge: Cambridge University Press, 1952 [1694]

221–2   Parkinson, Frank: *Science and Religion at the Crossroads*. Exeter: Imprint Academic, 2009. Reproduced by permission of the publisher

223–4   Sykes, Marjorie: *Friends and World Religions*. Hoshangabad, India: author's publication, 1957

224   Jashapara, Ashok: *Looking at the Light rather than the Lampshade*. London: *The Friends Quarterly*, vol. 37, no. 1, 2009. © *The Friends Quarterly*: reproduced with permission

225   Fryer, Jonathan: *Flirting with the Buddha* in *Patterns and Examples* (ed. Jarman, Peter and Tucker, Eva). York: Sessions, 2005. Reproduced by permission of the author

225–6   Pym, Jim: *The Pure Principle*. York: Sessions, 2000. Reproduced by permission of the author

226   Jarman, Peter: *Quaker Way, Buddhist Way*, in *Patterns and Examples* (ed. Jarman, Peter and Tucker, Eva). York: Sessions, 2005. Reproduced by permission of the author

227   Dunston, John: *Special Expressions: A Jewish Childhood*, in *Patterns and Examples* (ed. Jarman, Peter and Tucker, Eva). York: Sessions, 2005. Reproduced by permission of the author

227–8   Gillman, Harvey: *A Deeper Membership*. London: *The Friends Quarterly*, Volume 37, No 1, 2009. © *The Friends Quarterly*: reproduced with permission

228–9   Leonard, Alison: *A Goddess-Loving Quaker Ponders Her Dilemmas*, in *Patterns and Examples* (ed. Jarman, Peter and Tucker, Eva). York: Sessions, 2005. Reproduced by permission of the author

229–30   Unnamed Quaker: Article in *Twelve Quakers and Jesus*. London: Quaker Quest, 2007. Reproduced by permission of the publisher. (Note: all contributors to this series remain anonymous)

231   Fox, George: *To all that would know the way to the Kingdom. The Works of George Fox*: State College, PA: New Foundation Publications, 8 volumes, 1990 [1831]

AUTHOR INDEX